THE NONALCOHOLIC BAR

The Nonalcoholic Bar

CLASSIC AND CREATIVE COCKTAILS FOR EVERYONE

John deBary

Illustrations by LOZO Illustration

UNION SQUARE & CO.
NEW YORK

U
UNION
SQUARE
& CO.
NEW YORK

UNION SQUARE & CO. and the distinctive Union Square & Co. logo are trademarks of Hachette Book Group, Inc.

Text © 2025 John deBary
Illustrations © 2025 LOZO Illustration

All rights reserved. No part of this publication may be reproduced, stored in a retrieval system, or transmitted in any form or by any means (including electronic, mechanical, photocopying, recording, or otherwise) without prior written permission from the publisher.

ISBN 978-1-4549-6260-1
ISBN 978-1-4549-6261-8 (e-book)

Library of Congress Control Number: 2025941925

Union Square & Co. books may be purchased in bulk for business, educational, or promotional use. For more information, please contact your local bookseller or the Hachette Book Group's Special Markets department at special.markets@hbgusa.com.

Printed in China

2 4 6 8 10 9 7 5 3 1

unionsquareandco.com

Editor: Amanda Englander
Designer: Renée Bollier
Illustrator: LOZO Illustration
Project Editor: Ivy McFadden
Production Manager: Terence Campo
Copy Editor: Terry Deal

This book is dedicated to everyone in need of deliciousness

TABLE OF CONTENTS

9	Introduction
19	The Equipment
23	The Techniques
25	The Ingredients
35	The Back Bar

45
HERBAL

47	Garden Soother
48	Cucumber Collins
50	Lychee Hugo Spritz
53	Moderate Mule
55	Chamomile-Saffron Toddy
56	A Definitive Nonalcoholic Martini
59	Vernal Equinox Punch
60	Honeysuckle 75
63	Green Lightning

107
EARTHY

109	Cider Shandy
110	Vinegar Fizz
113	Barley Bomber
114	Pineapple Elixir 2.0
117	Cameron's Kiss
118	Honeydew Old Fashioned
121	Jaggery Sour
122	Mugi Manhattan
125	Pumpkin Spice Margarita
126	Mugi Punch

129
BITTER

131	Tart Negroni
132	Monaco
135	Digestivo Shots
136	Proxy Blush
139	Negroni Sbagliato (for Two)
140	A Definitive Manhattan
143	Darth Spritz
144	A Definitive Nonalcoholic Gin & Tonic
147	Polyberry Daiquiri

65
TART

67	Deep Purple
69	Verjus Daiquiri
70	Basil Smash
73	Honey Sidecar
74	Amoxicillin
77	Golden Gimlet
78	Corpse Reviver Reviver
80	Fermented Passion
83	Senchu-Hi
84	Arctic Cooler

87
FRUITY

89	Rocking Chair Punch
90	Cherry-Cola Temple
93	Citra Collins
94	Apricot Spritz
97	Berry Michelada
98	Vetiver Blush
101	"Midori Sour"
102	Slushy Minty Mary
105	Kitchen Sink Sling

149
SMOKY

151	Mugi Toddy
153	Lapsang-Luxardo
154	Berry Bramble
157	Smoked Cola Old Fashioned
158	New New York Sour
160	A Not-So-Definitive Old Fashioned
163	Dirty Old Fashioned
164	Pickup Toddy
167	Hot Curcu
168	Fireplace Punch

171
VELVETY

173	Miso Flip
174	Bocce Boule
177	Lost-and-Found Lake
178	Ethereal Angel
181	Coco-Coffee
182	Tahini Dreamsicle
185	Blood Orange Ramos
186	Nog of Virtue
188	Acknowledgments
189	Index

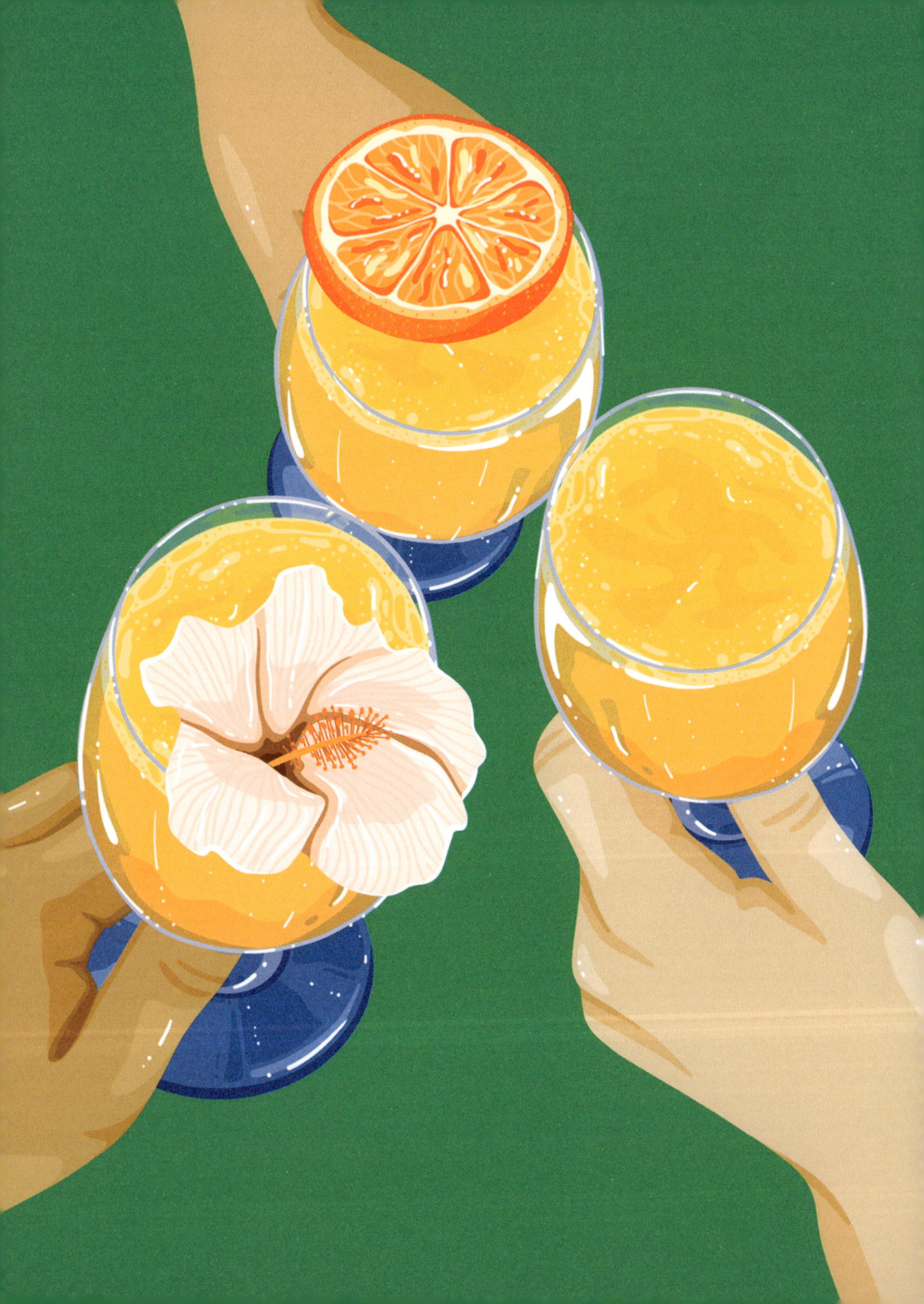

INTRODUCTION

WHO AM I?

In case you skipped over the cover of this book, my name is John deBary. People also call me "JdB," and if you write my name with a capital "D," I will correct you every single time. My career as a bartender began at the New York City cocktail bar Please Don't Tell, perhaps better known as PDT, where I spent about five and a half years behind the bar. Following that, I worked for the Momofuku restaurant group, first as a bartender at the East Village restaurant Momofuku Ssäm Bar, then later as the group's corporate bar director. During my tenure with Momofuku, I helped open about ten restaurants all over the country, designing the physical bars, creating distinctive menus, and training expert staff.

Eventually I came out from behind the bar and began writing about what I knew best. In 2012, my boss from PDT and longtime mentor, Jim Meehan, brought me on to help him edit *Food & Wine*'s annual cocktail book, which I had the honor of participating in for the next three years. While the magazine no longer issues this small paperback, it featured recipes contributed by some of the country's top bartenders. I oversaw testing them alongside the *Food & Wine* test kitchen team. One year—around 2014—I thought it would be fun to "convert" some of the recipes into nonalcoholic cocktails, and for that year's issue we included a separate chapter dedicated to my re-creations.

That chapter was my first experience seriously engaging with how to concoct nonalcoholic drinks that tasted as interesting and delicious as "regular" cocktails, and it taught me that nonalcoholic cocktails are as challenging as they are rewarding. And that is basically what this book is all about.

But before we get to that, it's worth mentioning that my career in the drinks and hospitality industry has led me to some other pretty cool places, too. I have been the resident drinks expert for Food52, where I made a very enjoyable series of drinks videos that you can find on YouTube (like and subscribe!). And I've had the pleasure and honor of writing for such storied publications as *PUNCH*, *Bon Appétit*, *New York* magazine, Food Network, and *Full Pour*, among others.

Oh, and I also started my own nonalcoholic drinks company, Proteau. In 2018, after leaving Momofuku, I partnered up with a strategic investor who helped me secure funding to launch a line of nonalcoholic aperitifs, which were on the market for about two years before the impacts of COVID-19, along with the standard challenges that befall startups, caught up with me and I pulled the plug. The process was fascinating for many reasons, but most relevant to this book, I learned how to take all the experience I had making delicious nonalcoholic cocktails and bottle it—literally.

My first cocktail book, *Drink What You Want: The Subjective Guide to Making Objectively Delicious Cocktails*, was published in June 2020 (which was kind of an interesting time to publish a cocktail book, but hey). I wanted to empower readers with the idea that what tastes good to one person might be revolting to another, and neither of those people is wrong—no one's subjective experience of drinking a cocktail matters more than anyone else's. To help the reader understand why a certain cocktail might be more preferable to another, I described a number of objective balance points that cocktails can hit, including sweetness, acidity, temperature, dilution, and bitterness. More on those in a minute—they're important here, too (see page 13).

Then I wrote *Saved by the Bellini & Other '90s-Inspired Cocktails* in 2023, which swapped cocktail philosophizing for a manic pop culture tour through the decade during which I spent my formative years. The book was mostly a way for me to cleverly connect '90s iconography to cocktails by doing things like creating a nonalcoholic large-format drink for Kevin McCallister to drink by himself because his entire family went to Paris without him and they didn't have cell phones. I was also lucky enough to have Tiffani Thiessen, aka Kelly Kapowski from the iconic sitcom *Saved by the Bell*, write the foreword to the book. She is hands down one of the most genuinely nice people I have ever met—and she has some great cookbooks, too—so that was fun.

But as my career in the drinks industry barreled toward the middle of its second decade, I became more and more convinced that nonalcoholic drinks were a fascinating territory to explore. This was encouraged in no small part by my choice to become a "non-drinker" when I turned forty. I don't call myself sober, because, well . . . you can guess why; I just don't drink alcohol. It really works for me—especially now that I'm what some might call "old." I'm not an evangelist for teetotalism; you do you. But I've also found that many people who regularly consume alcohol are delighted to encounter nonalcoholic drink options, and I live to serve; that's why I've written this book.

WHO ARE YOU?

Identity is complicated, and you certainly don't need to have yourself all figured out in order to find this book useful. But what I do mean when I ask this question is more about *why* you might be interested in this book. Regardless of what substances you do or do not consume, if you're interested in drinks—and in cocktails specifically—this book is for you. You do not need to be a teetotaler or a sober person or anything else in particular in order to enjoy the beverages you'll find here.

I'm not an expert on sobriety or substance abuse disorders. This book does not contain any anti-alcohol propaganda, and you can use it 365 days of the year—it's not just for Dry January or Sober October or whatever else you can make kind-of rhyme! I believe all intoxicants have their time and place; some people can consume them their entire lives without causing significant harm, while others can't. I also believe viable nonalcoholic drink options, such as those in this book, do help people drink less, simply by providing more options. You can find plenty of books, podcasts, YouTube channels, and credentialed professionals devoted to the topic of examining one's relationship to alcohol, so I will not be offering any guidance on the topic here.

Simply put, no matter who you are or how much alcohol you do or do not drink, this book is for you!

And speaking of you, thank you for reading.

WHY NONALCOHOLIC COCKTAILS?

In recent years, the drinks industry has seen an explosion of interest in nonalcoholic drinks. In my view, this is the natural progression of the cocktail renaissance that began in the mid-to-late 2000s. As more people learned about cocktails, they naturally wanted to explore as many ways of making them as possible. Nonalcoholic cocktails represented an undiscovered country for people like me who spent most of their careers leveraging their creativity to devise novel drinks that kept their customers coming back. For me, this arena represented a "what's next" after admittedly getting a little bored trying to come up with the next big daiquiri variation. This territory answers the question of how we can deploy our extensive expertise in truly new ways.

It also allows us to reach people who have previously been left out of the fancy cocktail conversation. As a hospitality professional, my goal is to welcome as many people as possible and give them as many options as possible. If you are welcoming people into your space, whether it's a commercial bar or your own home, you want to be able to serve something all your guests can enjoy. There are many, many reasons why someone might want to skip the alcohol in their drinks, so being able to serve a beverage that has the same level of thought, care, and deliciousness as one with alcohol is vitally important. Nonalcoholic cocktails are inclusive and accessible—key tenets of hospitality.

Nonalcoholic cocktails are also about providing options. When given the choice between a mediocre glass of wine or a sugary soda, most people would choose the wine even if they're not particularly interested in the alcohol contained in the wine. Even a mid glass of wine is more interesting than ice water or a can of Diet Coke. I've heard from enthusiastic alcohol consumers—who, according to beverage analysts, make up about 80 percent of consumers of nonalcoholic drinks—that they relish the chance to choose a delicious drink without alcohol when they feel like it. I think this is thanks to the fact that drinks with alcohol tend to be more interesting from a flavor perspective. Let's get into that now . . .

What Does "Nonalcoholic" Actually Mean?

It is not unreasonable to assume the word "nonalcoholic" means "zero alcohol." But according to US laws, products labeled this way can contain up to 0.5% alcohol by volume (ABV). To put this in perspective, most beers are 3% to 5% ABV, and spirits are generally 40% ABV, sometimes higher. In order for a product to be labeled "zero alcohol," it needs to contain literally zero alcohol. Many beverages contain trace amounts of alcohol because the extracts used to give flavor are ethanol-based. Vinegar is made from re-fermented wine and can contain small amounts of leftover alcohol. Even raw fruits like bananas have small amounts of alcohol in them!

Most people—including many people who do not drink alcohol—consider trace amounts of alcohol to be acceptable. If you need to avoid alcohol entirely, be sure to carefully check the label of whatever you're buying.

The drinks in this book adhere to US labeling laws, meaning some of them might contain trace amounts far under the legal 0.5% threshold. Many products used in these recipes, such as nonalcoholic beers and nonalcoholic wines, do contain trace amounts of alcohol. I also like to use cocktail bitters like Angostura and Peychaud's, which have a similar ABV to regular spirits like gin or whiskey, though the quantity in which they're used—just a few dashes—does not increase a cocktail's ABV beyond 0.5%. You can find nonalcoholic alternatives to bitters if you prefer, or you can omit them entirely (the drinks will lack a certain something, but they will probably be at least decent).

WHAT MAKES A COCKTAIL A COCKTAIL?

When I was a teenager, I took apart just about every piece of electronics in my possession. I was usually able to put them back together again (though not always . . . sorry, Mom!), but the reason I did this was because I was curious about how they worked. This same curiosity is what drives my interest in nonalcoholic cocktails. Taking things apart and putting them back together is one of the best ways to figure out how something works, and nonalcoholic cocktails represent a "taking apart" of traditional cocktails and reconstructing them using different ingredients. By doing so you achieve structurally similar results while also learning how ingredients function on a structural level to come together as a delicious mixed beverage.

Nonalcoholic cocktails are also a superior way to help you learn about your own taste preferences: unlike alcohol-based cocktails, which can be enjoyable simply because they contain alcohol, nonalcoholic cocktails are all about flavor. The objective characteristics that determine the success or failure of a drink can be measured and quantified:

- **TEMPERATURE** is extremely important when it comes to cocktails. The proper temperature for most cocktails is super cold, which is why you'll frequently shake with ice and/or serve over ice—but others taste better at room temperature and others still are best served hot.

- **ACIDITY** gives cocktails vibrancy and a refreshing quality, but that acidity must be properly balanced. A margarita with too much lime juice is probably too intense for some people, and the puckering, mouthwatering sensation will overpower the other elements in the drink.

- **SWEETNESS** is often the counterbalance to acidity. Sticking with our friend the margarita, too much sweetener will create a drink that tastes cloying and syrupy. Acidity and sweetness work in opposition to each other. If a cocktail tastes too sweet, add something with acidity, and vice versa. Not all cocktails contain significant acidity, and in those cocktails sweetness is balanced out by other elements in the drink such as dilution, bitterness, and in the case of alcohol-based drinks, alcohol. (Sweetness and acidity are also affected by temperature, but that's too science-y and I don't want to get sidetracked more than I already have.)

- **DILUTION** refers to the amount of water a cocktail contains. Even a cocktail like a Manhattan that is essentially all spirits needs to be chilled and diluted down a bit in order to taste balanced. Ice absorbs heat and melts into water, which is why ice is so important to cocktails. With nonalcoholic cocktails, however, dilution is usually the enemy—so we need to think more about preserving concentration rather than trying to space it out.

- **BITTERNESS** is our only taste sense that helps us detect poison in our food. It's a warning! (And no wonder most kids hate coffee . . .) Bitterness usually comes from alkaloids such as caffeine—and, obviously, not everything that's bitter will kill you. In drinks, bitterness makes for an interesting and complex taste. It's often applied at levels low enough that the cocktail does not taste noticeably bitter while still leveraging the interestingness-enhancing properties of bitter ingredients.

- **AROMATIC BALANCE** is extremely difficult to quantify, but it can be measured by our olfactory bulbs. The olfactory bulb is a little piece of our brain that juts out on the roof of our sinuses and allows us to smell things. Aromas can approach our olfactory bulb from the front, via our noses, and from the back up the top of our throats. I could go on and on about olfaction and flavor, but the key goal to keep in mind with aromatics is that the best cocktails should taste somewhat of each individual ingredient *and at the same time* taste like something entirely new—more than the sum of their parts.

- **SUBJECTIVE SUCCESS** for a cocktail is way more complicated than each of these individual characteristics, but the explanation is shorter: The person drinking the cocktail has to like it. I'm repeating myself here because it is important: Cocktails must work on both an objective level and subjective level to be truly great. Each person might have innate preferences that apply no matter what, such as liking sweeter drinks or hating the flavor of blueberries. Those preferences are informed by genetics, memory, culture, and especially the setting in which those drinks are consumed. The same person might have wildly different preferences depending on their current situation—even the most die-hard eggnog lover is most likely not going to want to chug a glassful after running six miles in ninety-degree weather.

14 | THE NONALCOHOLIC BAR

THE SCIENCE OF NONALCOHOLIC DRINK-MAKING

Even the most mediocre bartender can throw together some rum, lime juice, and sugar and make a drinkable daiquiri. When you remove rum from the equation, the job gets much harder. This is for two main reasons: the fact that there are so many interesting alcohol-based products to work with, and the physical properties ethanol (the alcohol we can drink) contains.

Regarding the plethora of products, there's not much to say other than drink-makers have a huge amount of options when choosing ingredients. Although the number of fancy nonalcoholic spirits is growing, the alcohol industry has had a few centuries' head start. Nonalcoholic spirits may never catch up, and this is for one immutable reason rooted in the chemistry of these drinks: Ethanol is not water. (More on ingredients on page 25.)

I'm not going to pretend to know enough about the physical sciences to explain why, but there are a few crucial differences between ethanol and water that help to contextualize any discussion of nonalcoholic cocktails: Ethanol and water have different boiling points, different freezing points, and different densities, and ethanol is a much stronger solvent than water. All of this adds up to mean that ethanol feels very different on the palate than plain water—and it also means that ethanol is a much more efficient vehicle for flavors than water alone. A good demonstration of how deeply different they are is to compare equal amounts of vodka

Sidebar on the Word "Mocktail"

Many people in the drinks industry think the word "mocktail" should be retired—and I used to be one of them. Mocktail is seen as a less-than-ideal label for nonalcoholic cocktails because the word "mock" implies derision and lesser status. And, like, sure, it's not great to mock people, but we all seem fine with the term "mock trial." Also, words mean what we want them to mean. Their meanings shift and change over time and even region.

Regardless, I like the term "nonalcoholic cocktails," but I have no problem if you want to call them mocktails. It's not my favorite word, but its meaning is widely understood. Plus, "nonalcoholic cocktail" is a mouthful. We have other things to worry about.

and water, both at room temperature. Place a tea bag into each and watch how quickly the tea infuses into the vodka after just ten minutes. The vodka will be mostly tea-colored while the water might be subtly discolored. There is no way around the simple physical fact that ethanol soaks up more flavor, but understanding that is key to both managing expectations around and figuring out how to make the most satisfying nonalcoholic cocktails possible.

And then there's the fact that ethanol is a powerful psychoactive drug. Ethanol can alter our mood and relieve pain, both facts contributing to why people drink it. Many times people just want something that will relax them and maybe take their minds off the stresses of their daily lives—and this is completely fine. How many times have you finished off a shitty glass of wine or a poorly mixed cocktail because, hey, it's a drink? But when considering nonalcoholic cocktails, we only have the flavor experience to rely on, so we have to pay that much more attention to it.

To repeat a key difference between the structure of nonalcoholic cocktails and alcohol-based cocktails: Dilution is generally always beneficial to an alcohol-based cocktail, while the opposite is true for nonalcoholic cocktails. One of the most common ways nonalcoholic cocktails fall short is they lack the flavor density needed to make the drink satisfying. I will help you avoid this flaw by teaching you to identify and maximize every opportunity to cram flavor into your drinks.

There is really no way around the fact that to make a nonalcoholic cocktail on the same level of complexity and deliciousness as traditional cocktails, you'll have to put in a bit more work. But there is nothing quite like the joy of bringing a nonalcoholic cocktail to your lips and realizing you're tasting something delicious and interesting that just happens to not contain alcohol.

LET'S TALK ABOUT THE COCKTAILS IN THIS BOOK

Okay, sorry. That was a lot of jargon for someone who feels bartenders often overthink their cocktails. Regardless of your comfort level with the science or the jargon, you don't necessarily need to understand *why* drinks taste good in order to make them—although it does help.

All you need to do is follow the hopefully-very-clear (at least my editor said so) instructions in this book, starting on page 19, where I talk you through all of the tools, glassware, and ingredients you need to be successful in your endeavors. I'm sure you'll recognize a lot of what we're using, and some things might be obvious, but I find it's always helpful to start from the ground up when teaching people to make successful cocktails. But what might not be familiar to you are the ingredients specific to nonalcoholic cocktail–making. When working with exclusively nonalcoholic ingredients, there are two resource-related challenges: the breadth of nonalcoholic spirits is nowhere near that of their traditional counterparts, and many ingredients need refrigeration in order to stay fresh and usable.

While you'll be able to rely on some grab-and-go ingredients, you're also going to want to build up your back bar. In a typical bar, there are shelves on the wall behind the bar lined with all manner of spirits, hence the name (surely you've seen this), from which bartenders can easily pull ingredients as they mix. Here, I've developed the Back Bar of the Nonalcoholic Bar, fifteen core recipes for syrups and infusions that are used extensively throughout the book. Most, but not all, of the drink recipes in these pages employ elements from the Back Bar.

That said, *every* ingredient in this book was chosen specifically for its ability to help make up for what you "lose" by mixing cocktails without alcohol. These recipes exploit ingredients to their full potential so you'll make nonalcoholic cocktails that are great on their own rather than for their attempt to trick you into thinking you're drinking a traditional cocktail.

The drink recipes are arranged according to their general flavor profiles and the way we all tend to think and talk about drinks: Herbal, Tart, Fruity, Earthy, Bitter, Smoky, and Velvety. When I'm working service in a bar or restaurant, I often help guide guests toward a cocktail choice by asking what type of drink they're in the mood for. You can do the same thing here: Do you have a hankering for a moody, smoky drink on a chilly night? Or do you want something with refreshing fruit flavors for a fun vibe? Each chapter begins with an explanation of the star adjective, including where you might have found examples of it in traditional cocktails. To me, the most salient feature of any cocktail is the subjective experience of drinking it, which is why I like to categorize drinks with the end result in mind.

If you're just dipping your toes into the nonalcoholic water, you'll find plenty of recipes that echo familiar favorites, or at least familiar drinks you've heard of, like Corpse Reviver Reviver (page 78), Berry Michelada (page 97), Dirty Old Fashioned (page 163), and A Definitive Nonalcoholic Gin & Tonic (page 144). Others, like Vetiver Blush (page 98), Digestivo Shots (page 135), and Ethereal Angel (page 178), are expressions of drinks containing ingredients I'm loving right now and also show how I (sometimes) like to get weird behind the bar.

I've also ranked each recipe according to its difficulty level. I know this is an extremely white-guy-who-grew-up-in-Greenwich-Connecticut thing to reference, but you know when you go to a ski area and what they consider to be a difficult course varies wildly from place to place? Well, it's kind of the same for cocktails: What one person might consider easy to make could be very, very difficult for someone else. Over the years, I have learned a lot about what people are willing and able to do at home in order to make a drink—and more important, what they are not.

It's impossible for me to step out of my own bias, but I have tried to make even the "hard" cocktails here relatively easy. Long story short, I'm cribbing the universal ski resort system to give you a four-tiered effort rubric for the drinks in this book:

- 🟢 **GREEN CIRCLE:** You will not need to track down items from a specialty store, and the only advanced prep you might need to do is juicing a lemon or lime. The steps used to create each drink are standard: shaking, stirring, and building in the glass.

- 🟦 **BLUE SQUARE:** These drinks use, at most, one recipe from The Back Bar and may require a juiced citrus. The ingredients might be mildly off the beaten path but should be easily findable online. Equipment-wise you might need to employ a standard kitchen device such as a blender.

- ◆ **BLACK DIAMOND:** Requiring up to two recipes from The Back Bar and maybe also a fresh juice or two, these drinks are a fairly substantial project, but mere mortals should not be too intimidated.

- ◆◆ **DOUBLE BLACK DIAMOND:** These drinks call for three (or more) recipes from The Back Bar and might also ask you to bust out an extra kitchen appliance, or plan a little further ahead. I would characterize these drinks more as "projects," but they are well worth the extra effort.

THE EQUIPMENT

THE TOOLS

Shaker

Sometimes called a Boston shaker, the best versions are comprised of two metal tins, one small and the other large. You can use a shaker in which half the set is a pint glass, but I find those to be heavy and awkward. You'll also see three-piece shakers that have a built-in strainer, but I don't love them—they jam frequently and can be difficult to open. For stirring drinks, I use the small tin of the shaker instead of a fancy mixing glass. If you have a fancy mixing glass, that's great and you can use it, but you don't need to run out and buy one.

Jigger

Jiggers are essential tools for measuring drinks, especially when it comes to drinks that rely on precision. Even after fifteen-plus years of mixing drinks, I still wouldn't dream of making cocktails without jiggers. I recommend a small one that measures ½ ounce on one side (with a line for ¼ ounce) and ¾ ounce on the other, as well as a large one with 1 ounce on one side and 2 ounces on the other. There are all-in-one jiggers with internal graduation lines, but sometimes it's hard to see what you're doing.

Some drinks in this book call for larger measures, like a cup. For this, feel free to use whatever liquid measuring cups you have on hand. Or if you like suffering, you can jigger out 8 ounces, which equals 1 cup.

Strainer

Once you've shaken or stirred your drink, you usually need a way to separate it from the ice. Enter: the strainer. It's comprised of a metal paddle that sits on top, with a spring underneath that grips the inside of the shaking tin. You'll also sometimes see julep strainers, which some people believe are necessary for straining stirred drinks, but I think they're superfluous.

Knife

A sharp, good-quality knife is a crucial tool for drink-making, helping with tasks like cutting fruit for juicing or trimming garnishes. Get an all-purpose knife you're comfortable using and keep it sharp.

Barspoon

You need something to stir your drinks. I typically use a chopstick, but a dedicated barspoon is nice, too.

Peeler

A vegetable peeler is an essential tool for separating the skin and peels from various fruits so you can either use them for garnish or discard them before juicing. I like to think of vegetable peelers like disposable razors: They're really difficult to sharpen, so I buy a pack of cheap ones and replace them when they get dull. Even if you take care of them, no matter the quality, peelers will only last about a year with regular use.

Juicer

For the drinks in this book, you'll need something that can juice citrus, such as an elbow juicer or reamer, and something that can juice solid fruits, like a fancy centrifugal juicer. If you don't have the latter, you can blend the whole, peeled fruit in a blender or food processor and then strain out the solids. Note: For citrus, always use an elbow juicer or reamer. A juicer that shreds with a blade and then filters out the solids (such as a centrifugal juicer) will leave you with massive amounts of bitterness from the non-juicy parts of the fruit, and the juice will be gross.

Blender

I have come to see a blender as an essential tool for drink-making. You'll need it to make syrups and infusions as well as to make some of the drinks themselves. I love slushy, blended drinks, and there's really no other way to make them at home than with a blender.

Fine-Mesh Strainer

Straining solid bits from juices, infusions, and syrups is a critical step. To get the finest possible filtration, I use a gold coffee filter because it is durable and reusable. You can use a cheesecloth if you like, but gold coffee filters give the best results. Sometimes it can take a while for all the liquid to strain out, so I like to strain in small batches when possible and use a spoon to gently encourage the process by agitating the mixture.

Sieve

When you need to filter out solids but you don't need the high-resolution filtration of a gold coffee filter, a sieve has a less fine mesh, which allows you to more quickly strain out big, chunky solids from the liquid you want to retain. You can use a spoon or spatula to stir the mixture and help the filtering process along.

Big Ice Molds

Serving a drink with a big, muscular hunk of ice is one of the joys of cocktail-making. Fancy bars and restaurants buy super-clear cubes from specialty purveyors, and if you have access to one, go for it. If not, grab a large silicone mold and call it a day. When it comes time to use ice from these molds, be sure to let them sit out at room temperature for a few minutes so you can slide the cubes out easily; if you force the cubes out, you'll damage the silicone. Special gizmos that will give you super clear ice at home exist, and from what I hear they work great, but I haven't used them.

Containers

As a semi-former restaurant person, I have an affinity for Cambro's line of CamSquare containers for most of my storage needs. They're relatively inexpensive, durable, and available online, so buy some if you don't have a storage solution already. For smaller amounts, I like the circular deli containers used for take-out restaurant orders.

Straws

Plastic straws aren't great for the environment—nothing made from plastic is. But straws themselves are actually important to drinks, as they bring the drink into your mouth in a concentrated burst, plus they're good for avoiding a mouthful of ice when sipping drinks with lots of it. They're also great to have on hand for anyone who might not have the same level of physical ability that so many of us do. Get a few metal or borosilicate glass straws, and you won't have to feel guilty about the turtles.

THE GLASSWARE

Coupe

The coupe is the most ubiquitous cocktail glass. It has a bulb-like bowl at the top and a stem that allows you to hold the drink without the heat from your hands warming it up. (Martini glasses have straight edges—maybe it's because I have unsteady hands and a few mental health comorbidities, but I'm too nervous about spilling to use them.) Most coupes hold about five ounces of liquid, while a large coupe holds closer to ten. It's important to pre-chill your coupes in the freezer for about twenty minutes so that a warm glass doesn't heat up your drink.

Old Fashioned

Sometimes also called a rocks glass, these stemless glasses are large enough to hold a drink plus ice, typically about twelve ounces total. If you're serving the drink with ice, it's not as critical to pre-chill these glasses before using, but you can!

Tall

I'm lumping glasses like a water glass, pint glass, and Collins glass into one category: a tall drink of whatever you put in them. For drinks that call for a tall glass, use whatever you have handy, the only requirement being that the glass is large enough to hold drinks that contain a significant volume of liquid, about twelve ounces. Same as with the old fashioned glass, if the drink has ice in it, pre-chilling in the freezer is optional.

Wine

For all the drinks in this book that call for a wine glass, I'm referring to a white, or all-purpose, wine glass. Again, use whatever you have handy, except for flutes—they're too small and the narrow form does not allow you to nose the aromatics of your drink. Since wine glasses are typically made of very light glass, they don't have enough mass to worry about the temperature, but if you want, you can chill them.

Small

A few of the drinks here call for a small glass—it's not necessarily a common term, but its meaning shouldn't be mysterious. Use a glass small enough so the drink does not look comically small by comparison—but if you don't have anything that fits the bill, pick whatever you think works best. As you know by now, chill the glass if you're not serving the drink with ice.

THE TECHNIQUES

MEASURE

Measuring is critical to making great drinks. Yes, you can free-pour, but when you're measuring down to a quarter ounce, it's hard to eyeball precisely. When measuring with a jigger, you want to pour to the meniscus, meaning that the surface tension of the liquid keeps it from spilling over—this step will ensure accuracy with every measure.

SHAKE

Shaking accomplishes a few key tasks: It mixes the drink, chills it, dilutes it, and adds aeration. Perhaps you've seen people pontificating about the best technique for shaking; I'm not going to say one style is better than another, but I will say the key is violence. You want to shake the drink as hard as you possibly can for around fifteen seconds. This will give the drink enough time to reach proper levels of mixing, dilution, temperature, and aeration.

STIR

Stirring drinks accomplishes the same thing as shaking, minus the aeration, which we skip when we want to keep the original texture of the base ingredients. In contrast to the violence of shaking, gentleness is the name of the game here as you don't want the drink to be quite as cold or diluted as a shaken drink. As with shaking, a lot of people will regale you with the nuances of stirring, but for most drinks, about twenty seconds will do the trick.

STRAIN

Once the drink is at the right temperature, diluted, mixed, and (sometimes) aerated, you need to separate it from the ice you've used to do that. The tool for that is a strainer, and it fits over the rim of the shaker with a metal spring to help form a seal, allowing you to pour out the drink while leaving behind the used ice.

GARNISH

You might think a garnish is superfluous, but you'd be wrong. Some are a visual signifier of a completed drink, while others serve a vital, flavor-based purpose. Citrus peels contain delightful aromatics, and expressing (that is, forcing the essential oils out of pores in the skin) and perching them over the drink provides an added experience. Citrus wedges invite the drinker to squeeze it into the drink, supplementing the drink's acidity. Citrus wheels look nice and add a small degree of aromatics. Edible garnishes such as cherries, olives, and candied ginger both look nice and taste delicious.

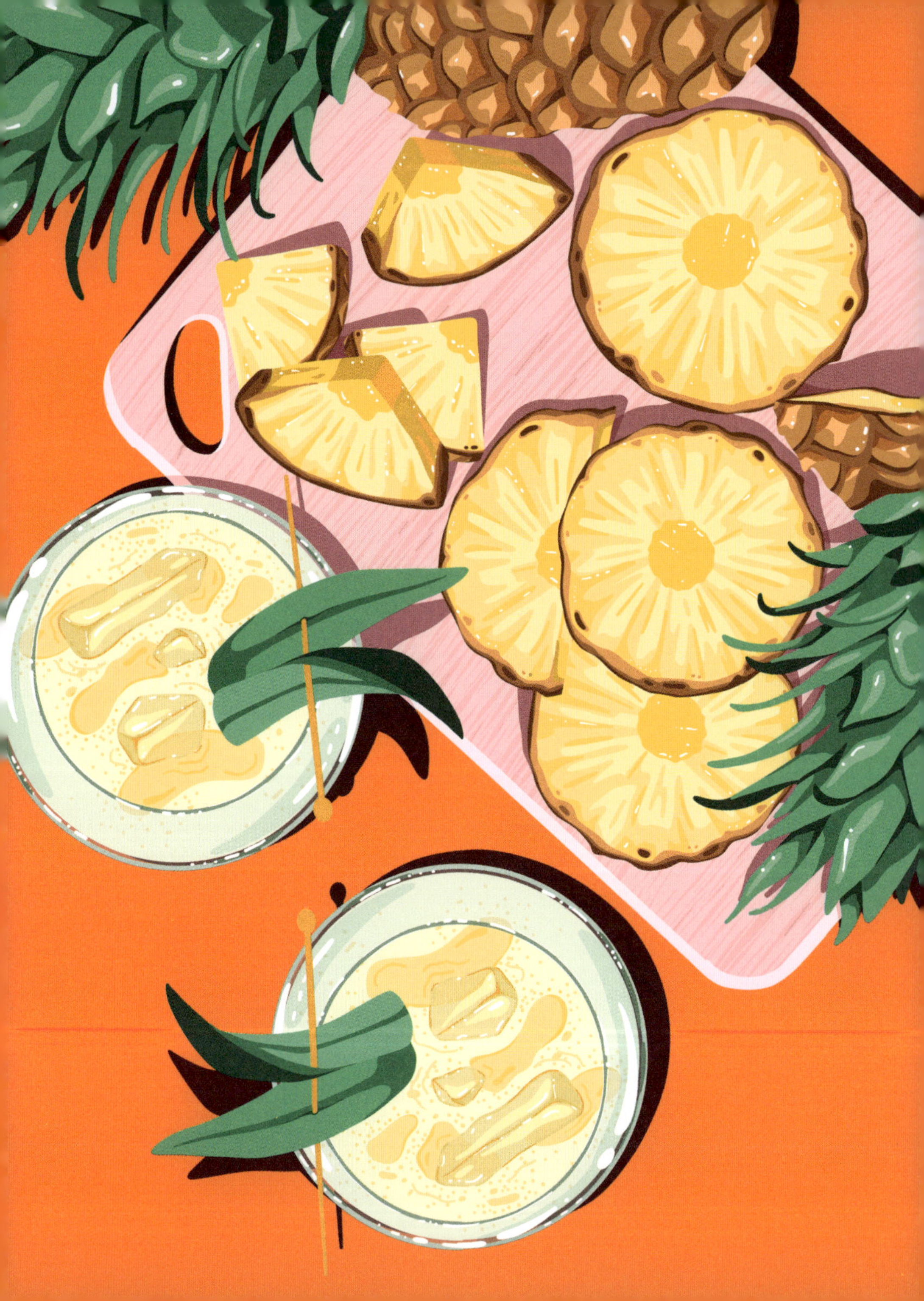

THE INGREDIENTS

NONALCOHOLIC BASE SPIRITS

Mimics

In standard cocktail vernacular, the term "base spirit" refers to the primary spirit that makes up most of the volume of the cocktail and gives the drink much of its character. For instance, when someone asks for a vodka martini, the vodka is the base spirit.

Structurally, nonalcoholic cocktails are different from classic cocktails in that they don't always rely on one big measure of a base spirit. Even so, it helps to think of ingredients in the same way, especially since many nonalcoholic spirits are what I like to call "mimics" of traditional spirits such as gin, whiskey, and tequila. Mimics certainly have their place, but I don't like to rely on them as much as I would traditional spirits. A significant volume of any spirit is ethanol—usually around 40%. When you replace that volume with water, as you would when making a nonalcoholic version of the spirit, you're not going to get the same result. Furthermore, because these products lack the preservative qualities of ethanol, they usually rely on an alternative preservative, which can give the spirit an acidic quality that, while not categorically unpleasant, is kind of weird when compared to whatever they are mimicking. Many mimics also include a spicy ingredient to replicate the burn you feel when drinking alcohol, which I also find kind of weird. Others have artificial sweeteners—yup, weird again. Drawing a direct line to the original spirit these products are mimicking just sets you up for disappointment; it reminds you of the thing you're not drinking.

In this book, I've relied on mimics that are fairly generic. Lyre's Spirit Co, Ritual Zero Proof, and Monday are some of the more common producers of nonalcoholic spirit mimics, and they will work well in the recipes in this book, though whatever you choose should be fine. Almave exclusively produces nonalcoholic tequila mimics that I find to be pretty credible.

Aliens

The take-it-apart-and-put-it-back-together nature of nonalcoholic cocktails applies not only to recipes but also to the ingredients we can use to make them. Some may pick and choose aspects of classic spirits and weave them together in new ways, while others are truly unlike anything else—they're aliens.

I find aliens to be some of the more successful products to come out of the recent boom in the nonalcoholic drinks industry, mostly because they are cool and delicious, but also because they have no baggage attached to them by virtue of the fact that they're not trying to remind you of something else—something better—that you're not drinking. Spirits from producers such as Ghia, Aplós, Tenneyson, and (parentheses) are some of my current favorites, and I've used them judiciously yet enthusiastically in the recipes here.

Whether mimics or aliens, I have tried to use nonalcoholic spirits conservatively because the industry is still maturing. It's hard to say if in ten, twenty, or a thousand years these products will still be around. So if you're reading this book far in the future and you can't find a specific product at your local bottle shop on Caladan, you should still be able to have some fun.

Nonalcoholic spirits, once opened, will generally keep for a few months in a cool dry place, but I, perhaps superstitiously, like to keep them in the refrigerator. Be sure to check the label for any specific storage instructions.

Nonalcoholic Vermouth

In the emerging world of nonalcoholic drinks, nonalcoholic vermouths are some of the most successful in terms of fidelity to the source material as well as just objectively tasting good. Vermouth is typically classified into two main categories: dry and sweet, and the nonalcoholic varieties tend to follow the same bifurcation with "dry" vermouths being clear or pale in color and "sweet" vermouths being deep red. Some of my favorites are made by Roots Premium Spirits; Martini & Rossi makes some, too, but whatever brand you go with should work well in every recipe in this book. I also keep opened bottles of nonalcoholic vermouth in the fridge to extend shelf life, and because I have an anxiety disorder.

Nonalcoholic Liqueurs

When I first encountered the term "nonalcoholic liqueur," I was like . . . so you mean just syrup? Liqueurs are traditionally vehicles for flavors like fruits and herbs, and the alcohol and sugar act as substrates carrying the flavor. Take out the alcohol and you have a syrup, right? Well, technically, yes, but producers of nonalcoholic liqueurs build a flavor profile that's a bit more interesting, complex, and less sweet than say, a pump-bottle syrup used to flavor coffee. Giffard makes some of the best nonalcoholic liqueurs, and their elderflower liqueur is used a bunch in this book. And, you guessed it, I keep opened bottles in the refrigerator, but you don't have to.

Nonalcoholic Bitter Aperitifs

There are a few producers that make nonalcoholic knockoffs of Campari and Aperol. I use Wilfred's, but there are offerings from producers such as Lyre's Spirit Co, The Pathfinder, and Figlia that all have unique profiles but should work fine in the drinks here. Again, I keep them in the refrigerator, but it's not a requirement.

Nonalcoholic Wine

Generally speaking, nonalcoholic wine is made by taking regular wine and removing the alcohol. The results of this process vary wildly. I find that high-acid nonalcoholic sparkling and still white wines are the best results of this process, while I still have not found a nonalcoholic red wine that I enjoy drinking on its own. Nonalcoholic reds are great as cocktail ingredients, though, and are used throughout this book. Whatever brand you choose should be fine. These should definitely go in the refrigerator even if you don't have anxiety because they have a shelf-life that's similar to traditional wine once opened.

Nonalcoholic Beer

Very low alcohol beer has been a concept for a while, but in the past five years many craft brewers have expanded their repertoire to include nonalcoholic beers and many brewers exist that only make nonalcoholic beer. This is a cause for personal celebration because I love beer.

Nonalcoholic beer is made a few different ways, including controlled fermentation and de-alcoholization. Most of them can contain up to 0.5% alcohol and still be labeled "nonalcoholic" so depending on your comfort level, you may want to track down some truly 0.0% beers, which do exist. Some recipes in this book will call for a full 12-ounce can or bottle of beer, so you don't have to worry about storage once opened, but if you have any left over you can keep it in the fridge for a day and it will still be decently fizzy.

Verjus

Up until somewhat recently, verjus, the juice of unripe wine grapes, was more commonly used as a food ingredient, sometimes taking the place of vinegar in sauces and dressings due to its high acidity and bone-dry lack of sweetness. It is for this same reason that it's a great ingredient in drinks. It's slightly different from nonalcoholic wine because it's not fermented, which means it has a bit more brightness and none of the weird burnt flavor that some nonalcoholic wines have. I haven't experienced that wide of a variation in terms of producers, so use what's available and keep it in the refrigerator after you open it.

Vinegar

You see vinegar a lot in nonalcoholic fancy drinks, both ready-to-drink and nonalcoholic cocktails. Vinegar is typically made by fermenting alcohol, such as wine. The fact that it is a product of fermentation means it has tons of complexity due to the biological process of microorganisms eating alcohol and producing a huge number of metabolites. The key metabolite for vinegar is acetic acid, which is what makes vinegar taste, well, vinegary. The challenge with using acetic acid is that it is very aromatic, or smelly. If you use too much of it, your drink will taste like salad dressing and you're going to have a bad time—so measure carefully.

THE INGREDIENTS | 27

Kombucha

Kombucha is a fizzy beverage made by fermenting tea using a colony of bacteria and yeast. Like vinegar, kombucha also has acetic acid in it, which is why it can be somewhat polarizing. (I personally love it, thanks for asking!) Store-bought kombuchas made by producers such as Health-Ade and GT's typically fall below the 0.5% ABV required to secure a "nonalcoholic" label, but some can be significantly higher, so be sure to pay attention to labels.

Citrus Fruits

Citrus fruits and their juices are used extensively in cocktails and extensively in this book. Lemon and lime juices are found in hundreds of cocktails and provide acidity, dilution, and aromatics. In the case of cocktails that don't contain alcohol, these juices are all the more essential since acidity is a great way to add vibrancy and texture. Lemon juice is somewhat rounder than lime juice, but often these two can be used interchangeably in a pinch—although some drinks just "work" better with one over the other.

Orange and grapefruit juices are less commonly used and they are structurally different from lemon and lime because they are less concentrated. Orange juice is sweeter while grapefruit juice has a nice bitter undercurrent that adds a degree of austere sophistication.

Before using any citrus, first soak the fruit in warm water to remove any physical debris it might have picked up en route to you. This step also warms the fruit, making it easier to juice.

Citrus juice is quite fragile and will only taste fresh for a day or two if you keep it in the refrigerator. It will be useable for far longer (up to two weeks, or one month in the freezer), but it will taste weirdly metallic.

Pineapple

I love pineapples and regularly eat a whole one for dinner. If you think that's weird, that's a you problem. Regardless, pineapple juice is a great ingredient in nonalcoholic drinks because it adds acidity, sweetness, and tropical honey aromatics. And when shaken, it gives a nice frothy texture. Fresh juice is preferable, but I have grace for people who want to use canned. If you have a fancy masticating or centrifugal juicer, use it to juice a pineapple. You can also purée chunks in a blender or food processor and strain the solids out with a sieve. Pineapple juice keeps well in the refrigerator and does not get stale-tasting as quickly as citrus juice, but it will settle so be sure to stir it before using. Store it in the refrigerator for up to two weeks or in the freezer for up to two months.

Watermelon

Watermelon is another fruit that I have a voracious appetite for, but only when it's in season—out-of-season watermelon is just mealy and gross. But when you juice it, the texture of the intact fruit is irrelevant, so even in the cooler months I've procured fine-tasting juice out of even the palest and mealiest of fruits. Use a centrifugal juicer to make watermelon juice or purée chunks in a blender or food processor and strain with a sieve. It will separate quickly, so if you're not using it immediately, be sure to stir it up before using. Watermelon juice can be stored in the refrigerator for up to one week or in the freezer for up to three weeks.

Honeydew

If you guessed that honeydew is another fruit that I eat with alarming volume, you'd be correct. I feel like this green melon is often derided (or maybe that's just cantaloupe, which I also enjoy but am not feral for). Perhaps it's because I love the Japanese melon liqueur Midori and honeydew tastes almost the same, but I have found some fun uses for it in nonalcoholic cocktails. Use a centrifugal juicer for honeydew juice or purée chunks in a blender or food processor and strain with a sieve. Honeydew juice can be stored in the refrigerator for up to one week or in the freezer for up to three weeks.

Water

Water is the base for every beverage, and I won't belabor the point of its importance in nonalcoholic cocktails. Most of us are fortunate to have reasonably tasty water coming out of our faucets, but tap water is typically treated with chlorine and I don't love how the residual amount makes the water taste a little chlorine-y. I recommend filtering all water used to make drinks, whether it ends up as ice or is the base for a syrup.

Ice

As a tool, ice is used to shake and stir drinks, getting them cold, mixed, diluted, and, in the case of shaken drinks, aerated. Some claim shaking with large ice cubes is better, but for mere mortals, any decent-size cubes will get the job done. As an ingredient in the drinks themselves, again most decent-size ice will do. Big ice, however, is very nice for Old Fashioned–style drinks, which you can make at home with a mold (see page 21).

Sparkling Water

I have a lot of feelings about sparkling waters. Seltzer, club soda, and sparkling mineral water are all subtly different, and some brands are better than others. I will not bore you with how I think the 1L bottle of Pellegrino hits very different from the 750mL bottle. You can use whatever sparkling water you want—just chill it before using.

Cola

Cola has an interesting flavor profile of clove, cinnamon, vanilla, caramel, and sometimes citrus oil, but people often overlook it because it's perceived as little more than a sugary mass-market beverage. Use whatever brand you prefer (I generally use Coca-Cola because you can find it anywhere), and be sure to chill it before using.

THE INGREDIENTS | 29

Lemon-Lime Soda

Sprite and 7UP are the two most popular brands of lemon-lime soda, though others exist out there. As a category, I like how this ingredient adds some citrus aromatics, sweetness, and bubbles. Chill before using.

Tonic Water

Tonic water is flavored with quinine, a bitter substance made from the bark of the Cinchona tree. Quinine has medicinal properties—most notably, it treats malaria—but the levels in tonic water are not enough to have any medicinal effect; it is only included for flavor. I have a preference for the more artisanal varieties that have a bit less sweetness and more acidity, such as Fever-Tree or Q Mixers, but use whatever brand you like. As ever, chill before using.

Hop Water

Have you ever wanted a La Croix that tastes like an IPA? Well, that's hop water. It's made by infusing water with hops and then carbonating it. It's not fermented or dealcoholized, meaning most are literally 0.0% alcohol and zero calories, although that may vary from brand to brand, so check the label if that's important to you. From a flavor perspective, hop waters are not identical, but for the purposes of this book, you can choose any hop water you like. Sometimes hop waters are flavored with things like mango or watermelon and others have functional ingredients like caffeine and adapogens, so check the label—and chill before using. HOP WTR and Hop Splash by Sierra Nevada are two of my go-tos.

Yuzu Juice

Yuzu is a Japanese citrus that looks and tastes like a lemon but is more fragrant and fruity-juicy with elements of tangerine. If you can find fresh yuzu fruit and juice it, great. But I've always found that to be tough, so I buy bottled juice and am partial to the Yakami Orchard brand, though quite frankly I have not noticed a huge amount of variation between brands. Yuzu juice is easy to order online or find in a Japanese specialty market. Just make sure it is 100% juice because there are some that have added salt. After you open it, the juice will keep in the fridge for about a month.

Bitters

Cocktail, or aromatic, bitters are concentrated liquids that add aromatics and bitterness to cocktails with only a few small dashes. The two most popular bitters brands are Angostura and Peychaud's. Angostura has a profile not all that dissimilar from cola, with clove, cinnamon, cardamom, and gentian, a bitter root. Peychaud's has an anise-cherry flavor and is bright red. Orange bitters are another type of bitters that should be fairly self-explanatory.

Most bitters are made with alcohol. Angostura, for instance, is 44.7% ABV! In the amount that you add to drinks, usually a few dashes, it does not significantly increase the alcohol concentration of the finished drink. Depending on your comfort level, you might want to seek out nonalcoholic alternatives to Angostura, Peychaud's, and orange bitters.

Cold Brew Coffee

I do not like fumbling with machinery first thing in the morning and I have a ravenous capacity for caffeine, so every morning I mix cold brew concentrate with water and put it in the microwave for ninety seconds, and it's amazing. I make my own concentrate using the Toddy system, but you can just buy a small bottle of premade concentrate because you are in control of your own life. Compared to regular coffee that's brewed with hot water, cold brew has a milder acidity but also a lighter, fruitier flavor with less bitterness. For reasons I cannot explain, the flavors of cold brew last longer than regular coffee, which can start to taste stale after a few hours. Homemade cold brew keeps in the fridge for up to two weeks or freezer for up to one month.

Luxardo Cherries

I love cocktail cherries. The bright red fakey ones are delicious in their own way, but Luxardo cherries are out of this world. Luxardo is an Italian spirits producer best known for making maraschino (aka cherry) liqueur, and they also make cherries soaked in syrup and I love them. (Did I say that already?) The cherries themselves are quite dark in color—and flavor—and still retain a robust al dente texture despite being mummified in sugar. I use them often to garnish drinks because they look pretty and, yes, they taste great. But! Don't overlook the syrup they're soaking in. I use it as an ingredient on its own because it is just a syrup version of the cherries, which, as I might have mentioned, are very delicious. If you have similar mental health conditions to me, you might be tempted to keep an open container of these cherries in the fridge—this is not advisable. You won't ruin the cherries, but the syrup will crystalize, and it's kind of a hassle to get it all back to liquid again. Keep in a cool, dry place and they won't go bad. I promise.

Eggs

I consume a considerable—perhaps alarming!—quantity of sketchy substances, and I do not consider raw eggs to be even remotely one of them. Raw eggs have a reputation for harboring salmonella, but many other seemingly more innocuous foods (like raw produce) have similar risk profiles and the same level of alarm is not associated with them. People who have no issue consuming raw eggs in alcohol-based cocktails might think the alcohol sterilizes the egg, but the alcohol percentage is not high enough to sterilize the egg in the time it takes to make and drink the drink, so the risk in nonalcoholic cocktails is the same: low. All eggs are not the same, though. When making drinks, I always use the fanciest, most expensive, pasture-raised, humane-certified, yada yada eggs. Animal welfare is important to me, but I choose these eggs mostly because they taste better.

Sugar

Next to alcohol, sugar syrups are an excellent substrate for flavors. This is why you often find too-sweet nonalcoholic cocktails that try to cram in flavor via syrups. Plain table sugar is fine for the recipes that call for it, but I like to play around with different types of sugar, particularly here. Jaggery, an unrefined sugar from Southern Asia most commonly made from raw sugar cane juice, is one of my favorites because it packs a wallop of rich caramel-molasses flavor along with some subtle smoky and savory notes.

Salt

Salt makes everything taste better because it makes everything taste more like itself. It has a remarkable ability to soften bitterness, and it's often used in cocktails at a level below what would make the drink taste noticeably salty, so don't be afraid of it. When you're dissolving salt in liquid, its texture is not that important. Kosher salt is my go-to for drinks because it also is the best for applying to a rim of a glass thanks to its finer texture; flakier salts do not have the same sticking power.

Black Pepper

A few turns of a grinder filled with black peppercorns over the top of a drink can be transformative; I have had many aha moments where it was the missing element in a glass I felt was lacking a certain something. Even though black pepper can be considered somewhat . . . basic, I find the woodsy, spicy, and floral notes in black pepper to be deeply intriguing.

Hot Sauce

While I do think capsaicin, the compound that makes things spicy, to be a bit of a cheap trick nonalcoholic spirit producers use to mimic the burn from alcohol, hot sauce is a go-to ingredient for nonalcoholic cocktails. When used sparingly, the spice, acidity, and sweetness in hot sauces can act in much the same way bitters do: They provide a bit of a backbone and structure to drinks. The drinks in this book will work with whatever normal hot sauce you want to use. And when I say "normal" I mean Valentina, Tabasco, Cholula, even sriracha. Avoid the "Dave's Anus Annihilator"–type sauces because they are way too spicy and names like that should only be used for gay porn.

Fruit Preserves

Despite not making a huge number of appearances in this book, fruit preserves, such as orange marmalade and apricot preserves, are great, semi-unexpected ingredients in cocktails. They, of course, add fruit flavor to cocktails, but they also help enhance the texture thanks to pectin, a substance similar to gelatin that occurs naturally in many fruits.

Maple Syrup

The nomenclature surrounding maple syrup is really confusing. When I first started using it in cocktails, it was in an Old Fashioned made with bacon-infused bourbon and sweetened with "Grade B" maple syrup, which is thinner and darker than regular "Grade A" syrup. Recently, though, "Grade B" has been retired . . . so just be sure the word "dark" is somewhere on the label. Unlike honey or agave nectar, maple syrup will dissolve readily in drinks, so you do not need to pre-dilute it before using.

Orgeat

Apparently, the word "orgeat" is derived from the French word for barley. This is funny to me because orgeat does not contain barley and is generally considered a Middle Eastern product, although many regions' culinary traditions use some version of it. Orgeat is commonly made from almonds, sugar, and rose water. Some producers also include orange blossom water and apricot kernels. It has a nutty, milky flavor, and it goes into a lot of classic cocktails like the mai tai and Cameron's Kick. The flavor can vary widely from producer to producer; some are more syrupy sweet and others are drier and more aromatic. I like the one from Lebanese producer Kassatly Chtaura, which they call "almond syrup," but you can use whatever brand you like.

Orange Blossom Water

Sometimes called orange-flower water, this clear, aromatic liquid is made from the flower petals of bitter orange trees infused into water. It has origins in Middle Eastern culinary traditions and is a critical ingredient in classic cocktails like the Ramos Gin Fizz. It can be found in specialty grocery stores or ordered online. I've used the Lebanese producer Cortas brand with much success but I haven't noticed massive differences between brands, so whatever brand you prefer—or are able to find—should work well.

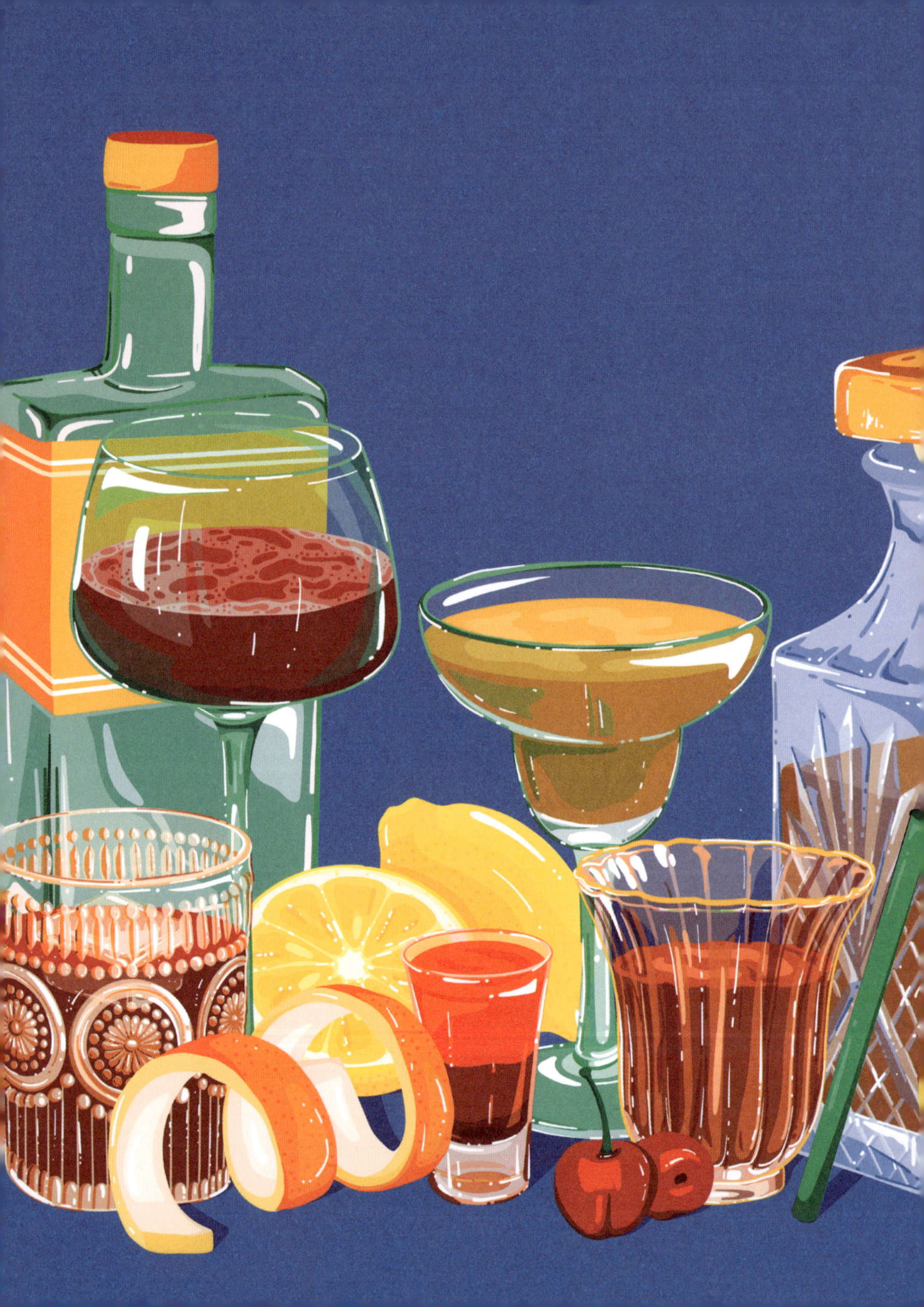

THE BACK BAR

In a typical bar, there are shelves on the wall behind the bar lined with all manner of spirits, hence the name. When mixing cocktails, bartenders pull ingredients from the back bar's shelves in order to whip up their creations. When working with exclusively nonalcoholic ingredients, we don't quite have the same resources. First, the breadth of nonalcoholic spirits is nowhere near that of their traditional counterparts, and second, many ingredients need refrigeration in order to stay fresh and usable. But I've structured the recipes in this book around the same basic idea of developing a collection of ingredients that you can draw upon over and over to create a wide array of different cocktails.

One of my cocktail book pet peeves is when a recipe asks you to make a big batch of syrup and then you only use a tiny amount of it in one drink. I have been guilty of that in the past, but I've done my best to avoid that here. In this book, each of the following elements is used enough that if you make one batch, you will get a good amount of mileage out of it.

I tried to keep the recipes for these back bar ingredients as straightforward and amateur-friendly as possible, but some are a little more involved than others. I give specific information on shelf life for each recipe, but, in general, they should last at least a week or two in the refrigerator and much longer if you decide to freeze them.

Jaggery Syrup

Jaggery is a type of sugar made from either sugar cane or palm tree sap that is a staple in many African and southern Asian cuisines. It has a deep, rich, caramel flavor that adds a lot of complexity to cocktails. Jaggery is widely available online, but feel free to use any dark sugar you like, such as Demerara or raw cane.

MAKES ABOUT 1 CUP

½ cup jaggery or other brown sugar
½ cup water

In a small saucepan over medium heat, combine the sugar and water. Cook, stirring, until the sugar is dissolved and the mixture is lightly boiling, about 10 minutes. As soon as the mixture begins to boil, remove the pan from the heat and let cool completely before using, at least 1 hour. Store in an airtight container in the refrigerator for up to 2 weeks or in the freezer for up to 1 month.

Citrus Syrups

Citrus juices are a key element in many great drinks, but the essential oils found in citrus peels are also a great source of flavor. Regardless of what type of fruit you're using, the technique is the same: blend peels with sugar, water, and a little bit of salt, then strain out the solids. Be sure to give the fruit a nice soak and scrub before using to remove any physical debris that might be lingering on its exterior. When peeling the fruits, avoid as much of the white pith as possible, since instead of containing flavorful oils, it will add a bitterness to your syrup.

MAKES ABOUT 1 CUP

- 5 medium oranges, 8 lemons, 9 limes, or 3 grapefruits (any variety)
- 1 cup granulated sugar
- ½ cup water
- ¼ teaspoon kosher salt

Gently wash the citrus and dry them with a clean kitchen towel. Using a vegetable peeler, peel the citrus, taking care to remove as little of the white pith as possible. Place the peels, sugar, water, and salt in a blender and blend on low speed until the sugar and salt are dissolved, about 30 seconds. Strain the mixture through a fine-mesh sieve and discard the solids.

Store the syrup in an airtight container in the refrigerator for up to 1 week or in the freezer for up to 1 month.

Saffron Honey

When using honey to sweeten cocktails, you'll need to dilute the honey with a bit of water so the thick, sticky stuff mixes properly with the rest of the drink. Here, saffron offers a mysterious semi-floral, semi-savory note—if you hate it or don't want to use it for any reason (I know, it's pricey!), omit the saffron; your drinks will taste fine.

MAKES ABOUT ¾ CUP

- ½ cup honey
- ¼ cup water
- ¼ teaspoon saffron threads

In a small saucepan over medium heat, combine the honey, water, and saffron. Cook, stirring, until well combined, about 5 minutes. Remove the pan from the heat and let cool completely before using, at least 30 minutes. Store in an airtight container in the refrigerator for up to 3 weeks or in the freezer for up to 2 months.

Ginger Syrup

Ginger is a staple in many amazing cocktails, both with and without alcohol. It brings an earthy, zingy, semi-floral note to cocktails. This syrup is a bit of a hassle to make if you don't have a juicer, but very much worth the effort.

MAKES A LITTLE MORE THAN 1 CUP

- 2 cups unpeeled ginger, washed and roughly chopped
- 1 cup granulated sugar

Using a juicer, juice the ginger according to the manufacturer's instructions. Alternatively, in a blender or food processor, pulverize the ginger on high speed for about 45 seconds, then pour the liquid through a fine-mesh sieve, pressing out the juice from the solids. Discard the solids. Using either method, you should have about ½ cup ginger juice.

In a medium saucepan over medium heat, combine the ginger juice and sugar. Cook, stirring occasionally, until the sugar is dissolved, about 10 minutes. Remove the pan from the heat and let the syrup cool completely before using, at least 2 hours. Store in an airtight container in the refrigerator for up to 1 month or in the freezer for up to 4 months.

Pepper Syrup

I rely on black pepper quite a bit for nonalcoholic cocktails, as its prickly piquancy replicates the "heat" that ethanol brings. This syrup contains three different types of pepper in order to create a multidimensional flavor experience, but if you want to replace the white and Sichuan peppercorns with more plain black peppercorns, I will allow it.

MAKES ABOUT 1½ CUPS

- 1 tablespoon whole black peppercorns
- 1 teaspoon whole white peppercorns
- 1 teaspoon Sichuan peppercorns
- 1 cup granulated sugar
- 1 cup water

Place all the peppercorns in a small saucepan over medium heat. Cook, stirring, until toasted and fragrant, about 5 minutes. Stir in the sugar and water. Bring the mixture to a gentle boil, then immediately remove the pan from heat. Let cool to room temperature, about 30 minutes, and then transfer the mixture to a blender. Blend on high speed until all the peppercorns are pulverized, about 30 seconds, then strain through a fine-mesh sieve and discard any solids. Store in an airtight container in the refrigerator for up to 2 weeks or in the freezer for up to 1 month.

Polyberry Syrup

I love the idea of a broad-spectrum berry syrup to cram as much complexity as possible into the flavors of these cocktails. Ideally you should use berries when they're in season, but since we're cooking them with sugar, the resulting syrup will be flavorful no matter the time of year you make it. You can also use frozen berries in a pinch.

MAKES JUST UNDER 2 CUPS

- 2 cups granulated sugar
- ½ cup water
- ½ cup fresh blackberries
- ½ cup fresh raspberries
- ½ cup fresh blueberries
- ½ cup chopped fresh strawberries

In a medium pan, combine the sugar, water, and all the berries. Bring to a boil over medium heat, stirring occasionally. Cover the pan and reduce the heat to low. Let simmer until the berries are infused, about 10 minutes. Remove from the heat and let cool completely, about 45 minutes. Strain the mixture through a fine-mesh sieve and discard the solids (or save for another use, such as topping pancakes). Store in an airtight container in the refrigerator for up to 2 weeks or in the freezer for up to 1 month.

Turmeric Syrup

Similar to ginger, turmeric provides drinks with a warm spicy-earthy quality. Its flavor is enhanced here with black cardamom pods, which are the smoky cousin to the classic green varieties more commonly found in baking and drink recipes. If left undisturbed for a while, some of the turmeric in this syrup will settle, so be sure to shake well before using.

MAKES ABOUT 1½ CUPS

- ½ cup whole black cardamom pods
- 1 cup granulated sugar
- 1 cup water
- 1 tablespoon turmeric powder

Place the cardamom pods in a medium pan. Cook over medium heat until toasted and fragrant, about 5 minutes. Stir in the sugar, water, and turmeric. Increase the heat to medium-high, bring the mixture to a light boil, and immediately remove from the heat. Let cool completely before using, at least 1 hour. Store in an airtight container in the refrigerator for up to 2 weeks or in the freezer for up to 1 month.

Mint Syrup

When used judiciously, mint gives drinks a bright lift, adding a bit of high-toned complexity and a pleasant cooling sensation. You can use any variety of mint you like, just be sure the leaves are dried and not fresh—fresh leaves contain too much water and the resulting syrup will lack concentration of flavor.

MAKES ABOUT 1½ CUPS

1 cup water
½ cup dried mint leaves
1 cup granulated sugar

In a medium pan, bring the water to a boil over high heat. Stir in the mint, then remove the pan from the heat. Let steep for about 10 minutes.

Place the sugar in a large heatproof bowl, then strain the mint mixture through a fine-mesh sieve into the sugar. Discard the mint. Stir until the sugar is completely dissolved, about 5 minutes. Let cool completely before using, at least 1 hour. Store in an airtight container in the refrigerator for up to 2 weeks or in the freezer for up to 1 month.

Green Tea Concentrate

Cold brew tea is one of my go-to tricks when making nonalcoholic cocktails because you can create a concentrated and complex ingredient using just tea and water. Green tea provides an earthy and sweet dimension, and this concentrated infusion packs a strong flavor—a little goes a long way. You do not need to spring for fancy green tea—feel free to use whatever you have on hand—but do not use matcha.

MAKES ABOUT 1¼ CUPS

½ cup loose green tea
1½ cups water

In an airtight container, combine the tea and water. Place in the refrigerator to infuse for at least 48 hours. Before using, strain the mixture through a fine-mesh sieve. Discard the solids. Return the tea to the airtight container and store in the refrigerator for up to 2 weeks or in the freezer for up to 1 month.

Lapsang Concentrate

Smoky Scotch whiskies are a great element in many drink-makers' back bars; finding a nonalcoholic way to incorporate that flavor is a challenge. Lapsang Souchong tea is traditional black tea, but it's dried over a smoky fire, similar to how barley is smoked to give certain Scotch whiskies such as Laphroaig and Ardbeg their characteristic medicinal smokiness. For the purposes of this recipe, you can use any Lapsang Souchong you like.

MAKES ABOUT 1¼ CUPS

½ cup loose Lapsang Souchong tea
1½ cups water

In an airtight container, combine the tea and water. Place in the refrigerator to infuse for at least 48 hours. Before using, strain mixture through a fine-mesh sieve. Discard the solids. Store in the refrigerator for up to 2 weeks or in the freezer for up to 1 month.

Mugi Concentrate

"Mugicha" is the Japanese word for tea made from an infusion of roasted barley into water. It has a roasty, earthy quality and when served cold, is surprisingly refreshing. In cocktails it provides a rounded counterpoint to citrus and other high-toned ingredients. Mugicha is available online and should also be on the shelf at any Japanese grocery store or specialty grocery.

MAKES ABOUT 1½ CUPS

2 cups water
½ cup loose mugicha (Japanese roasted barley tea)

In a small pan, bring the water to a boil over high heat, then remove the pan from the heat. Add the tea, cover the pan, and let cool completely, at least 1 hour. Strain through a fine-mesh sieve. Discard the solids. Store in an airtight container in the refrigerator for up to 2 weeks or in the freezer for up to 1 month.

Red Hibiscus Concentrate

Hibiscus is the petals of the roselle flower and is used in food and drinks all over the world. I love the vibrant acidity, subtle tannins, and bone-dry lack of sweetness when I want a refreshing, simple drink, which is always. It's kind of like a more interesting version of cranberry juice. For cocktails, I use a more concentrated version than what I'd drink straight in order to supply those same characteristics without adding too much dilution to my cocktail. You can find dried red hibiscus flowers online or in many specialty grocers.

MAKES ABOUT 1½ CUPS

1 cup dried red hibiscus flowers
2 cups water

In an airtight container, combine the hibiscus flowers and water. Place in the refrigerator to infuse for at least 48 hours. Before using, strain the mixture through a fine-mesh sieve. Discard the solids. Store in an airtight container in the refrigerator for up to 2 weeks or in the freezer for up to 1 month.

White Hibiscus Concentrate

The less common white hibiscus brings the same acidity as its red counterpart without the tannins. The honeysuckle-and-jasmine complexity of this infusion is meant to be on par with a high-acid white wine or verjus. White hibiscus is not easy to find at a brick-and-mortar store, but you can easily source it online.

MAKES ABOUT 1½ CUPS

1 cup dried white hibiscus flowers
2 cups water

In an airtight container, combine the hibiscus flowers and water. Place in the refrigerator to infuse for at least 48 hours. Strain the mixture through a fine-mesh sieve. Discard the solids. Store in an airtight container in the refrigerator for up to 2 weeks or in the freezer for up to 1 month.

Super Whiskey

Alas, I sadly do not find the crop of nonalcoholic whiskies currently on the market to be all that inspiring. They do a pretty good job of supplying the grainy, barrel-aged flavor that traditional whiskies do, but taste-wise, they leave a bit to be desired. So I amplify them with roasted dandelion root and cacao nibs, which add a bit of complexity and bitterness to the base flavors in nonalcoholic whiskey. The resulting liquid will be a bit cloudy, but the trade-off is more than worth it.

MAKES ABOUT 2 CUPS

- **2 cups nonalcoholic whiskey**
- **½ cup roasted dandelion root**
- **½ cup raw cacao nibs**

In a medium pan, combine the nonalcoholic whiskey, dandelion root, and cacao nibs. Bring to a boil over high heat, then immediately remove the pan from the heat. Cover and let cool to room temperature, at least 4 hours.

Transfer the mixture to a blender and blend on high speed until all solids are pulverized, about 30 seconds. Strain through a fine-mesh sieve. Discard the solids. Store in an airtight container in the refrigerator for up to 1 month. Do not freeze.

Ultra Gin

I feel the same way about nonalcoholic gins as I do nonalcoholic whiskies: They're okay, but I'm looking for a lot more flavor. Here, I dial up the gin botanicals with my own blend of cardamom, coriander, and lavender. The resulting gin will be cloudy, but the difference will not be noticeable in most of the cocktails in this book.

MAKES ABOUT 2 CUPS

- **1 tablespoon whole cardamom pods**
- **1 teaspoon whole coriander seeds**
- **½ teaspoon culinary-grade dried lavender flowers**
- **2 cups nonalcoholic gin**

In a medium pan, combine the cardamom, coriander, and lavender. Cook, stirring, over medium heat until toasted and fragrant, about 5 minutes. Add the nonalcoholic gin and increase the heat to high and bring to a boil. Immediately remove the pan from the heat, cover, and let cool completely, at least 4 hours.

Transfer the mixture to a blender and blend on high speed until all of the solids are pulverized, about 30 seconds. Strain through a fine-mesh sieve. Discard the solids. Store in an airtight container in the refrigerator for up to 1 month. Do not freeze.

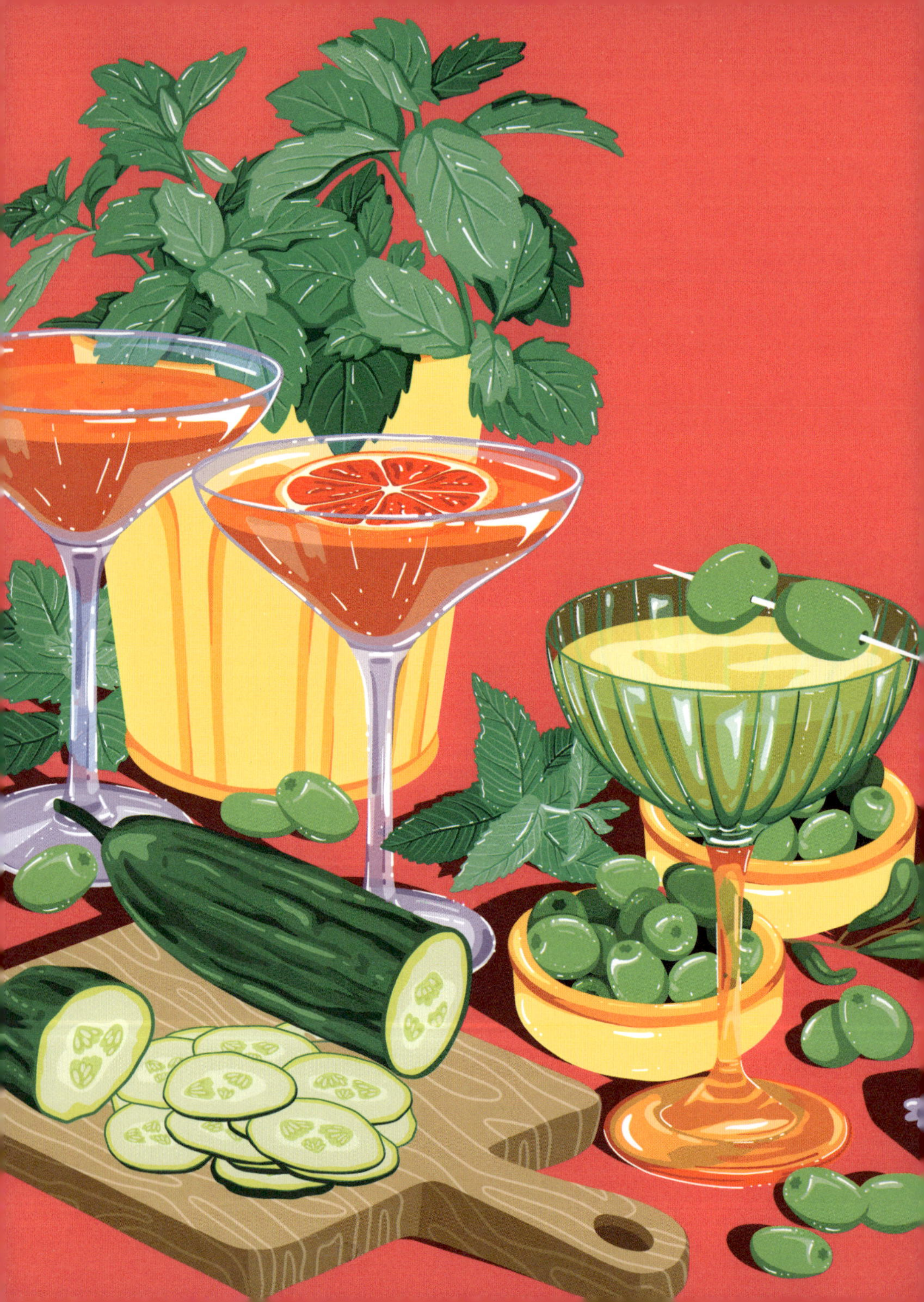

HERBAL

"Herbal" represents flavors that are subtly floral, grassy, vegetal, and, well . . . herbal. Classic cocktails such as the Corpse Reviver No. 2 and the Hugo Spritz are good examples of ethereally herbal cocktails. These drinks have the lightest flavor profile of all the drinks in this book; they are well enjoyed as aperitifs before a meal or make a perfect afternoon pick-me-up.

Garden Soother

MAKES 1 DRINK

●

When people complain about subpar nonalcoholic cocktails, I often hear them lament being served "something with pineapple" because for some reason it's a common choice when someone needs to mix up a nonalcoholic cocktail in a pinch. But I'm not afraid to use it here, where its honeyed, tropical notes pair well with the complex herbal notes in Aplós, a nonalcoholic spirit made with rosemary, gentian, and coriander, among other botanicals, that has a slightly absinthe-y quality. Additionally, pineapple shakes up with a nice foam, giving the texture that many nonalcoholic cocktails often lack. Hop water—a beer-like bitter drink made with hops and water (shocking, I know)—supplies some piney brightness as well as bubbles.

---

2 ounces Aplós Calme

1 ounce fresh pineapple juice

½ ounce fresh lime juice

2 ounces chilled hop water

Garnish: pineapple leaves

In a shaker, combine the Aplós, pineapple juice, and lime juice. Fill with ice and shake vigorously for 15 seconds. Strain into an old fashioned glass with one large ice cube or a few small ice cubes; top with hop water. Garnish with pineapple leaves and serve.

HERBAL | 47

Cucumber Collins

MAKES 1 DRINK

I'm going to come right out and say it: Cucumber is a hand fruit. Just like the apple, the cucumber comes packaged in its own edible wrapper and contains tons of hydration and flavor—and I would like for people to stop looking at me weird when I walk down the street happily munching on a green stick of goodness. If you're not brave enough to chow down on a whole cucumber in mixed company, fortunately you can juice one and combine it with a few additional ingredients to make this invigoratingly verdant Tom Collins riff that gives tons of green and herbal refreshment. I describe the flavor of this drink as like walking through an English garden during a misty morning.

---

4 ounces chilled lemon-lime soda, such as Sprite or 7UP

3 ounces fresh cucumber juice

1 ounce Ultra Gin (see page 43) or plain nonalcoholic gin

¾ ounce fresh lemon juice

2 dashes orange bitters or nonalcoholic orange bitters

Garnish: lemon wheel

Fill a tall glass with ice and add 2 ounces of the lemon-lime soda. In a shaker, combine the cucumber juice, gin, lemon juice, and orange bitters. Fill with ice and shake vigorously for 15 seconds. Strain into the prepared glass and top with the remaining 2 ounces soda. Garnish with the lemon wheel perched on the rim of the glass before serving.

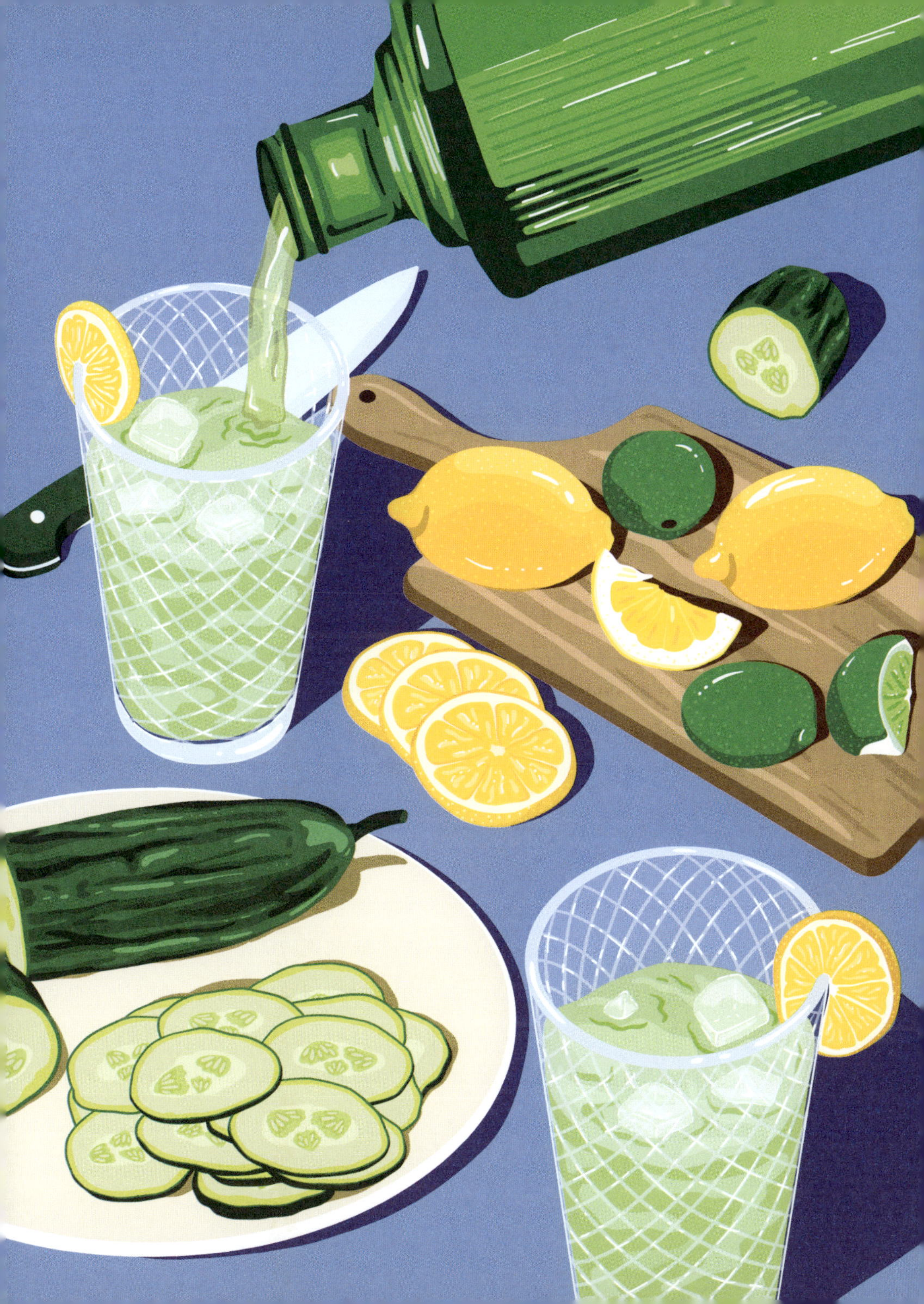

Lychee Hugo Spritz

MAKES 1 DRINK

This is a nonalcoholic and lychee-inflected version of the popular Hugo Spritz cocktail. Even though a nonalcoholic elderflower liqueur might seem identical to an elderflower syrup or cordial, the liqueur is a bit drier and contains additional botanicals that give it interest—so be sure you're using the liqueur, otherwise this drink will be a bit cloying. Combining sparkling wine and sparkling water might strike you as a bit redundant, but the water helps to lengthen the drink and gives the flavors in this glass room to breathe, making this an uber-refreshing summertime drink.

---

1 ounce chilled sparkling water

1 ounce nonalcoholic elderflower liqueur, such as Giffard

1 ounce liquid from a can of lychees

½ ounce fresh lime juice

2 ounces chilled nonalcoholic sparkling wine

Garnish: canned lychees

Fill a wine glass halfway with ice. In the glass, in this order, add the sparkling water, elderflower liqueur, lychee liquid, and lime juice, then top it off with the sparkling wine. Do not stir. Garnish by dropping as many lychees as you feel like into the drink, then serve.

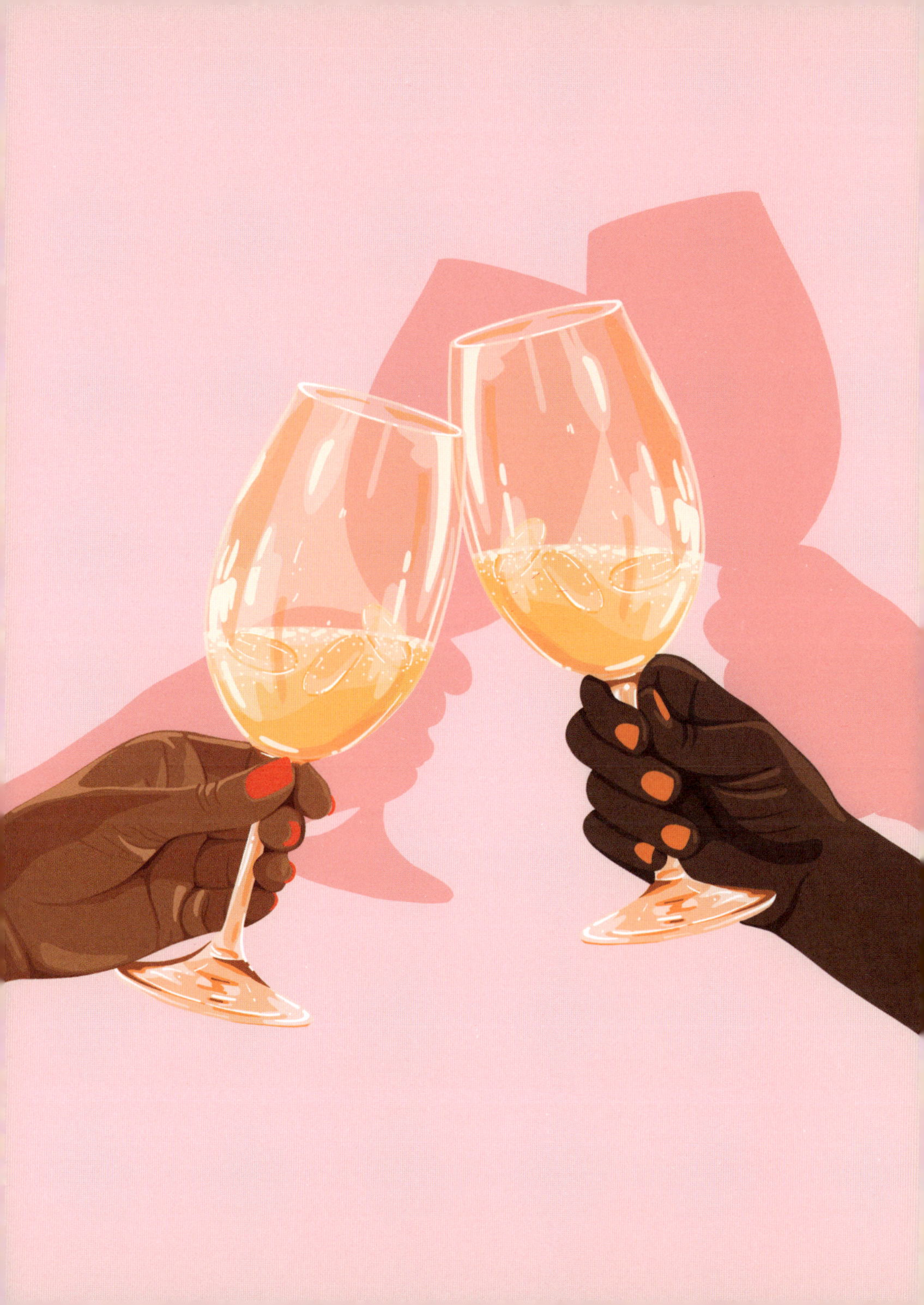

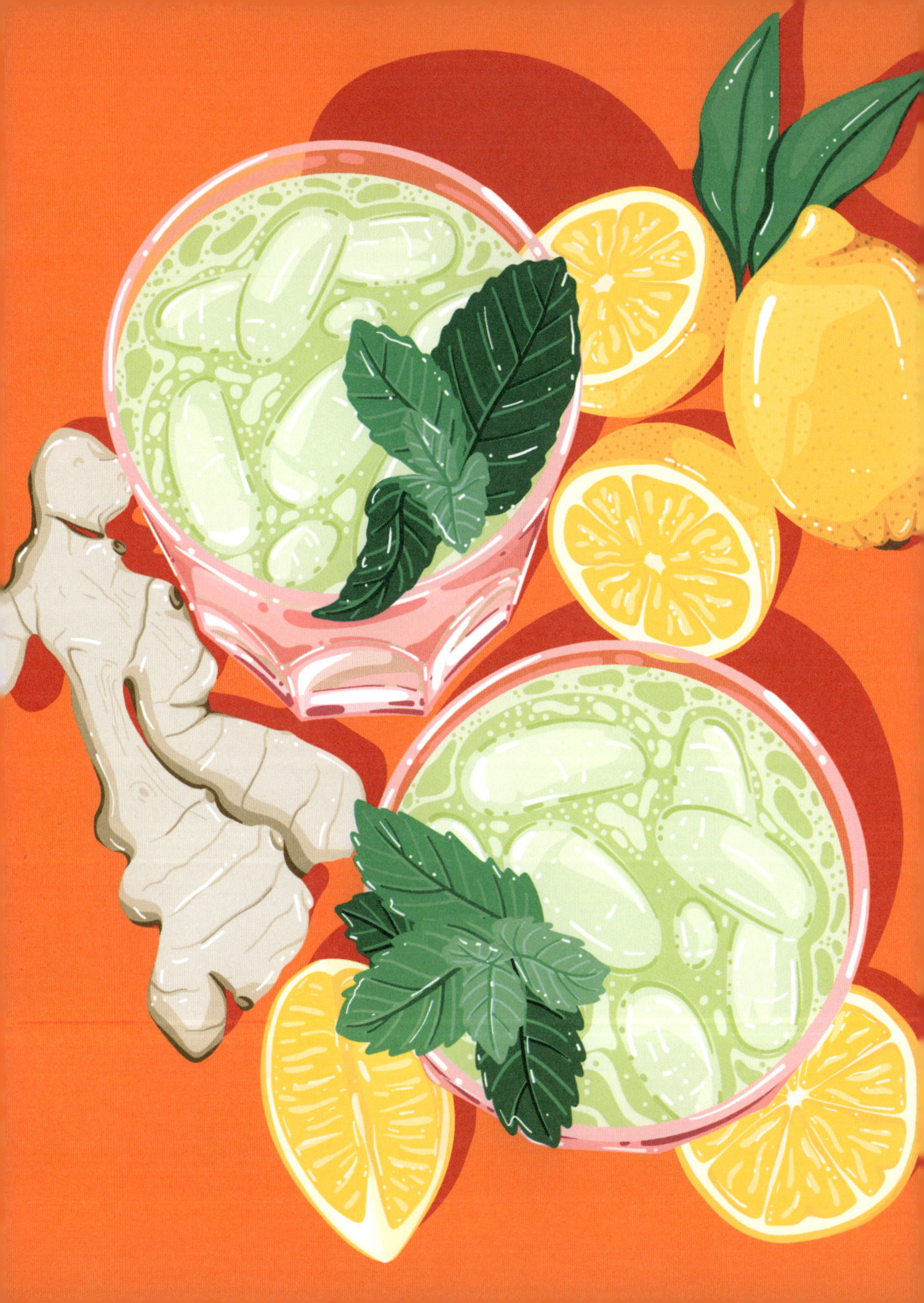

Moderate Mule

MAKES 1 DRINK

♦♦

A classic mule cocktail is a simple but mighty mixture of spirit, ginger, and lime—the most famous is probably the vodka-based Moscow Mule. This nonalcoholic version leverages augmented nonalcoholic whiskey to deliver a potent, spicy kick. If the idea of a supercharged whiskey substitute is not to your liking or you think it's too much work, I forgive you. Using off-the-shelf stuff will deliver a totally decent cocktail. Feel free to experiment with other nonalcoholic spirits here as well; the drink should work great with just about any option.

---

5 ounces chilled sparkling water

1½ ounces Super Whiskey (see page 43) or plain nonalcoholic whiskey

¾ ounce Mint Syrup (see page 40)

¾ ounce fresh lime juice

½ ounce Ginger Syrup (see page 38)

Garnish: fresh mint leaves

Fill a tall glass with ice and add 2 ounces of the sparkling water. In a shaker, combine the whiskey, mint syrup, lime juice, and ginger syrup. Shake without ice for 5 seconds, then pour into the prepared glass. Top with the remaining 3 ounces sparkling water and garnish with mint leaves before serving.

HERBAL | 53

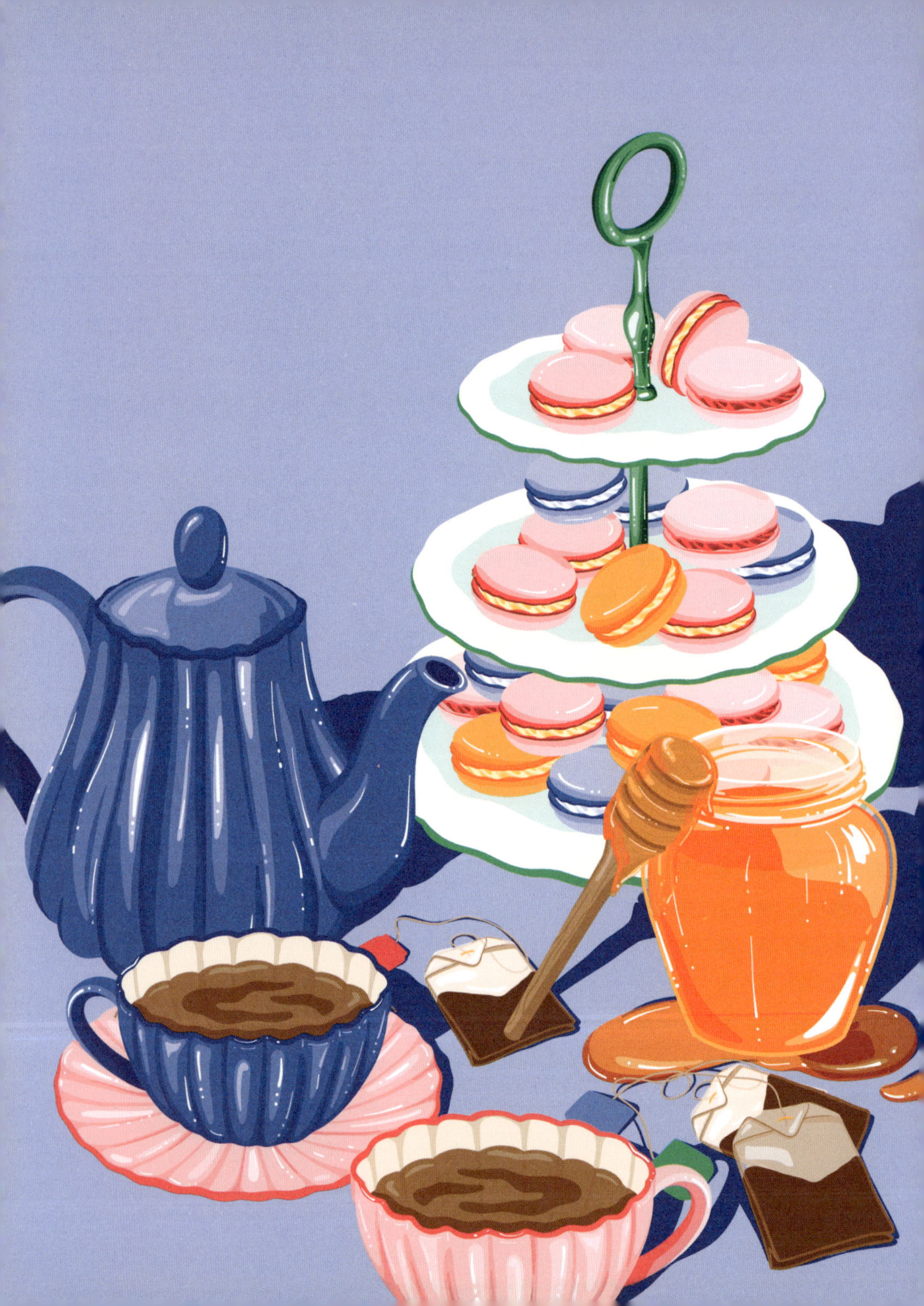

Chamomile-Saffron Toddy

MAKES 1 DRINK

While not obvious, heat is a great way to play with texture: Hot water is slightly less dense than cold or room temperature water, so higher heat encourages aromatics to vaporize more readily, making for a stronger-tasting drink. Here the earthy and mildly bitter notes from the chamomile tea are tempered by the sweetness from the saffron-infused honey syrup. Angostura bitters bring complex spicy notes of clove and cinnamon while offering an added hit of bitterness to dial up the complexity. The lemon juice adds a touch of vibrancy, making this an ideal sleepy-time sipper.

---

10 ounces boiling water

2 chamomile tea bags (or 1 tablespoon loose tea)

1¼ ounces Saffron Honey (see page 37)

½ ounce fresh lemon juice

4 dashes Angostura bitters or nonalcoholic bitters

In a heatproof mug, combine the boiling water and chamomile and let steep for 10 minutes. Remove and discard the chamomile.

Add the saffron honey, lemon juice, and bitters to the mug and stir briefly to combine before serving.

A Definitive Nonalcoholic Martini

MAKES 3 TO 4 DRINKS

I'm using the indefinite article here because I would never presume to tell anyone what "the" best martini is—it's a deeply personal drink that can be tweaked to suit a wide range of preferences. That said, when concocting a nonalcoholic version of this spirit-forward classic, I like to add a touch of spice and saltiness via hot sauce and olive brine. This recipe is an example of a "freezer martini," whereby all ingredients, including the dilution, can be premixed and chilled so all you have to do is pour when the time comes. But without alcohol, this thing will totally freeze, so it's best to consider it a "refrigerator martini."

1 cup (8 ounces) Ultra Gin (see page 43) or plain nonalcoholic gin

4 ounces water

4 ounces nonalcoholic dry vermouth

1 ounce olive brine

¼ teaspoon hot sauce

4 dashes orange bitters or nonalcoholic orange bitters

Garnish: olives

In an airtight container, combine the drink ingredients and chill in the refrigerator for at least 6 hours.

To serve, pour 4 to 5 ounces into a coupe and garnish with olives. Store any remaining martini in the refrigerator for up to 2 weeks. Do not freeze.

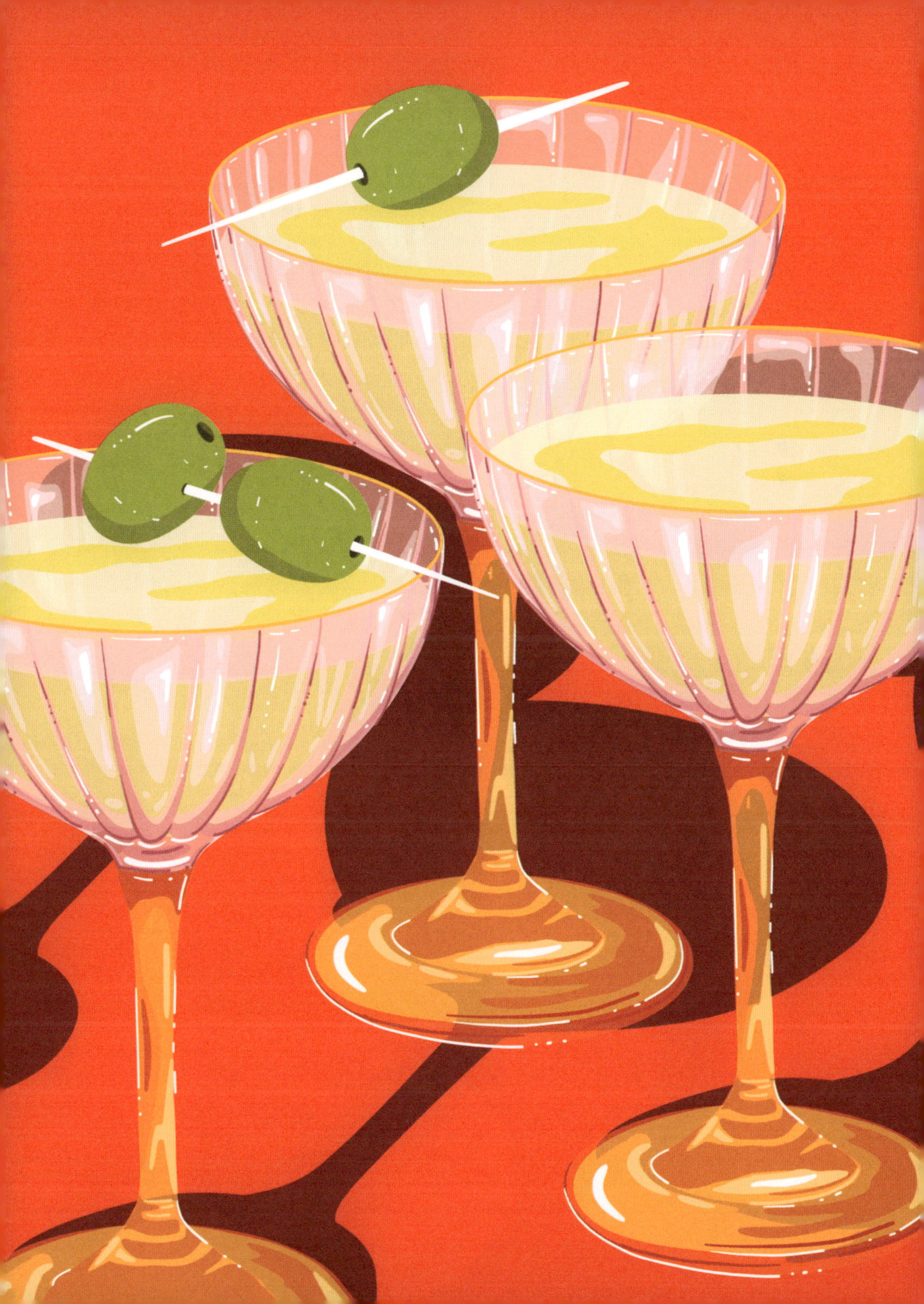

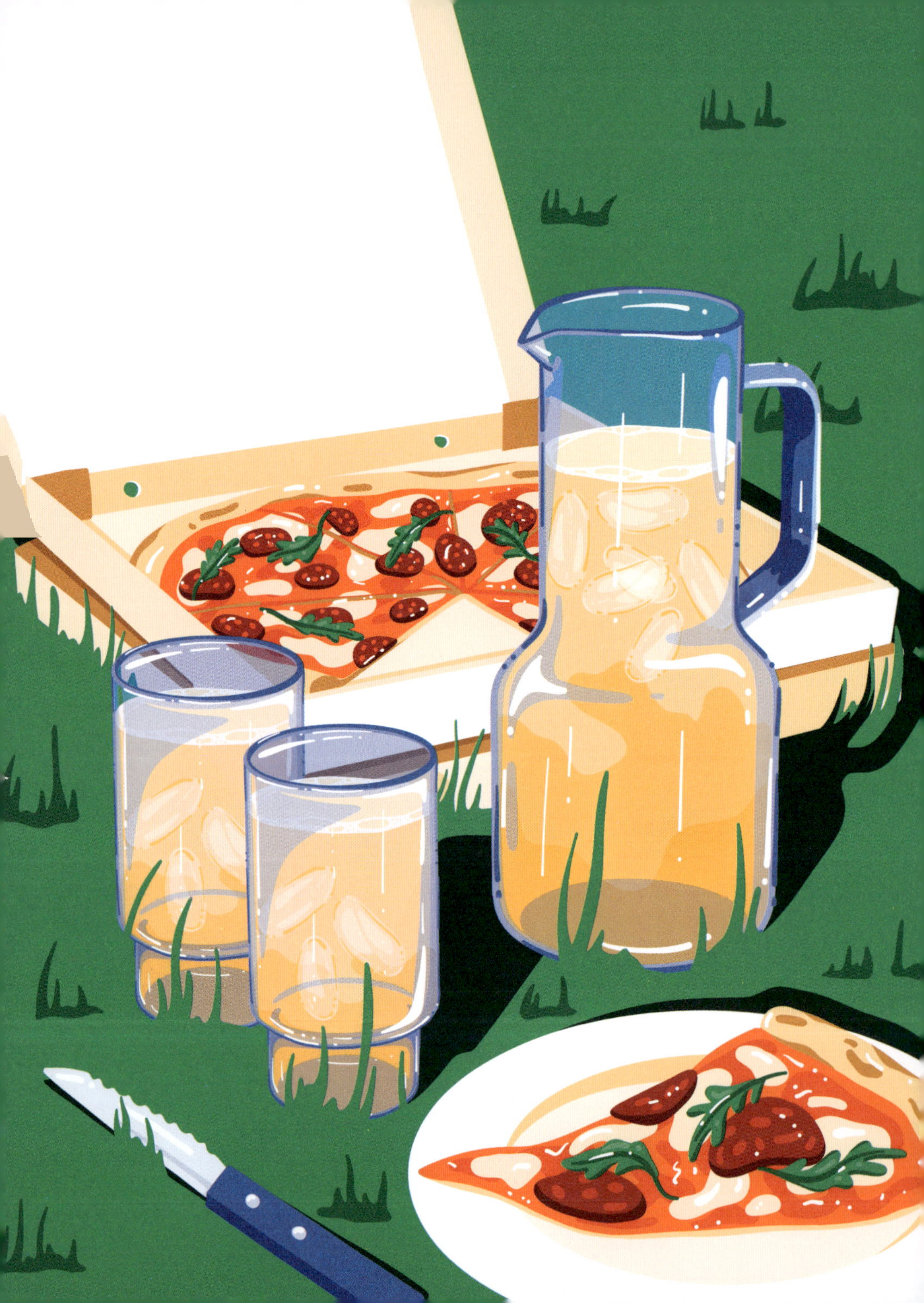

Vernal Equinox Punch

MAKES 7 TO 8 DRINKS

Nothing says springtime quite like a bowl—or pitcher, if you prefer—filled with a floral, citrusy punch. This drink feels like those last few days of winter when the idea of spring fills our hearts and glasses, but there is still an austerity in the air. Unless climate change renders seasons obsolete, in which case you can drink this whenever, wherever. Like the Lychee Hugo Spritz on page 50, the soda water acts as a spacer, allowing the lavender and elderflower space to blossom. Grapefruit and yuzu supply acidity and nuanced aromatics while you wait for warmer weather. When sourcing lavender, make sure it's culinary grade; the kind used for crafting is too perfumed.

LAVENDER INFUSION

½ tablespoon culinary-grade dried lavender flowers

2½ cups water

PUNCH

1 cup chilled nonalcoholic sparkling wine

1 cup chilled sparkling water

4 ounces Ultra Gin (see page 43) or plain nonalcoholic gin

4 ounces nonalcoholic elderflower liqueur, such as Giffard

2 ounces fresh grapefruit juice

1 ounce yuzu juice

Make the lavender infusion. In a small pot, combine the lavender flowers and water. Place over high heat and bring to a rolling boil for 30 seconds, then remove from the heat. Cover the pot and let the lavender steep for about 5 minutes. Remove and discard the lavender. Let the liquid cool slightly, then transfer it to an airtight container and chill in the refrigerator for at least 4 hours or up to a week.

Make the punch. Fill a large bowl with 6 to 8 large ice cubes or about 3 cups regular ice. Add the lavender infusion, sparkling wine, sparkling water, gin, elderflower liqueur, grapefruit juice, and yuzu juice. Stir to combine. Ladle into whatever glassware you like and serve.

Honeysuckle 75

MAKES 1 DRINK

◆

The French 75 is one of my all-time favorite cocktails and, in fact, the first drink I ever put on the menu at PDT was an apple-y riff on the classic. While this version does not contain any actual honeysuckle, the combination of white hibiscus and elderflower gives rise to an emergent honeysuckle-like flavor that I love to drink when I'm in the mood for something elegant, complex, and enlivening.

---

2 ounces White Hibiscus Concentrate (see page 42)

½ ounce nonalcoholic elderflower liqueur, such as Giffard

½ ounce Lemon Syrup (see page 37)

½ ounce fresh lemon juice

2 ounces chilled nonalcholic sparkling wine

Garnish: thin lemon wheel

In a shaker, combine the white hibiscus concentrate, elderflower liqueur, lemon syrup, and lemon juice. Fill with ice and shake vigorously for 15 seconds. Strain into a large coupe, top with the sparkling wine, and garnish with the lemon wheel floated on the surface of the drink before serving.

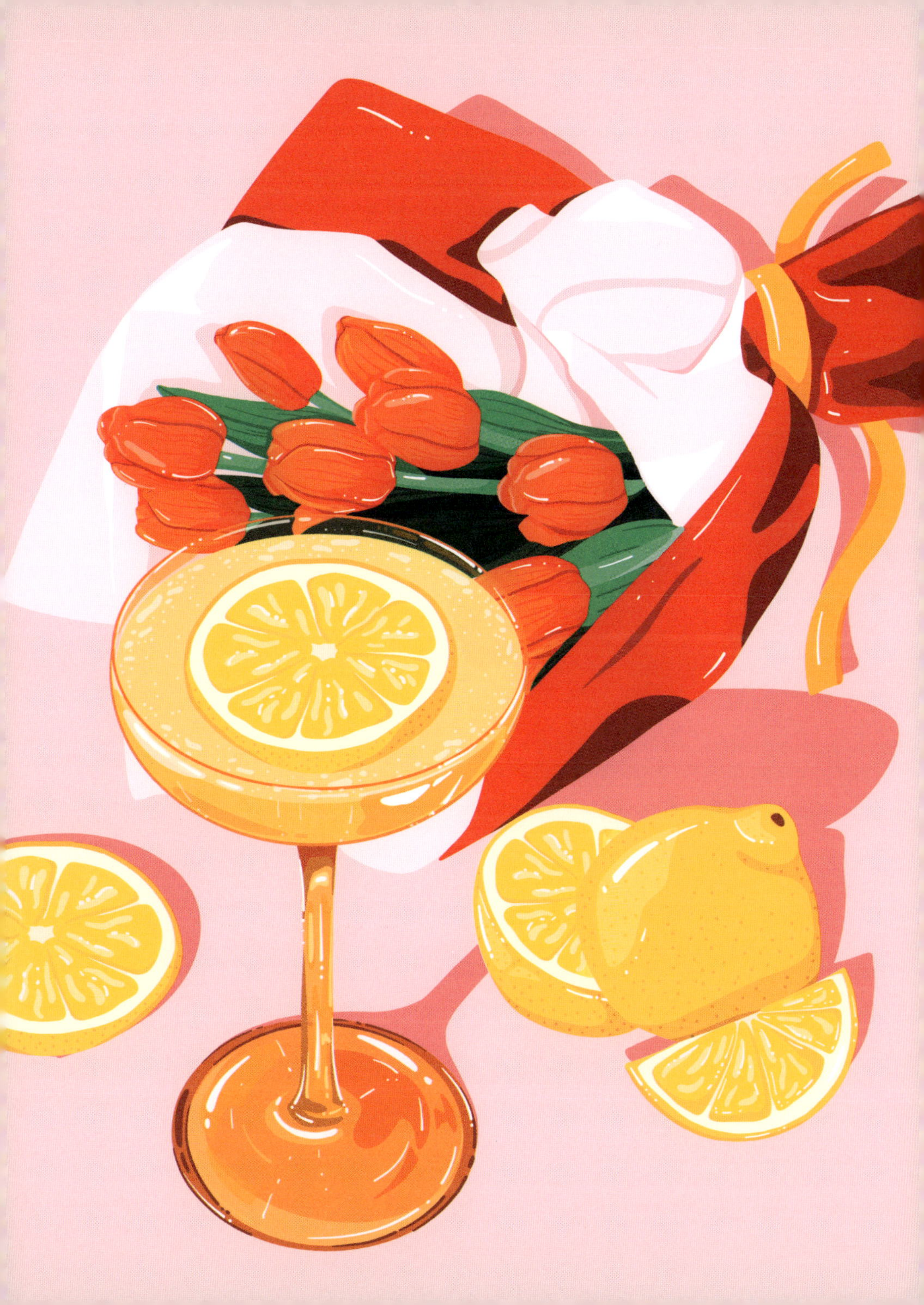

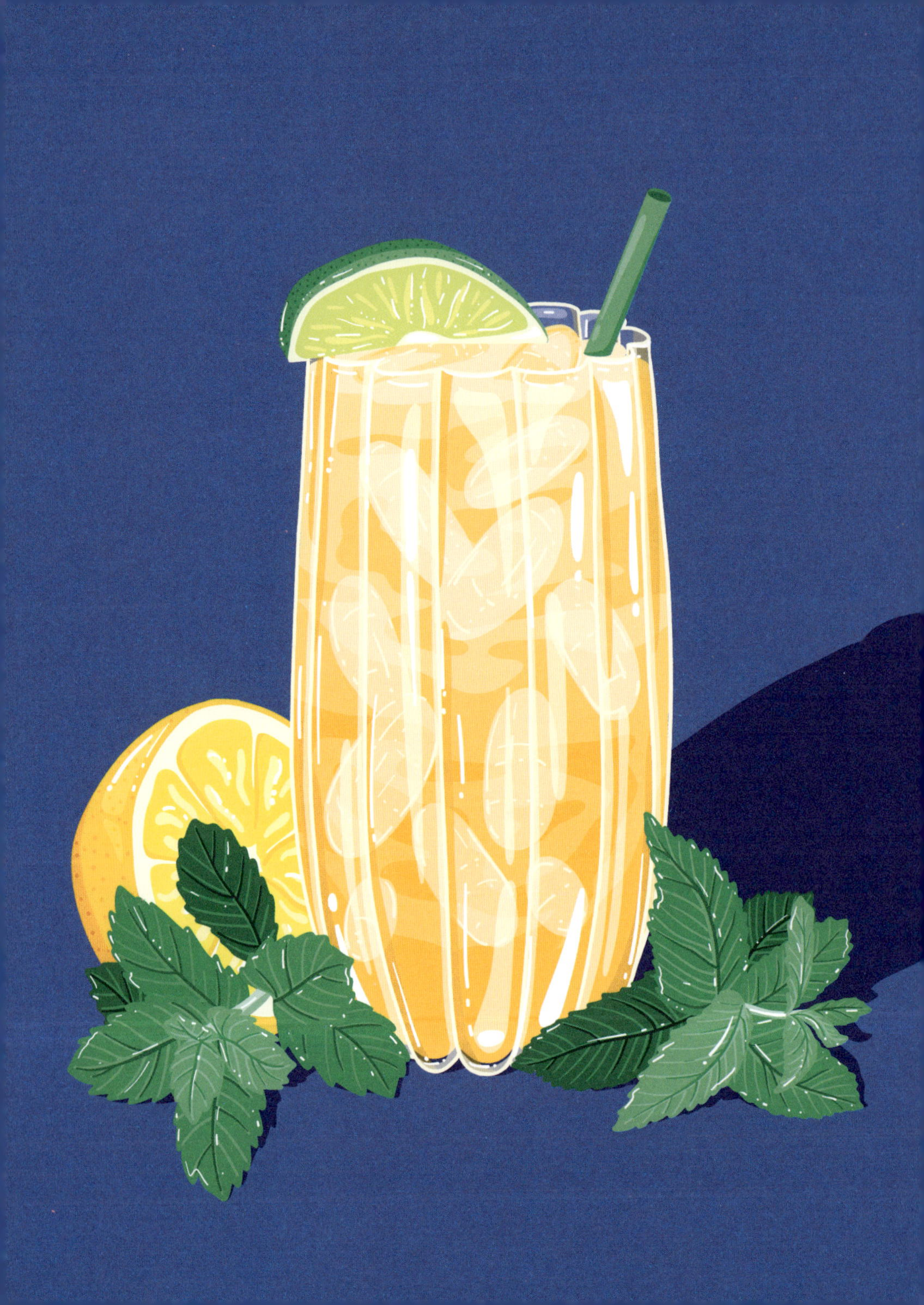

Green Lightning

MAKES 1 DRINK

◆

4 ounces chilled lemon-lime soda, such as Sprite or 7UP

3 ounces Green Tea Concentrate (see page 40)

1 ounce Mint Syrup (see page 40)

1 ounce fresh lime juice

Garnish: lime wedge

This drink is zingy, bright, and refreshing . . . kind of like what I would imagine a bolt of lightning would feel like if it didn't risk killing you. The green tea acts as an anchor with its earthy, grassy notes while the acidity from the soda and lime juice prickles the palate. For the acid junkies among us (me!), the lime wedge lets you ramp up the acidity even more while adding aromatics from the peel. The mint syrup provides a cooling sensation—something sorely needed after a lightning strike.

Fill a tall glass with ice and add 2 ounces of the lemon-lime soda. Add the green tea concentrate, mint syrup, and lime juice, then top with the remaining 2 ounces soda. Stir gently to combine. Garnish with a lime wedge.

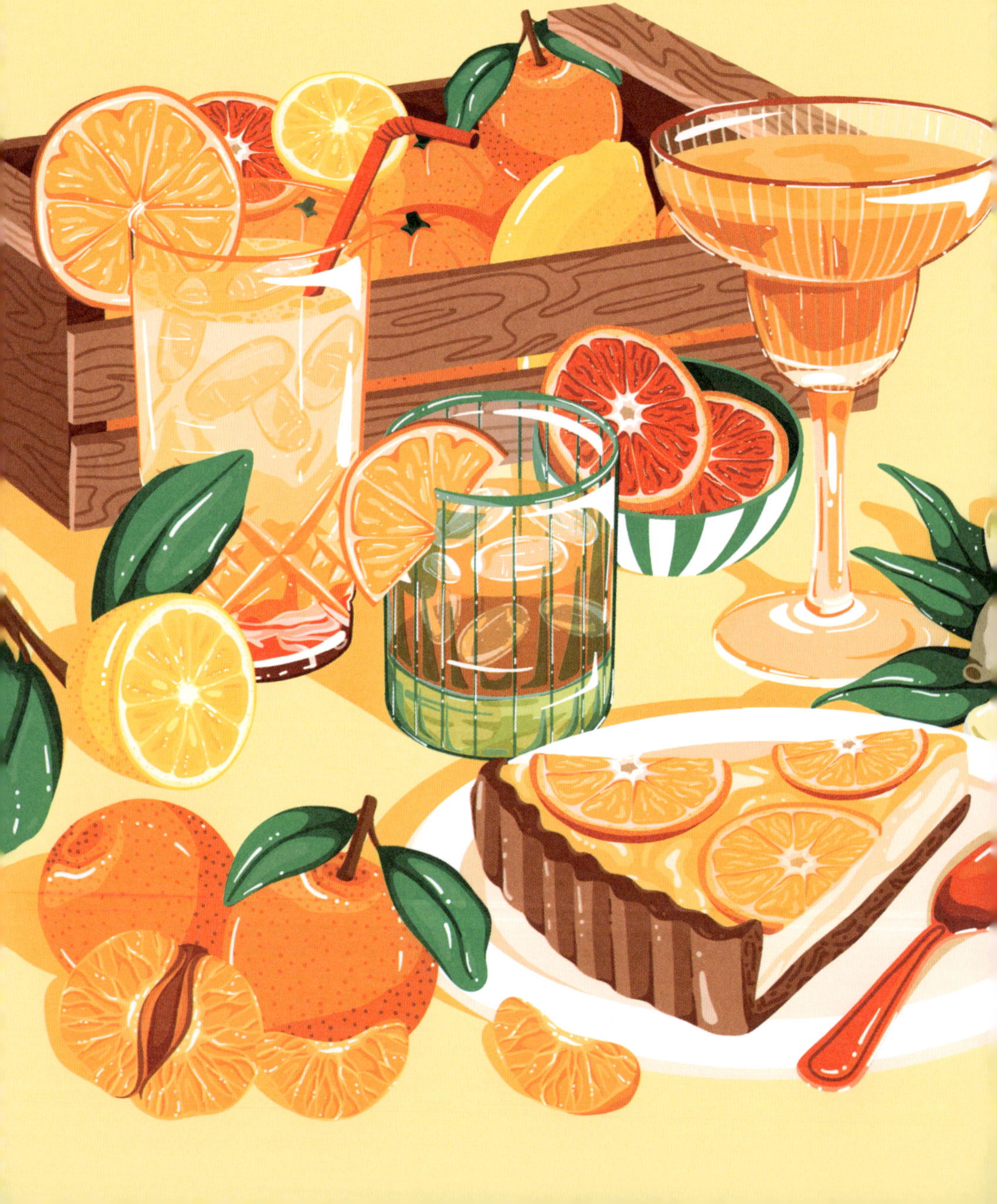

TART

Acidity is a cornerstone of many great cocktails: The spark of vibrancy helps to balance out a drink's sweetness and wake up our senses. This flavor is all the more essential in nonalcoholic cocktails, where you want to include as much zing as possible to excite the palate and help replicate some of the texture that alcohol provides. The margarita, the Sidecar, and the Tom Collins are all classic examples of drinks that deliver it in spades. Acidity is most frequenty added to cocktails by way of citrus juices, so the flavor of lemon often goes hand in hand with the sensation of acid on the palate. The drinks in this chapter make wonderful palate cleansers, deriving their citrus notes from conventional fruits like lemons and limes but also from less common fruits like yuzu and tangerines as well as less common acids, such as those found in vinegar and kombucha.

Deep Purple

MAKES 1 DRINK

I originally was going to call this recipe "Purple Drink," but that didn't seem appropriate for a few reasons. Name aside, the combination of vibrant red Sanbittèr soda and a few drops of blue food coloring render this drink a moody, opaque purple. Sanbittèr is an Italian soda that comes in cute little bottles—it's basically a mixture of nonalcoholic Campari and soda. Here, its intensity is tempered a bit by a healthy pour of sparkling water while the grapefruit juice provides acidity and bitterness.

---

5 ounces chilled sparkling water

1 (100mL) bottle Sanbittèr

2 ounces fresh grapefruit juice

½ ounce Orange Syrup (see page 37)

2 drops blue food coloring

In a tall glass filled with ice, combine the drink ingredients and stir gently to combine. Serve.

TART | 67

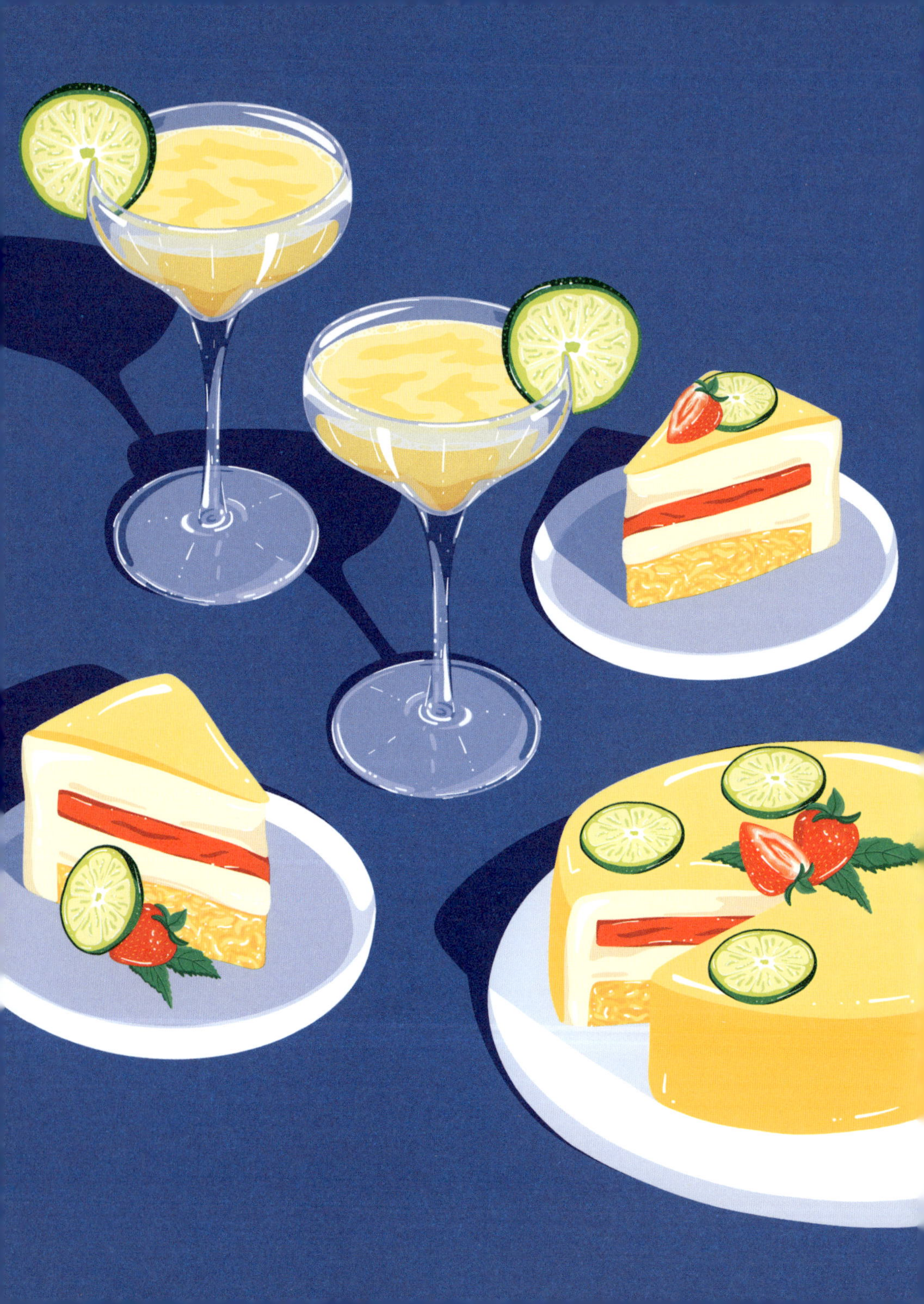

Verjus Daiquiri

MAKES 1 DRINK

The daiquiri is known for being a simple drink that showcases the brilliant combination of rum and lime juice. This nonalcoholic variation adds a few elements to this pairing with the addition of orange marmalade and verjus. The marmalade also adds a bit of texture thanks to the pectin that gives it its jelly-like consistency. Using lime juice *and* lime syrup might strike you as redundant, but the bitterness from the peels helps to make this drink taste like a cocktail as opposed to a glass of juice. When used judiciously, rum extract can give a cocktail the right amount of "rumminess" while taking up a lot less space in your house than a whole bottle of nonalcoholic rum. It does contain alcohol, but like bitters, the small amount you're adding to the drink will not raise the ABV significantly.

1½ ounces verjus

¾ ounce Lime Syrup (see page 37)

½ ounce fresh lime juice

1 tablespoon orange marmalade

¼ teaspoon rum extract

Garnish: lime wheel

In a shaker, combine the drink ingredients. Fill with ice and shake vigorously for 15 seconds. Strain into a coupe and garnish with the lime wheel perched on the rim before serving.

Basil Smash

MAKES 1 DRINK

◆

A culinary workhorse, fresh basil also makes fantastic drinks. I love how the herb's complex licorice-clove aromatics are delivered alongside a subtle savory note. The lime syrup here gives a nice bitter oomph, thanks to the fact that lime peels are probably the most bitter among the most common citruses. The term for when you pour the entire contents of the shaker into the glass is "dirty dumping," which I think is hilarious. The technique gives the drink a feral, messy vibe and the rough chunks of ice make for a seriously refreshing drinking experience—here especially.

---

1 ounce Ultra Gin (see page 43) or plain nonalcoholic gin

1 ounce verjus

¾ ounce Lime Syrup (see page 37)

5 fresh basil leaves

In a shaker, combine the drink ingredients. Fill with ice and shake vigorously for 15 seconds. Pour the entire contents of the shaker into an old fashioned glass and serve.

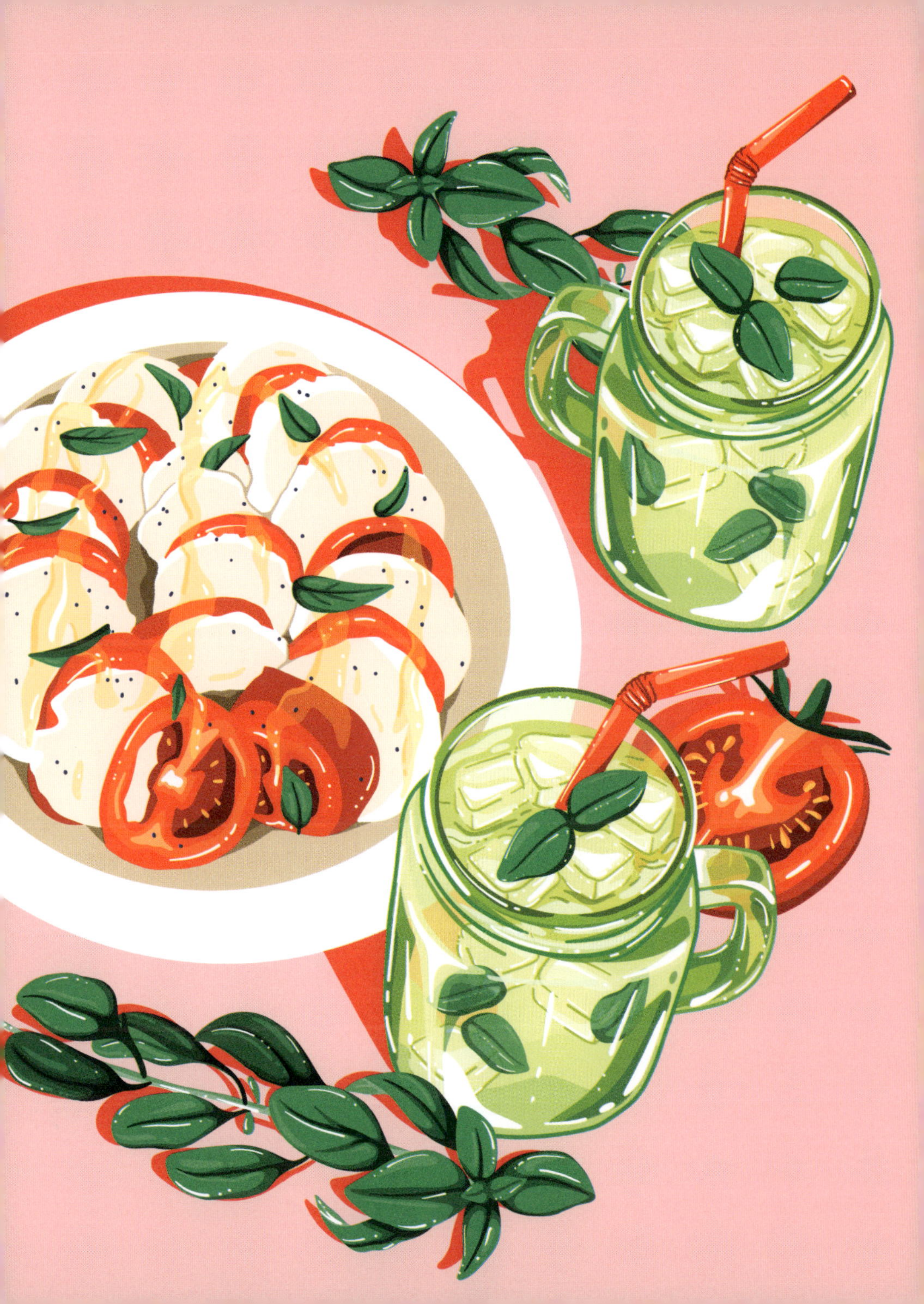

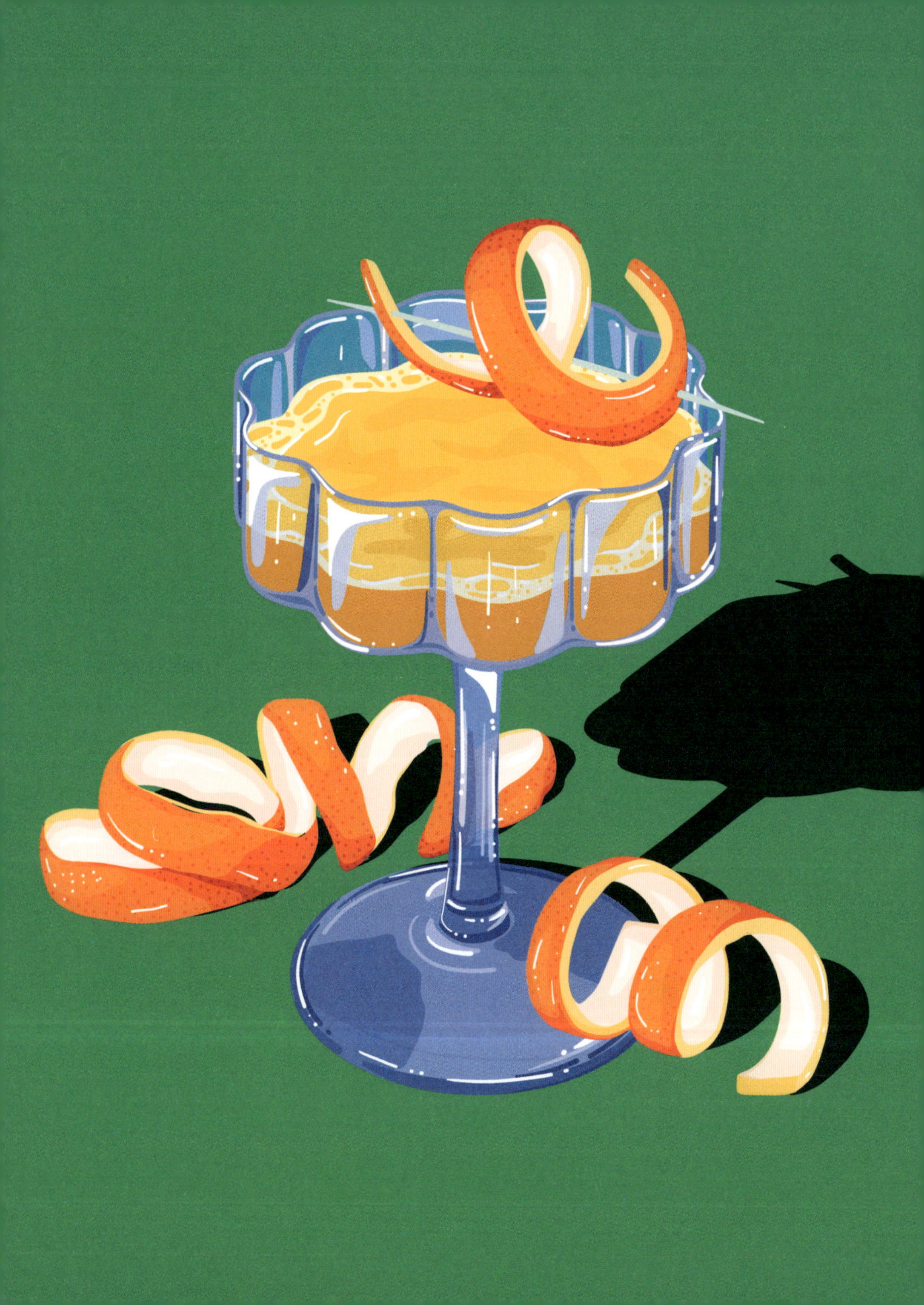

Honey Sidecar

MAKES 1 DRINK

◆

Okay, I'll admit this drink really bears no resemblance to the classic combination of brandy, orange liqueur, and lemon juice known as the Sidecar. But the complexity of the saffron honey infuses this drink with some depth that's reminiscent of the original. It also helps that the classic Sidecar is a very citrus-forward drink, just like this one. The lemon juice and orange syrup risk pushing this drink into citrus overload territory— but what's life without a little danger?

---

1 ounce chilled sparkling water

1 ounce fresh pineapple juice

¾ ounce fresh lemon juice

½ ounce Saffron Honey (see page 37)

½ ounce Orange Syrup (see page 37)

Garnish: orange peel

In a shaker, combine the drink ingredients. Fill with ice and shake vigorously for 15 seconds. Strain into a coupe. Express the orange peel over the drink, then perch it on the rim and serve.

Amoxicillin

MAKES 1 DRINK

♦♦

Bartender Sam Ross is responsible for some of the most iconic drinks of the twenty-first century. His Penicillin, a mixing of two kinds of Scotch plus honey, lemon, and ginger, feels like it's been around for centuries since the ingredients are so ubiquitous and the combination of honey and ginger is so iconic. To replicate the smoke found in many Scotch whiskies, we're using the Lapsang concentrate coupled with augmented nonalcoholic whiskey to supply some bitter, grainy notes. As always, you can use unaugmented nonalcoholic whiskey and I won't be offended, but I will be a little sad.

1½ ounces Lapsang Concentrate (see page 41)

1 ounce Super Whiskey (see page 43) or plain nonalcoholic whiskey

¾ ounce Ginger Syrup (see page 38)

¾ ounce Saffron Honey (see page 37)

¾ ounce fresh lemon juice

Garnish: candied ginger

In a shaker, combine the drink ingredients. Fill with ice and shake vigorously for 15 seconds. Strain into an old fashioned glass filled with one large ice cube or a few small ice cubes. Garnish with the candied ginger on a pick and serve.

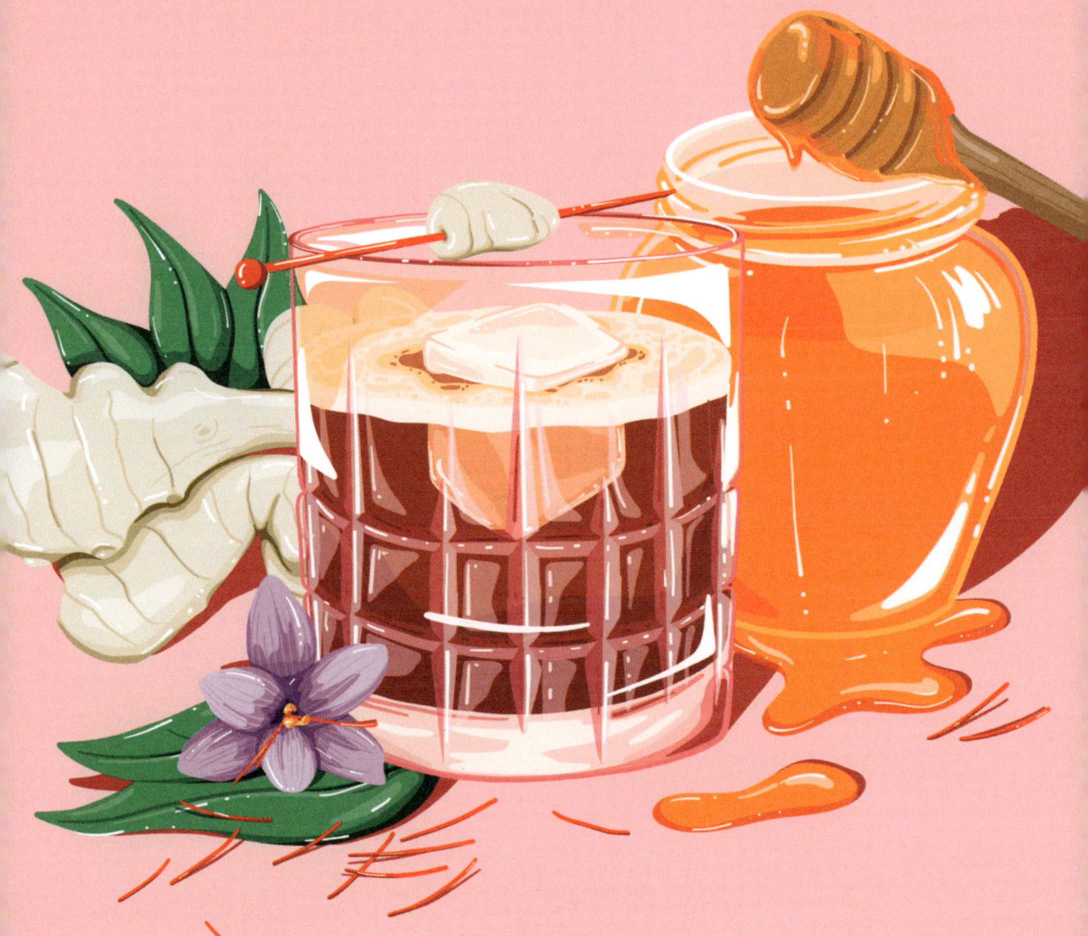

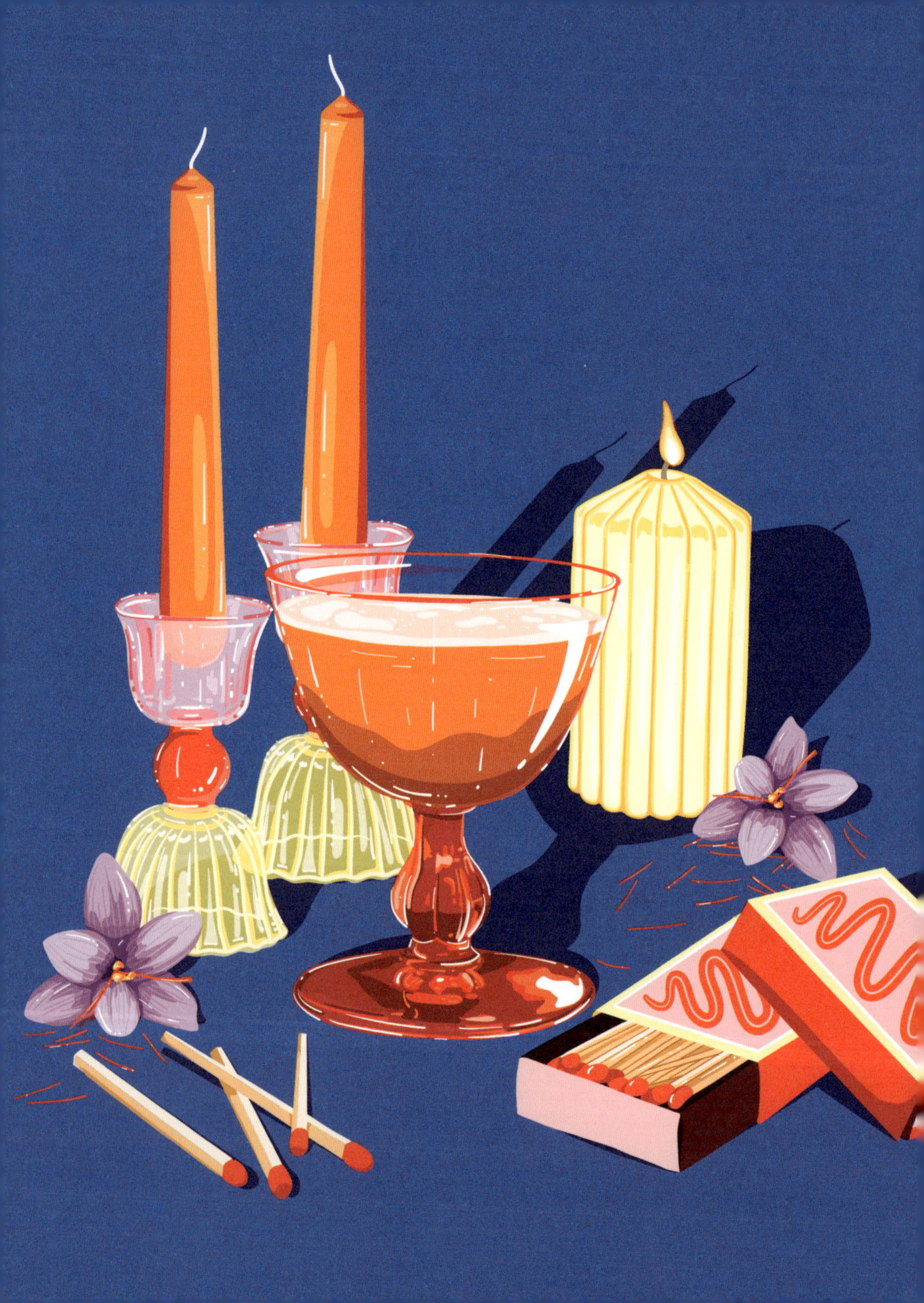

Golden Gimlet

MAKES 1 DRINK

♦♦

If you think this drink is named after Kylie Minogue's slightly underrated 2018 album *Golden*, you are right—and also probably gay. The cover art features a seated Minogue bathed in supple gold-yellow-red lighting, and it's the first thing that came to mind when I poured this drink for the first time. The turmeric syrup is an earthy counterpart to the bright notes from the orange syrup and lemon juice. And in case you were wondering . . . yes, I'm gay.

1½ ounces Super Whiskey (see page 43) or plain nonalcoholic whiskey

1 ounce fresh lemon juice

½ ounce Turmeric Syrup (see page 39)

½ ounce Orange Syrup (see page 37)

½ ounce Saffron Honey (see page 37)

In a shaker, combine the drink ingredients. Fill with ice and shake vigorously for 15 seconds. Strain into a coupe and serve.

TART | 77

Corpse Reviver Reviver

MAKES 1 DRINK

The classic Corpse Reviver No. 2 is a lovely concoction of gin, aperitif wine, orange liqueur, and lemon juice accented with a rinse of absinthe. (There is also a Corpse Reviver No. 1, but we don't talk about him.) Like the classic, this cocktail features subtle herbal absinthe-y notes thanks to the Aplós and the nonalcoholic gin, plus big hits of acidity and fruitiness thanks to the citrus and nonalcoholic white wine. When you're in need of something vibrant and interesting to bring you back to life, drink two and call me in the morning.

1½ ounces nonalcoholic gin

1½ ounces Aplós Calme

1 ounce nonalcoholic white wine

½ ounce Orange Syrup (see page 37)

½ ounce fresh lemon juice

In a shaker, combine the drink ingredients. Fill with ice and shake vigorously for 15 seconds. Strain into a large coupe and serve.

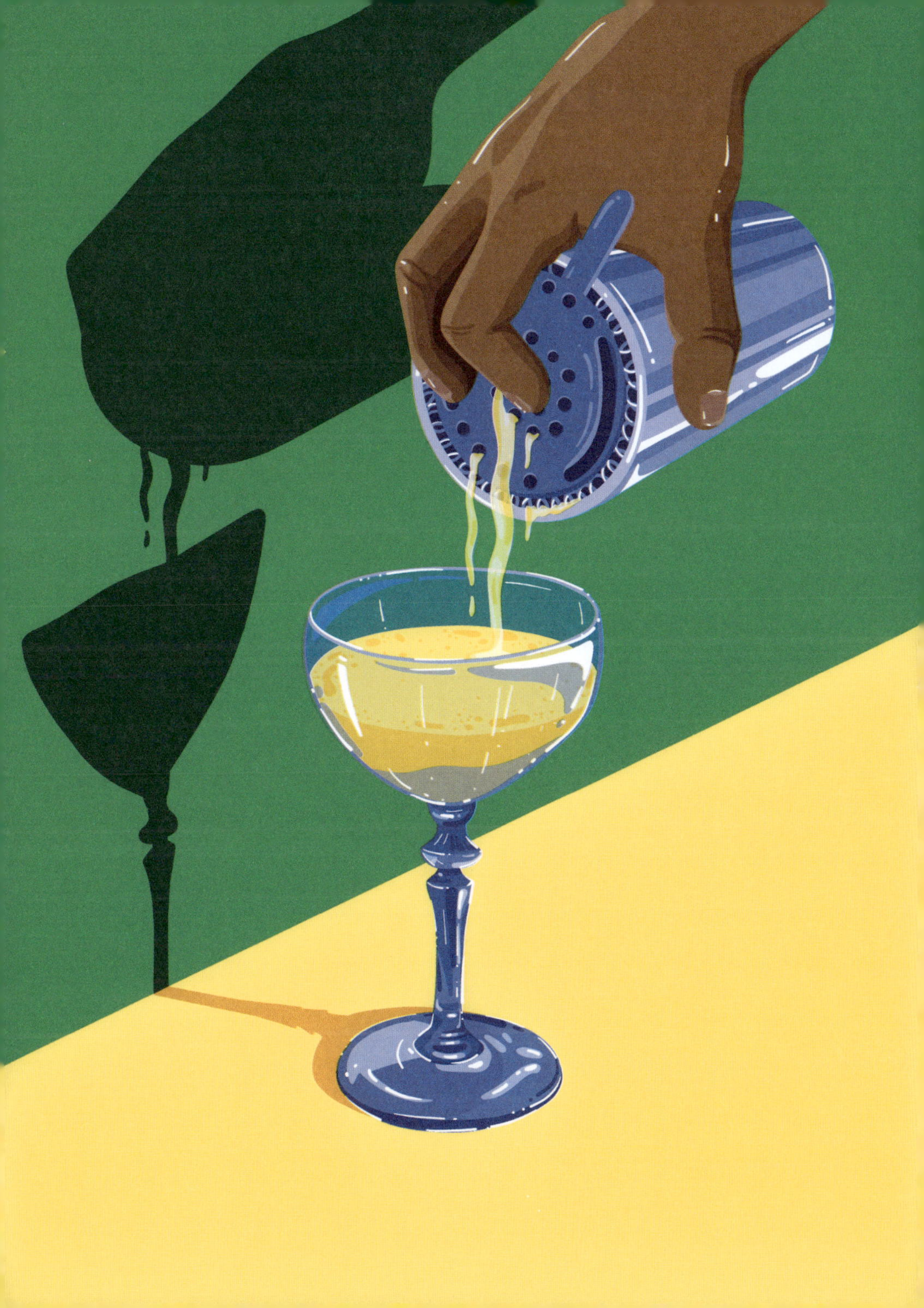

Fermented Passion

MAKES 1 DRINK

●

3 ounces nonalcoholic sweet vermouth

6 ounces passion fruit–tangerine kombucha, such as Health-Ade (see Note)

Garnish: orange half wheel

NOTE: While kombucha is generally considered nonalcoholic, it does contain trace amounts of alcohol, up to 0.5% ABV.

Fermentation is one of humanity's greatest allies: It's responsible for such delights as cheese, pickles, and all manner of alcoholic beverages. Fortunately for those among us who are skipping the alcohol, we can use a nonalcoholic fermented product like kombucha to satisfy our cravings for a deliciously complex drink. This semi-tropical drink is tart, mildly bitter, and far more interesting than you might think given that it's only two ingredients.

In a tall glass filled with ice, pour in the vermouth followed by the kombucha. Garnish with the orange half wheel before serving.

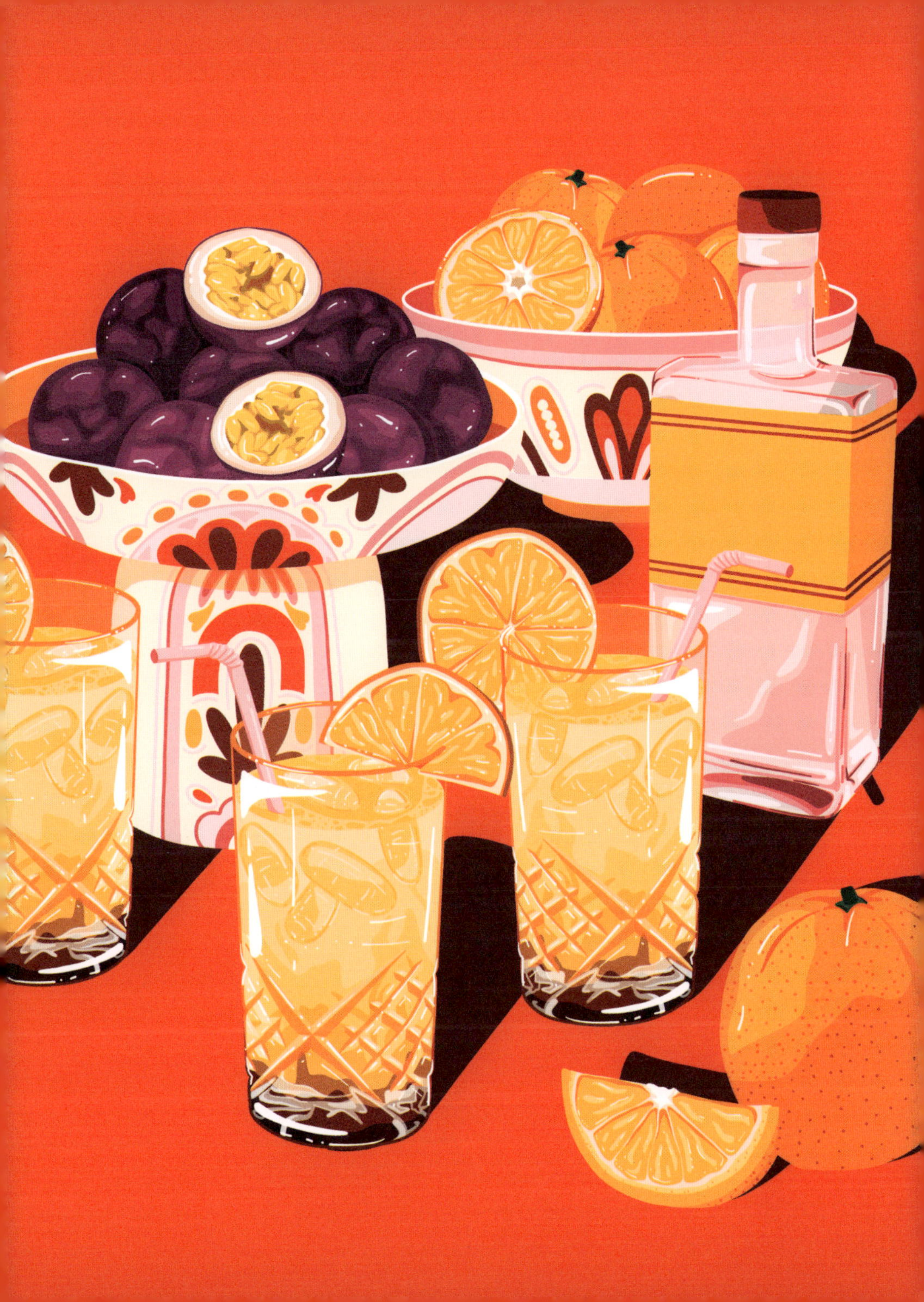

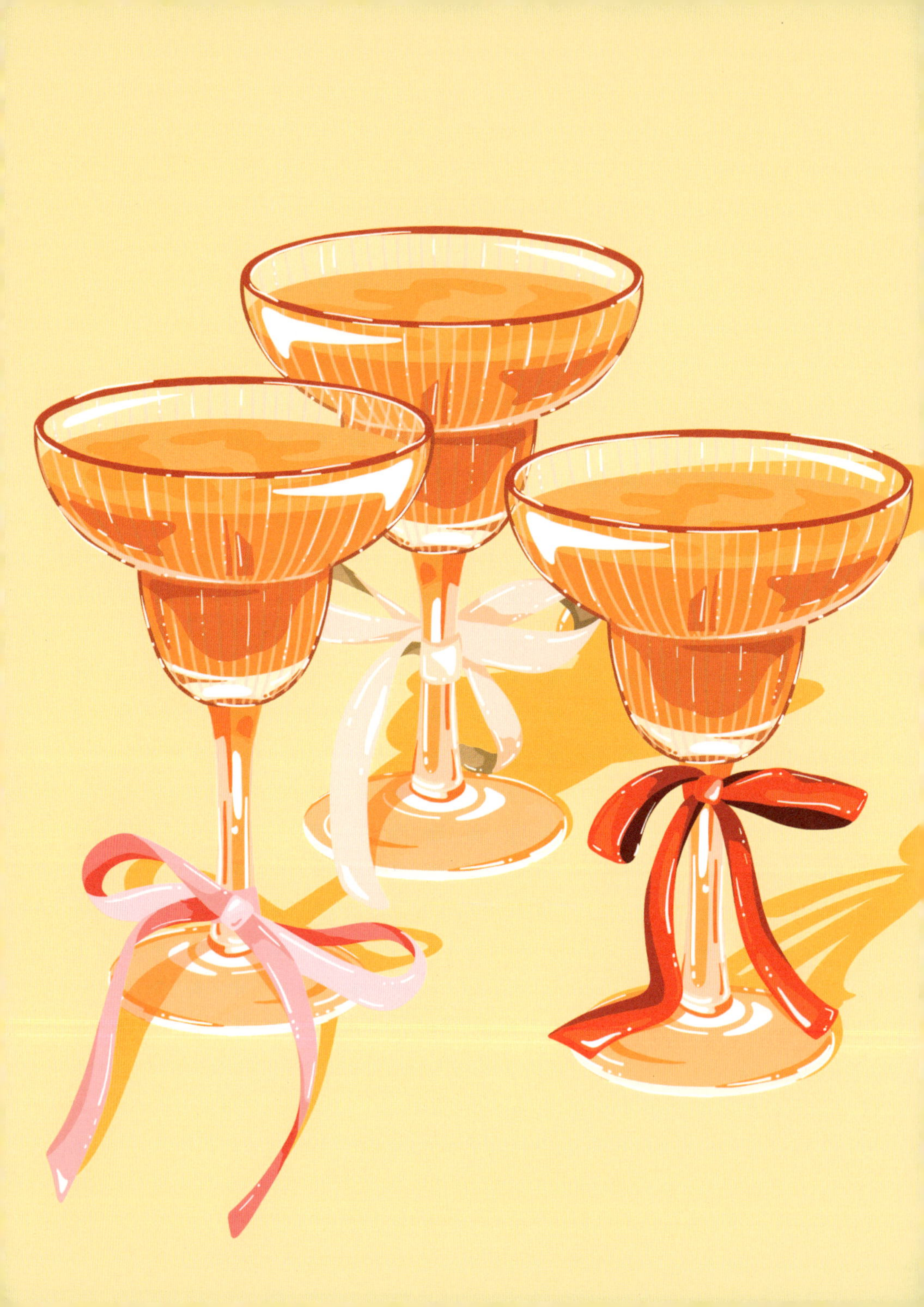

Senchu-Hi

MAKES 1 DRINK

◆

Chu-Hi is a canned Japanese alcoholic beverage that's a carbonated mixture of shochu and some kind of fruit like lemon or lychee. That name is an abbreviation for "shochu highball," and here we achieve the same vibe by mixing green tea and hop water. The tea gives an earthy grounding while the hop water lends piney top notes. The drink is named after sencha, a Japanese variety of green tea, but any type of green tea will do. Lemon juice and grapefruit syrup are the final pieces in the puzzle that make this drink bright and refreshing. Now, who do I talk to about getting this thing into a can?

---

3 ounces Green Tea Concentrate (see page 40)

¾ ounce fresh lemon juice

½ ounce Grapefruit Syrup (see page 37)

2 ounces chilled hop water

In a shaker, combine the green tea concentrate, lemon juice, and grapefruit syrup. Fill with ice and shake vigorously for 15 seconds. Strain into a large coupe, add the hop water, and serve.

Arctic Cooler

MAKES ABOUT 3 DRINKS

♦♦

I love blue drinks and I also love Gatorade, so, obviously, my favorite type of Gatorade is blue. There are a few different blue Gatorade varieties, including some that feature a vague berry flavor. I've done my best to replicate the experience of drinking this azure sports drink by using some slightly more "sophisticated" ingredients like white hibiscus and a syrup made from fresh berries. But, because I think sophistication is overrated, blue food coloring gives this shareable drink an authentic silliness we all need.

---

2 cups chilled water

2 ounces White Hibiscus Concentrate (see page 42)

2 ounces Lemon Syrup (see page 37)

2 ounces fresh lime juice

2 ounces Polyberry Syrup (see page 39)

2 drops blue food coloring

Pinch sea salt

Garnish: orange wedges

In an airtight container, combine the drink ingredients and stir. Chill in the refrigerator for at least 3 hours and up to 3 days. To serve, divide the drink among old fashioned glasses filled with ice. Garnish with orange wedges and serve.

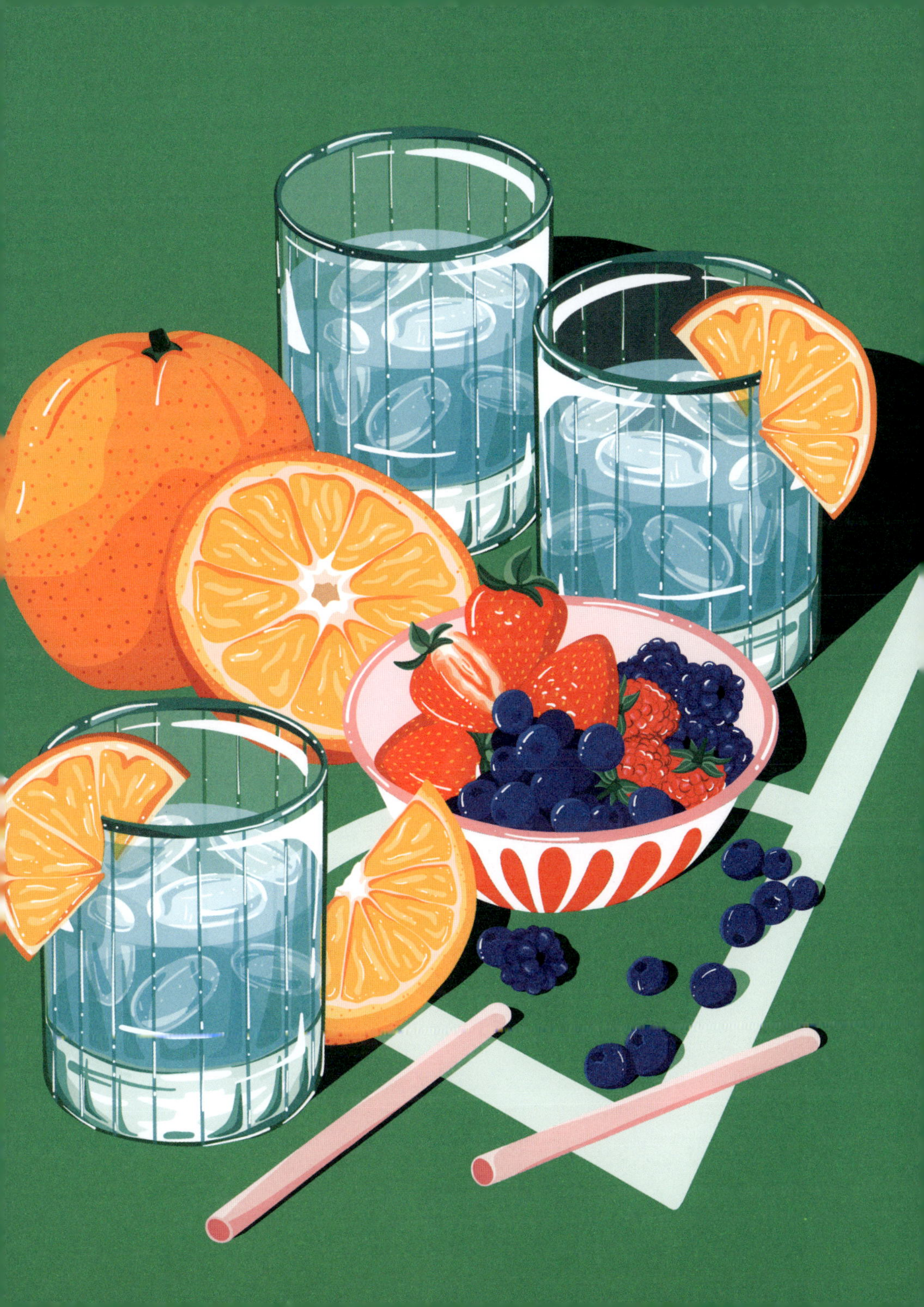

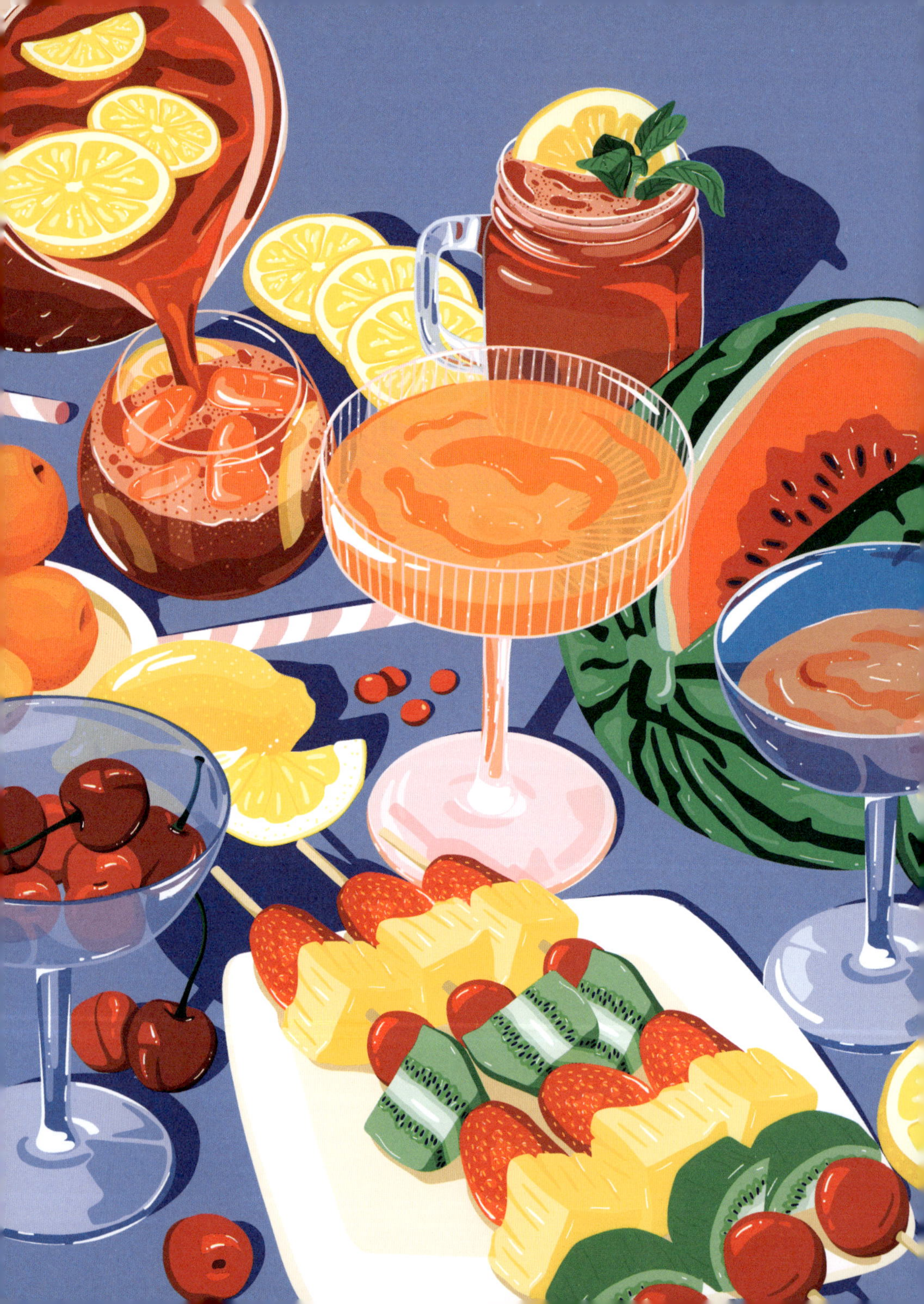

FRUITY

Non-citrus fruits are a great way to incorporate diverse, complex flavors into your nonalcoholic cocktails. Cherries, watermelon, and pineapple are just a few you'll see used here, but even though this chapter is dedicated to non-citrus fruits, those reliable guys also show up a bunch. Fruits bring summery freshness to cocktails and contain respectable amounts of aromatic complexity. Some of my favorite classic fruity cocktails are the Singapore Sling, the Midori Sour (it's a good drink!), and the Bloody Mary—because the tomato is a fruit. You'll find solid alternatives here that are delicious on their own or as accompaniments to light hors d'oeuvres and appetizers.

Rocking Chair Punch

SERVES ABOUT 8

◆

If you don't have a screened-in porch with a couple of rocking chairs upon which to while away an afternoon, you are still allowed to make this drink. As a culinary professional, I have a hard time working with fresh peaches because they are only in season for like ten minutes a year and an out-of-season peach is worse than worthless. Fortunately for all of us, canned peaches are always in season. Here you'll blend them up along with their sweet syrup for a rich and smooth purée that's paired with Earl Grey tea, mint, nonalcoholic whiskey, and some bubbles. You can use regular black tea here if you feel like it, but the bergamot flavor of Earl Grey gives this woodsy late-afternoon punch some nice high tones to go along with those from the mint syrup and lemon juice.

2½ cups water

2 Earl Grey tea bags

1 (8½-ounce) can peaches in syrup

1 cup chilled sparkling water

1 cup chilled nonalcoholic sparkling wine

3 ounces Super Whiskey (see page 43) or plain nonalcoholic whiskey

2 ounces Mint Syrup (see page 40)

1 ounce fresh lemon juice

Garnish: lemon wedges and fresh peach pieces, if available

In a medium pan, bring the water to a boil over high heat. Remove the pan from the heat, wait for 10 seconds, then add the tea bags. Let steep for about 5 minutes, then remove the tea bags, squeezing out any excess moisture, and discard tea bags. Let the tea cool completely before using, at least 30 minutes.

Meanwhile, pour the canned peaches and their syrup into a blender and blend on high speed until completely smooth, about 30 seconds.

In a large punch bowl or pitcher, combine the cooled tea, peach purée, sparkling water, sparkling wine, whiskey, mint syrup, and lemon juice. Stir gently to combine. Add lemon wedges, peach pieces, and 6 to 8 large ice cubes or 2 cups regular ice. Serve in whatever glassware you like.

Cherry-Cola Temple

MAKES 1 DRINK

When I was growing up, my parents would take my brother and me to the local Chinese restaurant, where I would order a Shirley Temple and feel preciously grown-up (even if I simultaneously thought ordering the pu pu platter was hilarious). The classic Shirley Temple combines ginger ale with grenadine, a syrup made from pomegranate juice, and is a lovely shade of red. Its simple pairing of fruit and ginger is easy enough for most palates while also being slightly more sophisticated than most people give it credit for. While Shirley is an excellent nonalcholic beverage all on her own, this rendition maintains the spicy-fruity setup of the classic but switches out the ginger for cola and aromatic bitters. Instead of pomegranate, we're using Luxardo cherry syrup that, while still deep red, is a bit more rich and satisfying than most grenadines. To bring this drink back from the brink of cloying, we throw in some acidic lime juice for balance. Sure, you could just go buy a cherry cola, but I assure you this version is way better.

7½ ounces chilled cola (or 1 cup; I won't call the cops)

¾ ounce Luxardo cherry syrup

½ ounce fresh lime juice

4 dashes Angostura bitters or nonalcoholic bitters

Garnish: Luxardo cherries

In a tall glass filled with ice, combine the drink ingredients. Stir gently to mix well. Garnish with the cherries on a pick and serve.

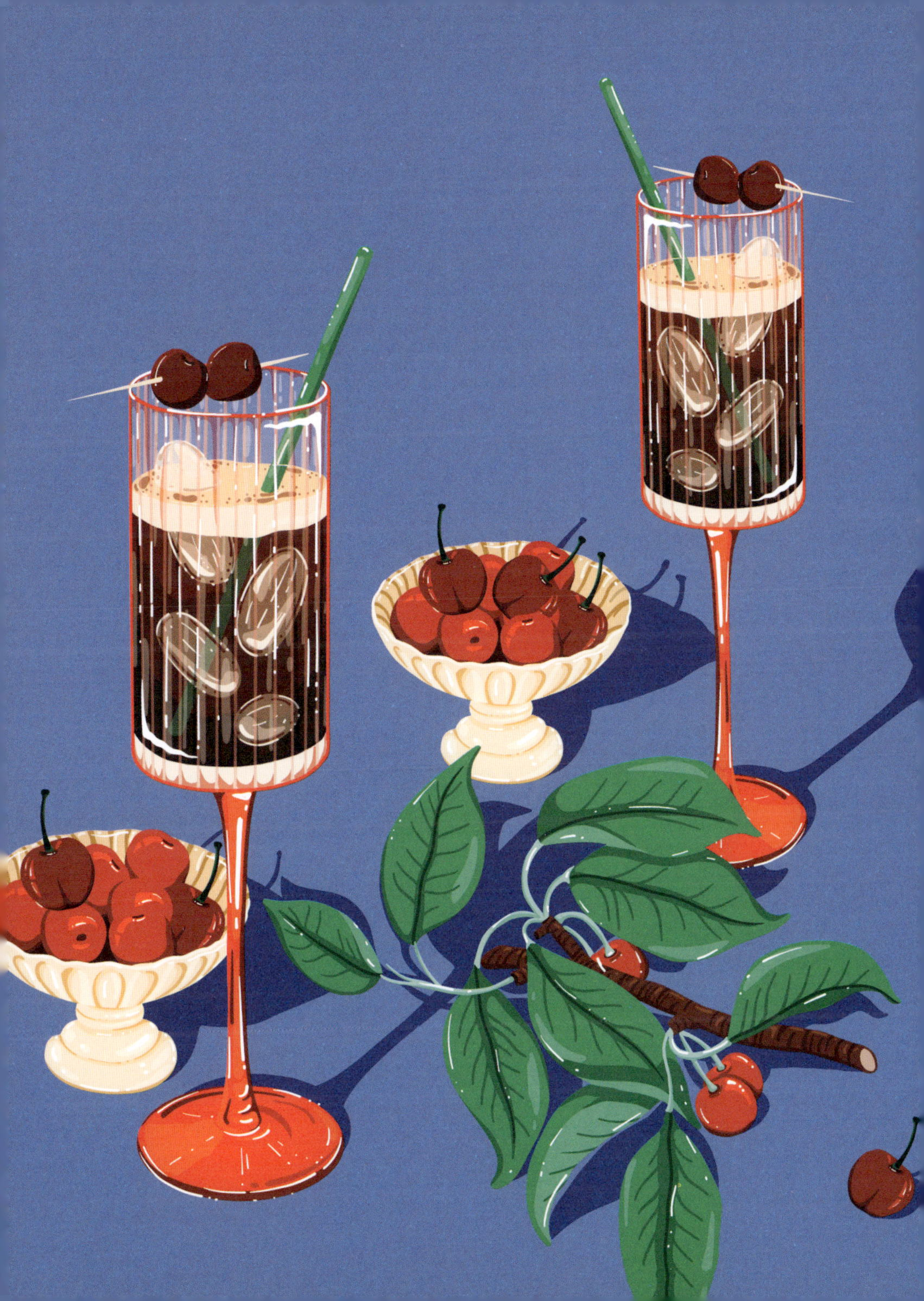

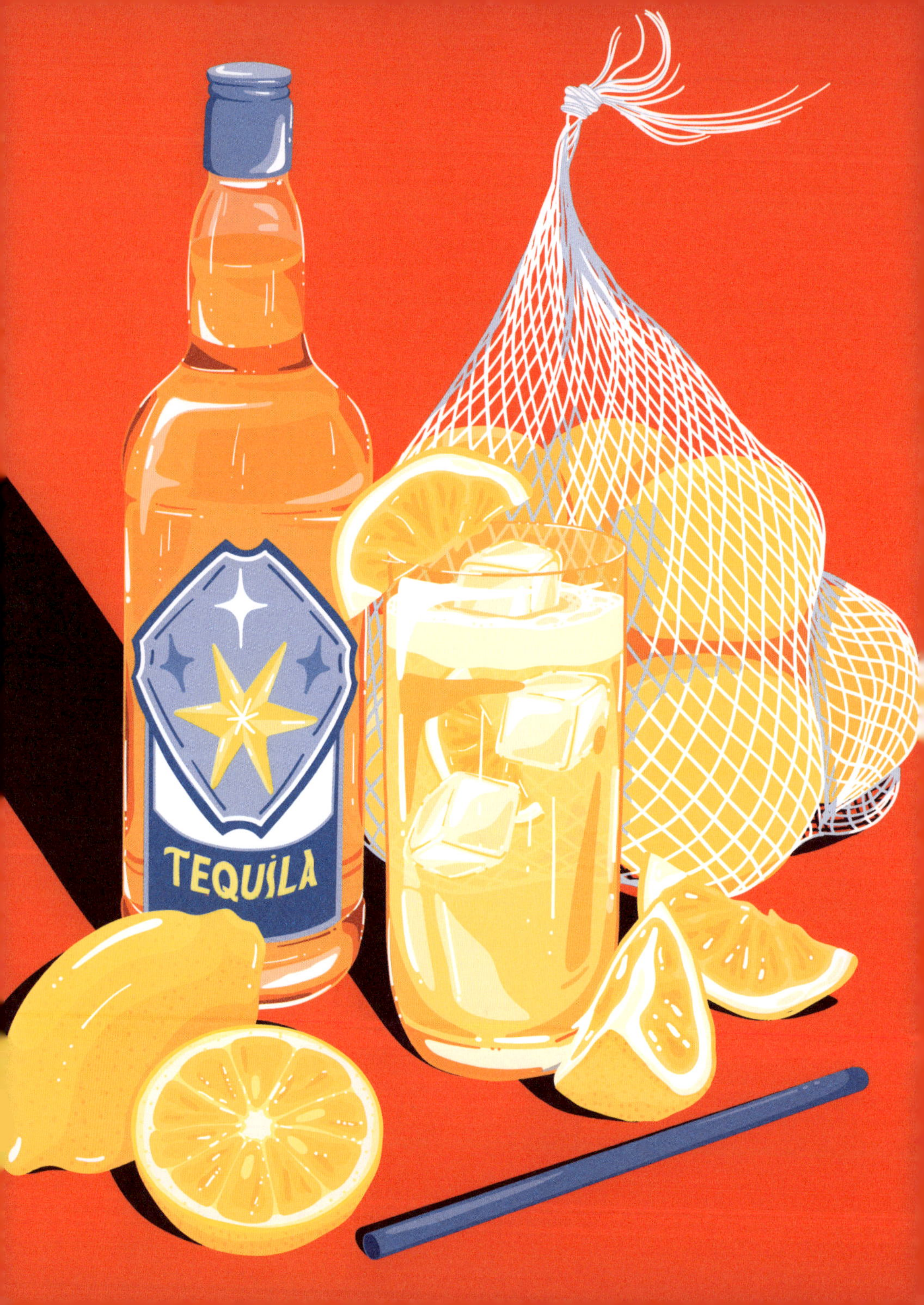
TEQUILA

Citra Collins

MAKES 1 DRINK

Dating back to the nineteenth century, the classic Tom Collins is a simple, refreshing, and subtly herbal combination of gin, lemon juice, and soda water. This riff reconstructs that premise using bright, pine-y hop water mixed with pineapple juice and yuzu standing in for lemon juice. Instead of the traditional gin profile, this drink gets some additional roasty and sweet notes from the non-alcoholic tequila. "Citra" refers to a variety of hops that often makes its way into hop waters. It's prized for its tropical, citrus, and resiny notes. Not every producer indicates the hop varieties used in their waters, so if you can't find one that explicitly mentions it, don't sweat it.

---

3 ounces chilled hop water

1½ ounces nonalcoholic blanco tequila

¾ ounce fresh pineapple juice

¼ ounce yuzu juice

Garnish: lemon wedge

In a tall glass filled with ice, pour in 1 ounce of the hop water. In a shaker, combine the tequila, pineapple juice, and yuzu juice. Fill with ice and shake vigorously for 15 seconds. Strain into the prepared glass and top with the remaining 2 ounces hop water. Garnish with the lemon wedge and serve.

Apricot Spritz

MAKES 1 DRINK

It's easy to rely on the acidity and aromatics of citrus juice when throwing together a sparkling wine–based cocktail. And for good reason: The bright acidity of citrus matches well with bubbles. But this drink sidesteps the usual coupling in favor of stone fruit and bubbly. It's an attempt at making a more spirit-forward drink inasmuch as it is possible in a book full of nonalcoholic cocktails. The apricot preserves amplify the lush texture while the orange blossom water delivers vibrant floral tones on the nose. Don't overdo it with the orange blossom water, though: Your drink will be too perfume-y. This cocktail is one where I won't urge you to use Super Whiskey because the unmodified nonalcoholic whiskey gives just the right amount of flavor.

---

5 ounces chilled nonalcoholic sparkling wine

1½ ounces nonalcoholic whiskey

2 tablespoons apricot preserves

¼ teaspoon orange blossom water

Fill a wine glass with about ½ cup of ice and add the sparkling wine. In a shaker, combine the remaining ingredients. Shake without ice for 5 seconds and pour into the prepared glass. Serve.

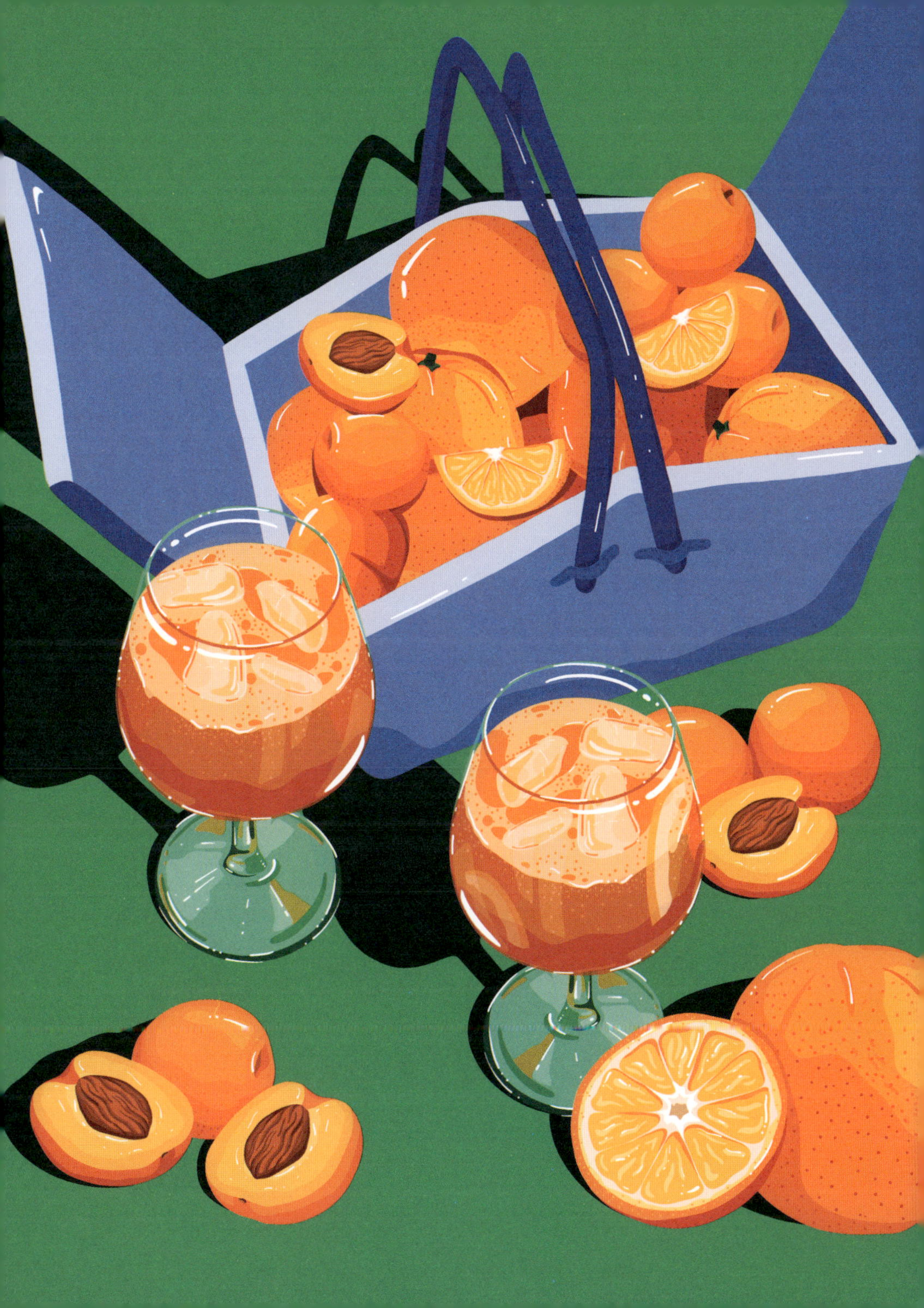

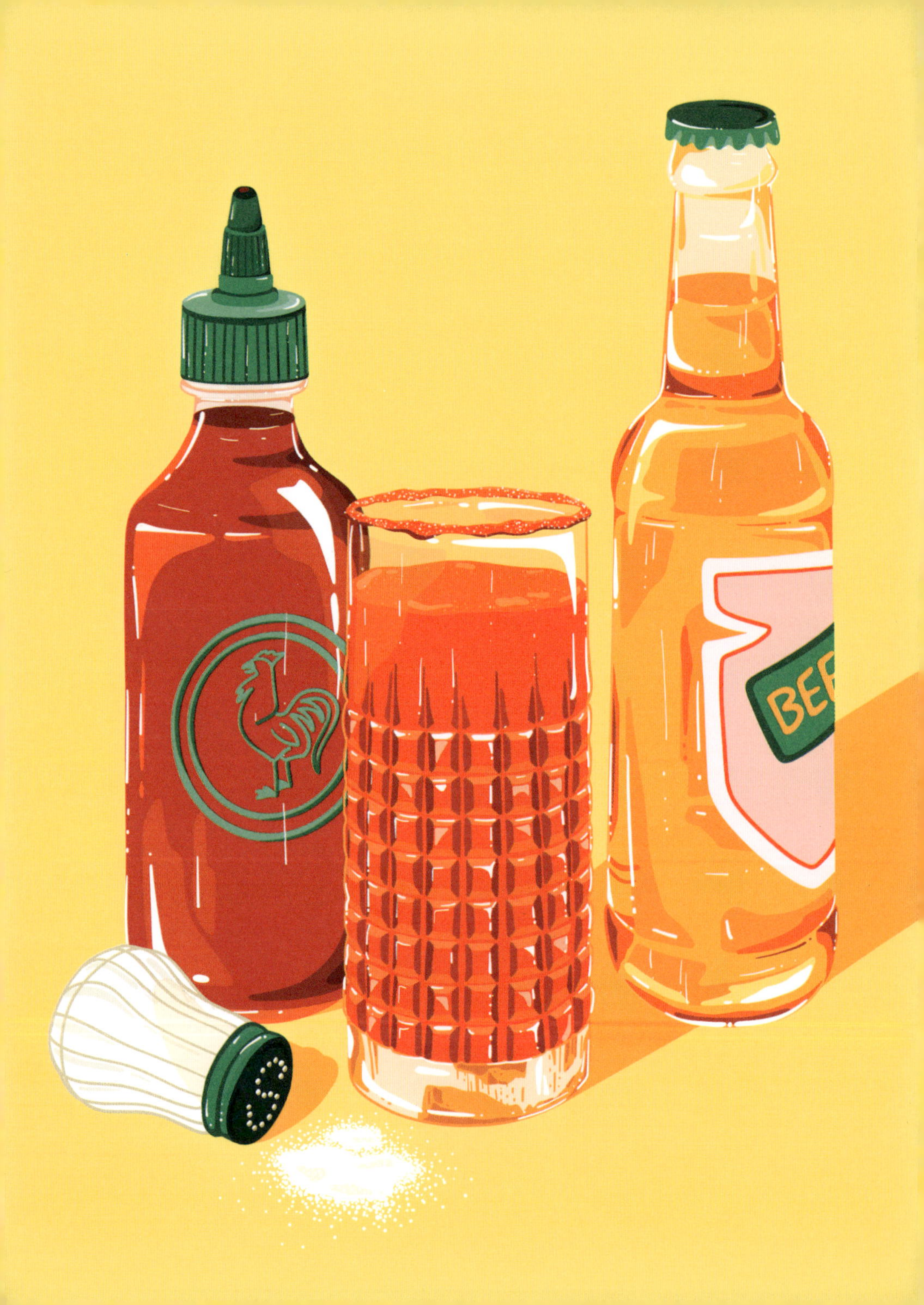

Berry Michelada

MAKES 1 DRINK

Beer is one of my favorite beverages, and non-alcoholic beers have come a long way since the dark days when O'Doul's ruled. In recent years, the category has exploded, offering a diverse array of nonalcoholic options from dark porters to bright wheat versions. The classic michelada is a simple mixture of beer and hot sauce, and this version is sweetened with a bit of Polyberry Syrup to give added layers of flavor. When salting the rim, be sure to use kosher salt, as it has the best texture to grip onto the rim. Use whatever type of hot sauce you like as long as it's not obscenely spicy.

Kosher salt

1 ounce Polyberry Syrup (see page 39)

6 ounces chilled nonalcoholic light beer

½ ounce fresh lime juice

½ ounce hot sauce

Pour about 2 tablespoons salt onto a small plate. Dip the rim of a tall glass into the polyberry syrup and then into the salt to coat the rim. Pour the beer, lime juice, and hot sauce into the prepared glass, stir gently to combine, and serve.

Vetiver Blush

MAKES 1 DRINK

I was introduced to Rooh Afza syrup while recording an episode of the podcast *Recipe Club*, where my fellow guests and I make recipes according to various randomly selected requirements. My task was to make a super luxurious (read: expensive) version of Rooh Afza, an Indian syrup made from a long list of ingredients like borage, coriander, screwpine, and vetiver. Fortunately for you, you do not need to spend hundreds of dollars to make your own Rooh Afza; it can be purchased for a reasonable sum at a specialty store or ordered online. I find it pairs wonderfully with watermelon. Topped off with a little lime juice and nonalcoholic sparkling wine, this one is as complex as it is refreshing.

1½ ounces fresh watermelon juice

¾ ounce Rooh Afza syrup

¾ ounce fresh lime juice

2 ounces chilled nonalcoholic sparkling wine

In a shaker, combine the watermelon juice, Rooh Afza syrup, and lime juice. Add ice and shake vigorously for 15 seconds. Strain into large coupe or wine glass and add the sparkling wine. Serve.

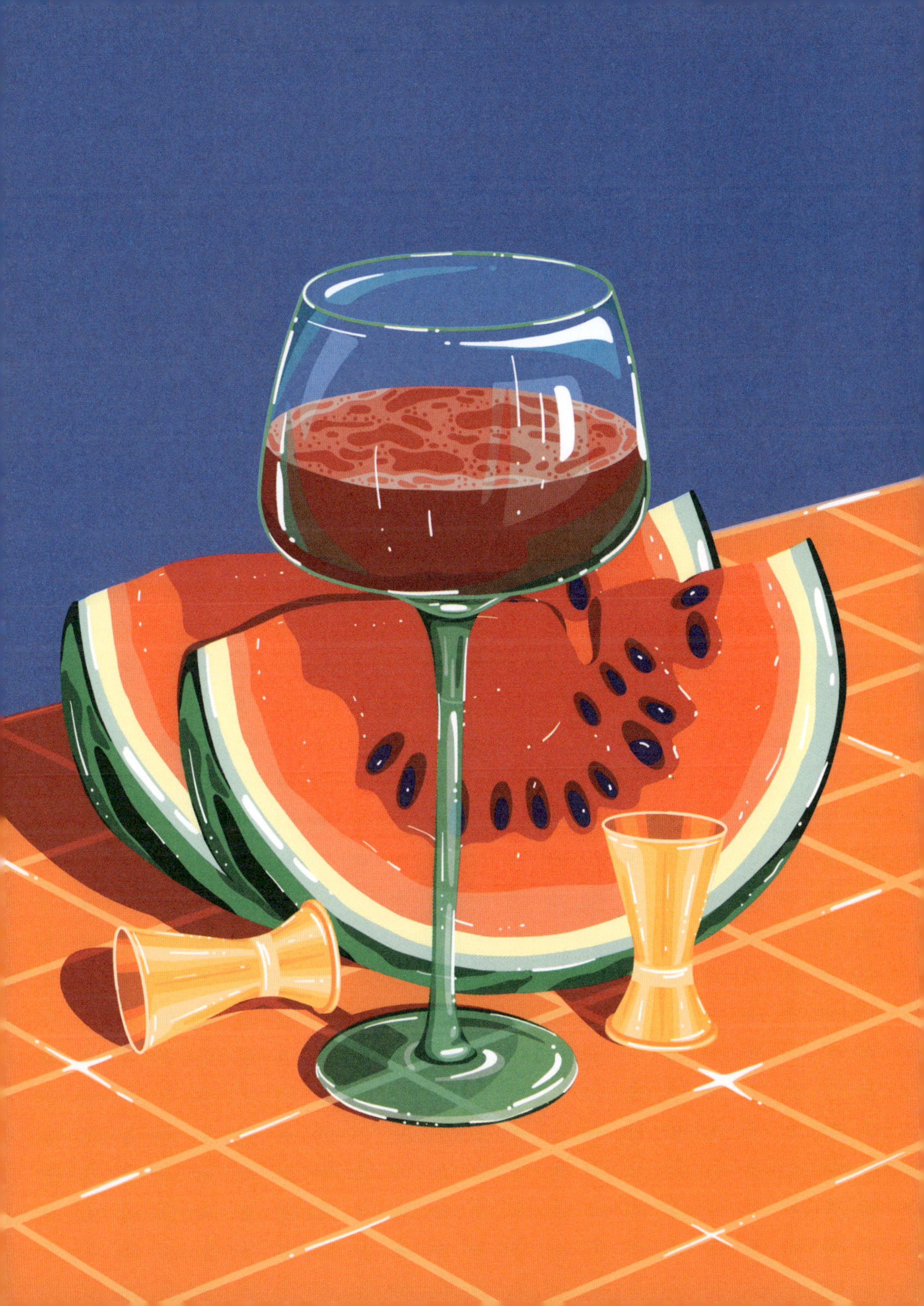

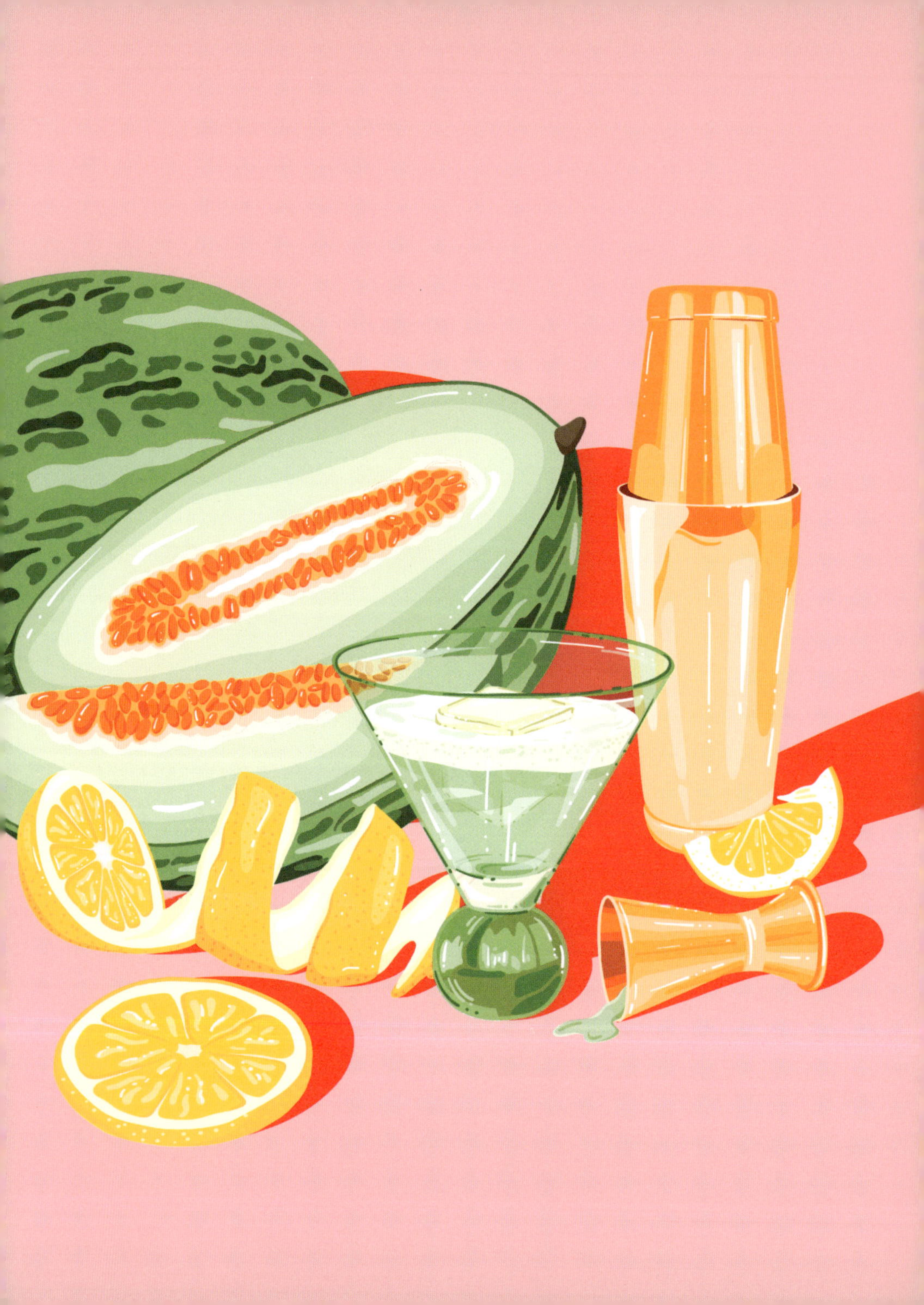

"Midori Sour"

MAKES 1 DRINK

This drink's name is in quotation marks because it obviously does not use Midori, the Japanese melon liqueur that gives the classic cocktail its iconic verdant hue. Instead, fresh honeydew juice and verjus stand in, while the rest of this drink hews pretty closely to the original, with the lime syrup bringing some added depth and bitterness. The orange bitters on top helps balance out some of the barnyard-y smell of the egg whites while also adding a hit of aromatic complexity. If you're squeamish about using raw egg white, I get it, but in the grand scheme, eggs are not much more likely to contain dangerous levels of pathogens than any other raw food. Also, I hate to burst your bubble, but even in alcohol-based drinks, the concentration of alcohol is not sufficient to kill germs. Sorry!

---

2 ounces fresh honeydew juice

½ ounce verjus

¼ ounce fresh lime juice

¼ ounce Lime Syrup (see page 37)

1 large egg white

Garnish: orange bitters or nonalcoholic orange bitters

In a shaker, combine the drink ingredients. Shake without ice for 5 seconds. Fill with ice and shake vigorously for 15 seconds. Strain into an old fashioned glass with one large ice cube or a few small ice cubes. Dash orange bitters over the top before serving.

Slushy Minty Mary

MAKES 2 DRINKS

♦♦

In this drink, frozen watermelon chunks cleverly (if I do say so myself) take the place of plain ice, which keeps the flavor density of this drink as high as possible. Combined with red hibiscus and bitter aperitif, this drink is a deep, satisfying red, which is as good of a connection to the Bloody Mary as any. Since this drink is on the more labor-intensive end of the spectrum, we're going to make two—because who wants to drink alone?

---

4 cups chopped watermelon

4 ounces nonalcoholic blanco tequila

3 ounces Red Hibiscus Concentrate (see page 42)

5 ounces Mint Syrup (see page 40)

2 ounces nonalcoholic bitter aperitif, such as Wilfred's

½ ounce hot sauce

Kosher salt

Place the watermelon in a resealable plastic bag and chill in the freezer until frozen, at least 6 hours.

Transfer the frozen watermelon to a blender and add the tequila, red hibiscus concentrate, 3 ounces of the mint syrup, the aperitif, and the hot sauce. Let the mixture sit in the blender for 10 to 15 minutes to thaw the watermelon a bit.

Meanwhile, place about 2 tablespoons salt on a small plate. Dip the rim of a tall glass into the remaining 2 ounces mint syrup, then into the salt to coat, shaking off any excess. Repeat with a second glass.

Blend the watermelon mixture on medium speed until smooth, about 30 seconds. Pour into the prepared glasses and serve.

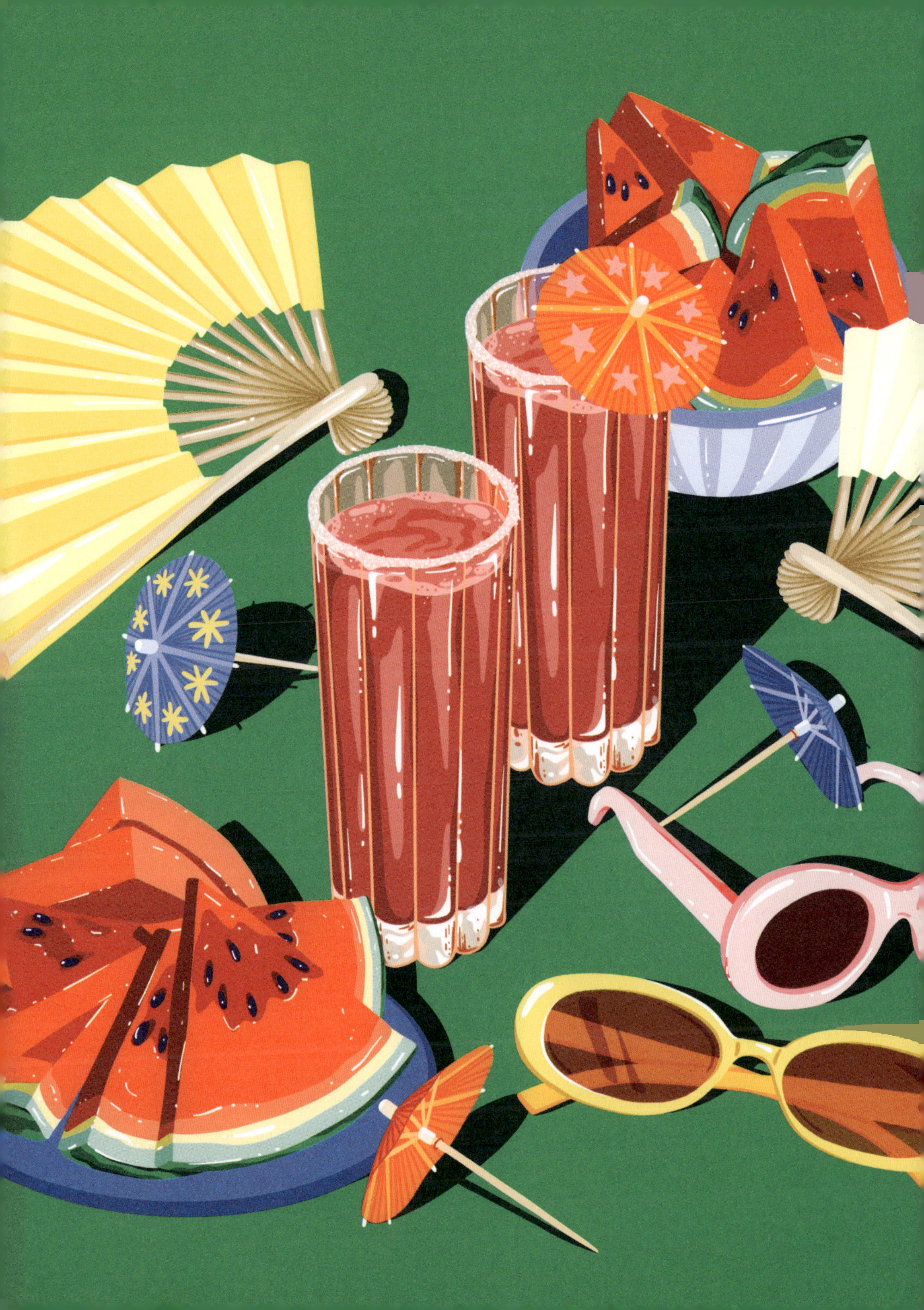

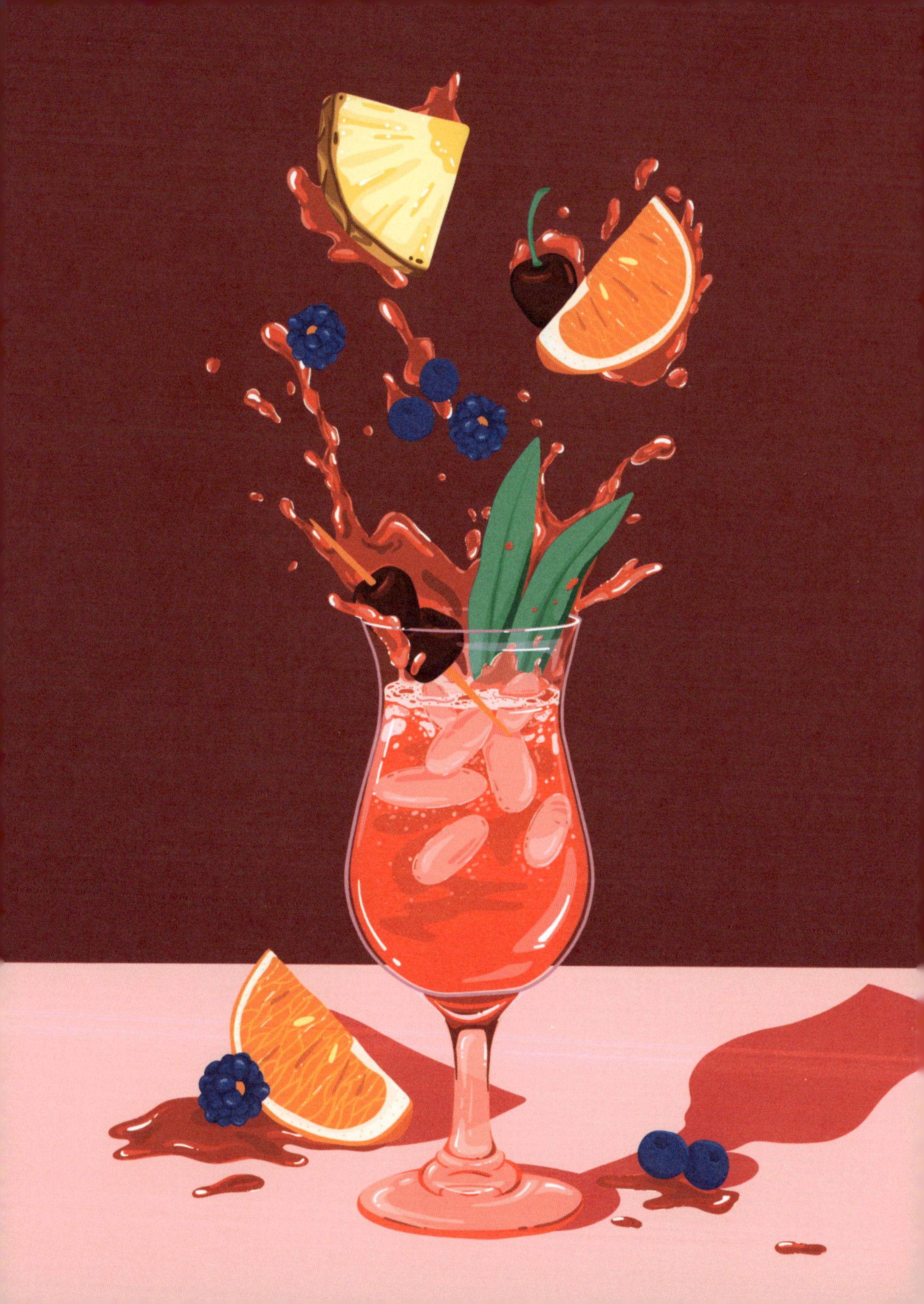

Kitchen Sink Sling

MAKES 1 DRINK

◆

As the name might imply, this drink has a lot going on. It's loosely based on one of my all-time favorite cocktails, the Singapore Sling, which is a delightfully fruity mix of gin, pineapple juice, cherry liqueur, orange liqueur, and lime juice. Here I use flavor-enhanced nonalcoholic gin to punch through the rest of the ingredients. And no, that's not a typo, I am indeed asking you to put ketchup in this drink. I feel like ketchup, while ubiquitous, is not prized for its non-savory applications in the way it should be. Here it offers a savory-salty counterbalance to the sweet ingredients while still being fruity. (Yes, tomato is a fruit!) Thanks to the tomatoes, ketchup contains a nice amount of glutamates, which are the titular ingredient in MSG (monosodium glutamate). Glutamates are great because they make everything taste better, and the idea that MSG makes you sick is just that, an idea—there's no scientific evidence to support it.

---

2 ounces fresh pineapple juice

1½ ounces Ultra Gin (see page 43) or plain nonalcoholic gin

¾ ounce Polyberry Syrup (see page 39)

½ ounce ketchup

½ ounce fresh lime juice

1 tablespoon orange marmalade

2 dashes Angostura bitters or nonalcoholic bitters

Garnish: Luxardo cherries and pineapple leaf

Fill a shaker with ice and shake vigorously for 30 seconds until the ice is crushed. Pour the crushed ice into a tall glass. Combine the drink ingredients in the shaker and shake vigorously with fresh ice for 15 seconds. Strain over the crushed ice. Garnish with cherries and pineapple leaf on a pick, then serve.

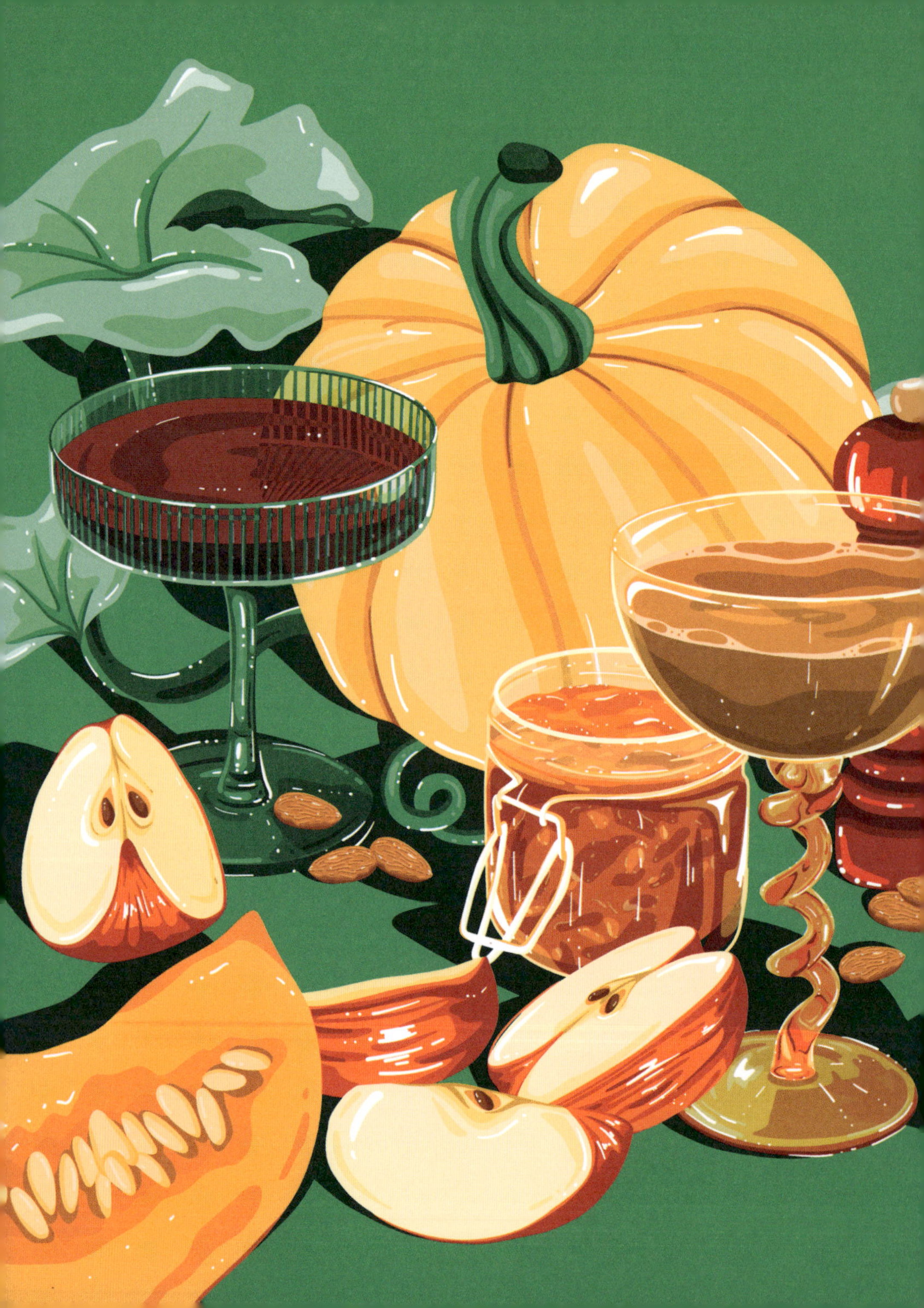

EARTHY

Since it's so easy to end up with "fancy lemonade" when you're making nonalcoholic cocktails, it's important to try to broaden your repertoire to include drinks that offer some of the same depth and savoriness that many traditional cocktails do. Dark maple syrup, barley tea, and bitters are some of the ways to find earthiness in nonalcoholic cocktails. Earthy flavors are dark and robust and typically work well when incorporated into cocktails enjoyed during cooler months. Manhattans, Old Fashioneds, and Flips made with a whole egg are all classic cocktails that I deem to be earthy. The alternatives here are applicable in a wide variety of situations from refreshing long drinks to more digestif-style sippers.

Cider Shandy

MAKES 1 DRINK

Technically a Shandy is equal parts beer and lemon-lime soda—a wonderful, simple cocktail. In case you haven't noticed already, I take a pretty broad license when it comes to naming drinks that only vaguely resemble their classic counterparts, so I'm calling this woodsy blend of cider, cola, and bitters a Shandy, and you're just going to have to play along. It's easy to sideline cola as a sugary, insipid beverage, but I find it has great aromatics of clove, cinnamon, and, depending on the brand, citrus. Tempering cola's sweetness with cider brings those aromatics to the forefront while the bitters further underlines the cola's aromatic qualities.

---

6 ounces chilled cola

4 ounces chilled apple cider

2 dashes Angostura bitters or nonalcoholic bitters

In a tall glass filled with ice, combine the drink ingredients, stir gently, and serve.

Vinegar Fizz

MAKES 1 DRINK

I want vinegar to be more of a thing that people drink, but the fact that it is so . . . well, smelly, makes it a tricky substance to want to ingest. It provides vibrant acidity and tons of complexity thanks to fermentation, but if you use too much, your drink just tastes like salad dressing. A small dose of rice vinegar is just enough to make this cocktail bright and complex while the dark maple syrup balances it with sweetness and depth. Without the lemon-lime soda, this drink is rather small, so I pour the soda into the shaker in order to eke out every last drop of flavor before pouring.

½ ounce rice vinegar

½ ounce dark maple syrup

½ ounce fresh lime juice

4 ounces chilled lemon-lime soda, such as Sprite or 7UP

In a shaker, combine the vinegar, maple syrup, and lime juice. Fill with ice and shake vigorously for 15 seconds. Open the shaker and pour in the soda. Strain into a small glass and serve.

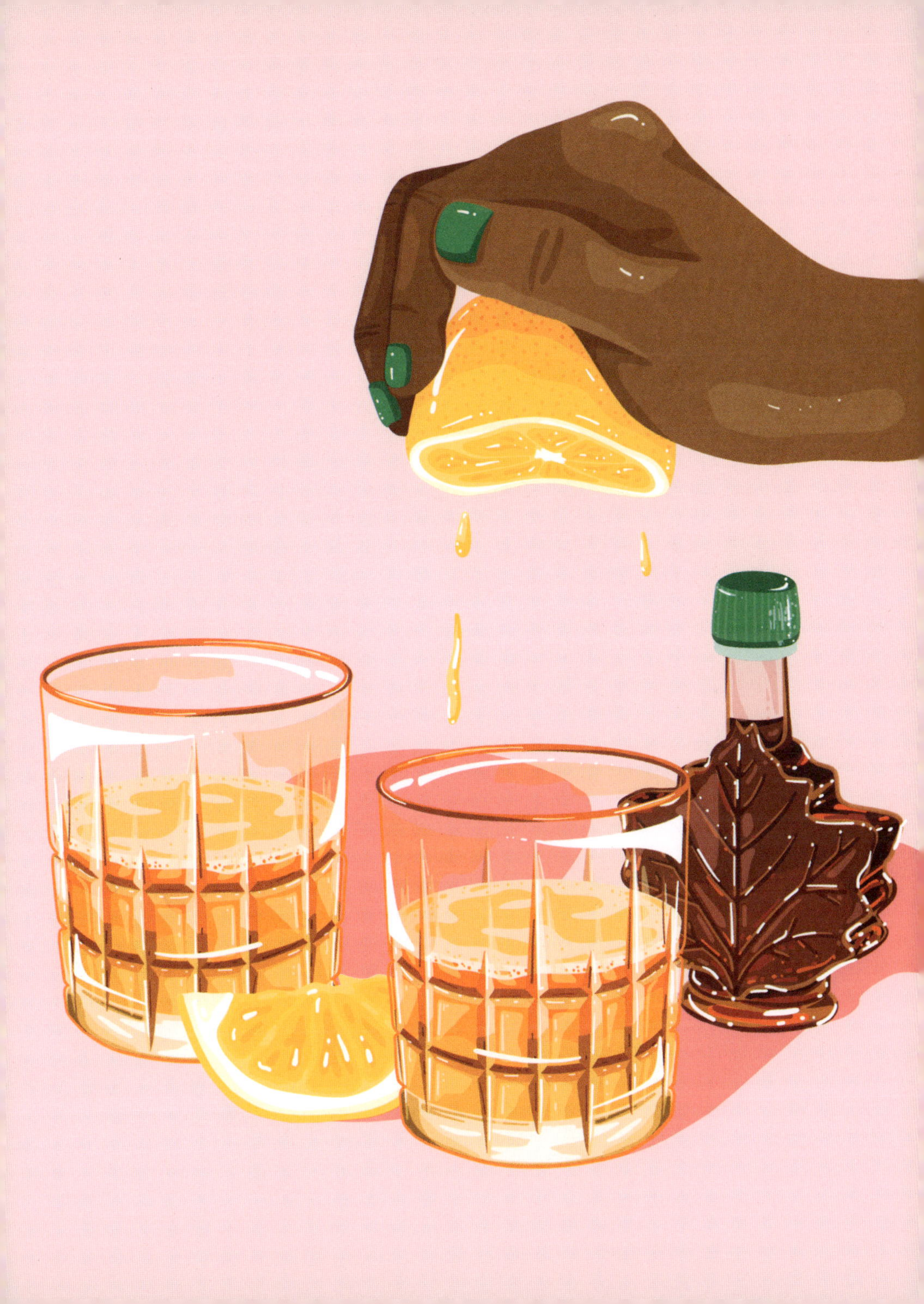

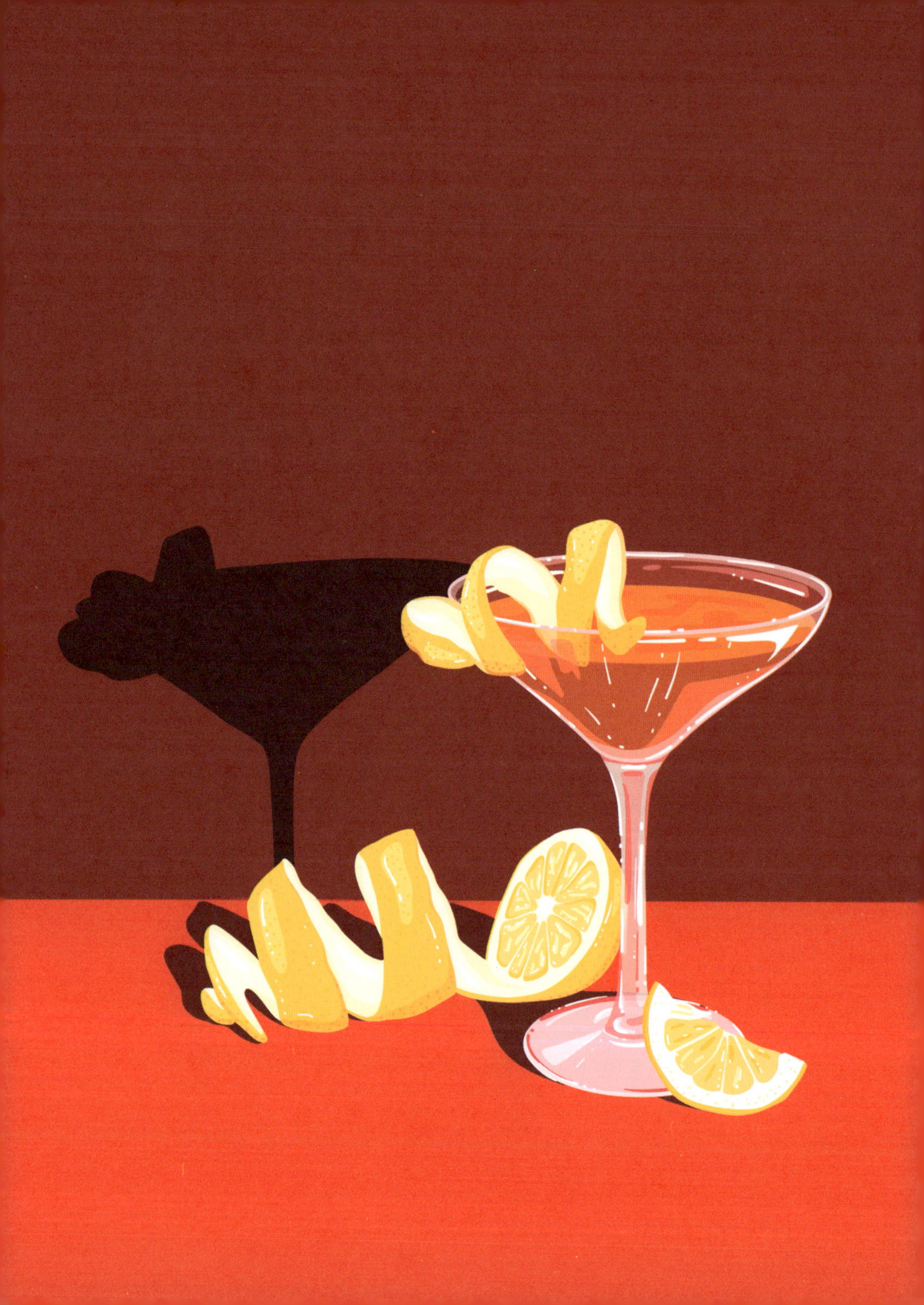

Barley Bomber

MAKES 1 DRINK

The Brown Bomber, a mix of Tennessee whiskey, wine-based aperitif, and gentian liqueur, was one of the first cocktail recipes I memorized when I began my career as a bartender. The drink was invented by industry legend Don Lee, at the cocktail bar PDT in the late 2000s. I've re-created the overall vibe—with some liberties, of course. Barley tea and nonalcoholic whiskey serve as stand-ins for Tennessee whiskey, while ginger and elderflower make this a bright but silky sipper. Tenneyson Black Ginger is a nonalcoholic spirit made with botanicals like ginger, lemon balm, and dandelion. You can use Super Whiskey here if you want, but I find an unadulterated liquid is best for preserving the drink's clarity and aromatic balance.

---

1 ounce Mugi Concentrate (see page 41)

½ ounce Tenneyson Black Ginger nonalcoholic spirit

½ ounce nonalcoholic elderflower liqueur, such as Giffard

½ ounce nonalcoholic whiskey

Garnish: lemon peel

In a small shaking tin or mixing glass, combine the drink ingredients. Fill with ice and stir gently for 20 seconds. Strain into a coupe. Express the lemon peel over the top of the drink, then perch it on the rim of the glass and serve.

EARTHY

Pineapple Elixir 2.0

MAKES 1 DRINK

◆

Having the privilege of writing multiple cocktail books means you have the opportunity to revise your previously published drinks to make them easier—and, more important, tastier. This is my upgraded version of the Pineapple Elixir from my first book, *Drink What You Want*, which adds a hit of jaggery syrup for depth and complexity. Meanwhile, the kaleidoscopic pepper syrup lights up your palate.

---

6 ounces chilled tonic water

1 ounce fresh pineapple juice

½ ounce Jaggery Syrup (see page 36)

½ ounce Pepper Syrup (see page 38)

In a tall, ice-filled glass, combine the drink ingredients. Stir briefly to combine and serve.

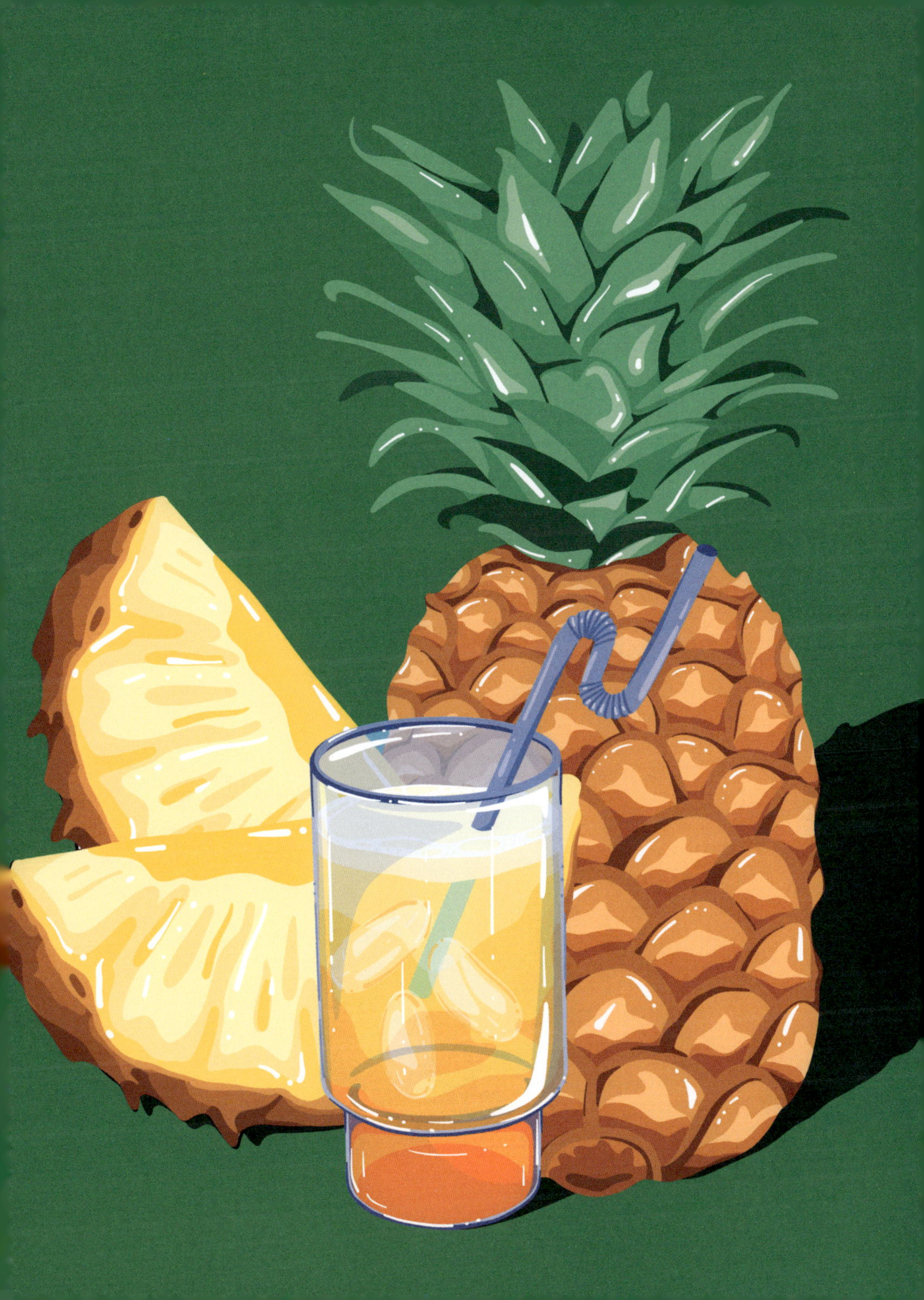

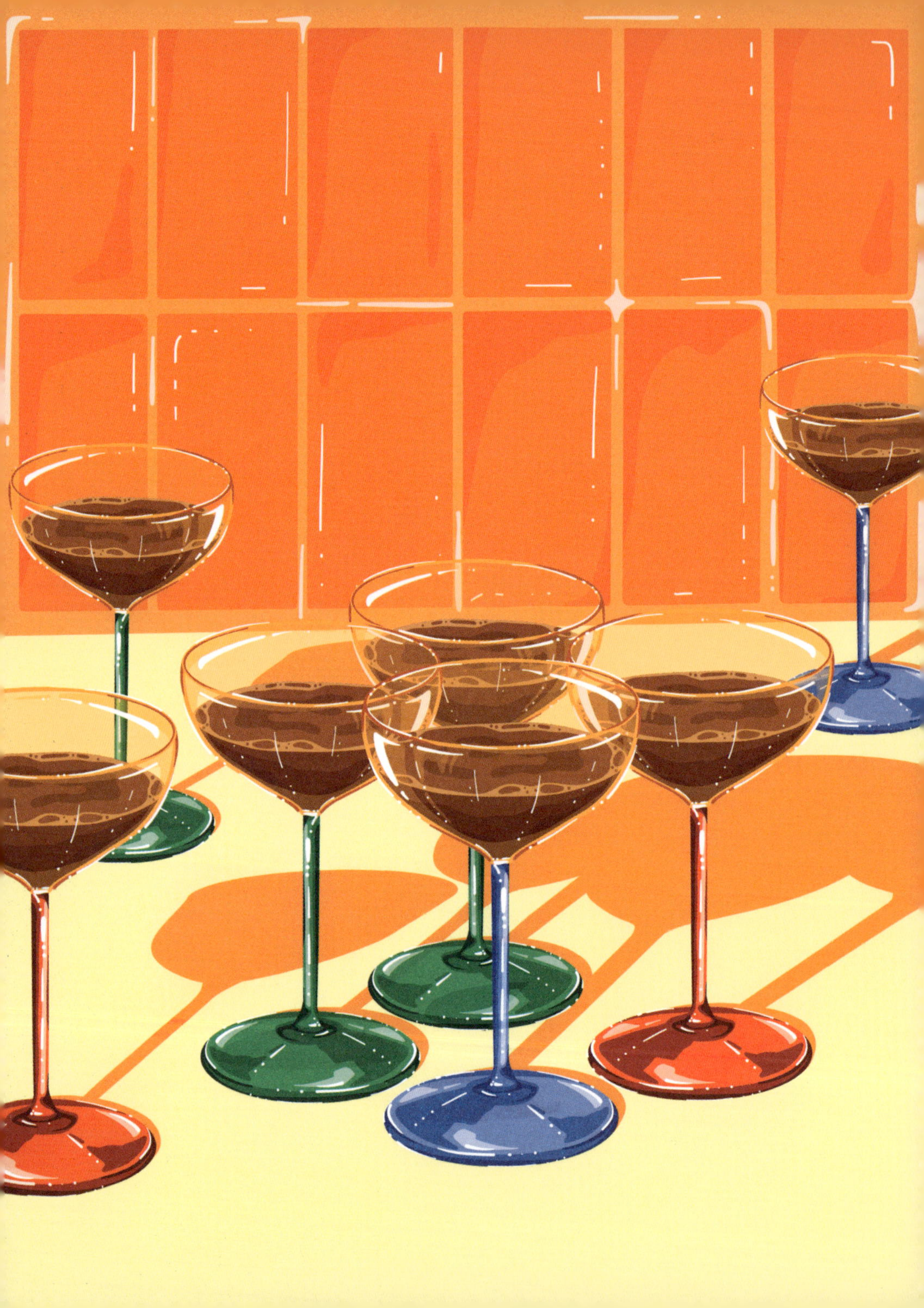

Cameron's Kiss

MAKES 1 DRINK

■

1½ ounces Super Whiskey (see page 43) or plain nonalcoholic whiskey

¾ ounce orgeat syrup

¾ ounce fresh lime juice

The Cameron's Kick is an off-the-beaten-path classic cocktail made with Irish whiskey, lime juice, and orgeat, a Middle Eastern almond (sometimes apricot kernel) syrup. This version is a pretty faithful re-creation of that simple classic. Given how few ingredients it uses, the Super Whiskey is essential for delivering a satisfying drink. You can use whatever type of orgeat you prefer, just know the "artisanal" varieties tend to be slightly less sweet and more subtle in terms of the almond aromatics. I have respect for all makers of orgeat, but I usually choose a more conventional one, like from Kassatly Chtaura, to make this drink really pop.

In a shaker, combine the drink ingredients. Fill with ice and shake vigorously for 15 seconds. Strain into a coupe and serve.

Honeydew Old Fashioned

MAKES 1 DRINK

◆

It would be absurd (but maybe delicious) to try to make a classic Old Fashioned using Midori. The drink would be insanely sweet and too melon-y perhaps even for my overstimulated palate. Fortunately for us, by ditching the alcohol, we can mix up a melon-based Old Fashioned using mugi concentrate to cut through some of that sweetness and balance out the fruit aromatics. I like to build my Old Fashioneds in the glass, skipping the step of stirring in a separate vessel, because I like drinks that are intended to be sipped slowly to be a bit more concentrated because over time, the ice will melt into the drink, making it more diluted.

---

1 ounce fresh honeydew juice

1 ounce Mugi Concentrate (see page 41)

¼ ounce Pepper Syrup (see page 38)

2 dashes Angostura bitters or nonalcoholic bitters

Garnish: orange peel

In an old fashioned glass with one large ice cube or a few small ice cubes, combine the drink ingredients. Stir gently for 20 seconds. Express the orange peel over the top of the drink, then perch it on the rim of the glass and serve.

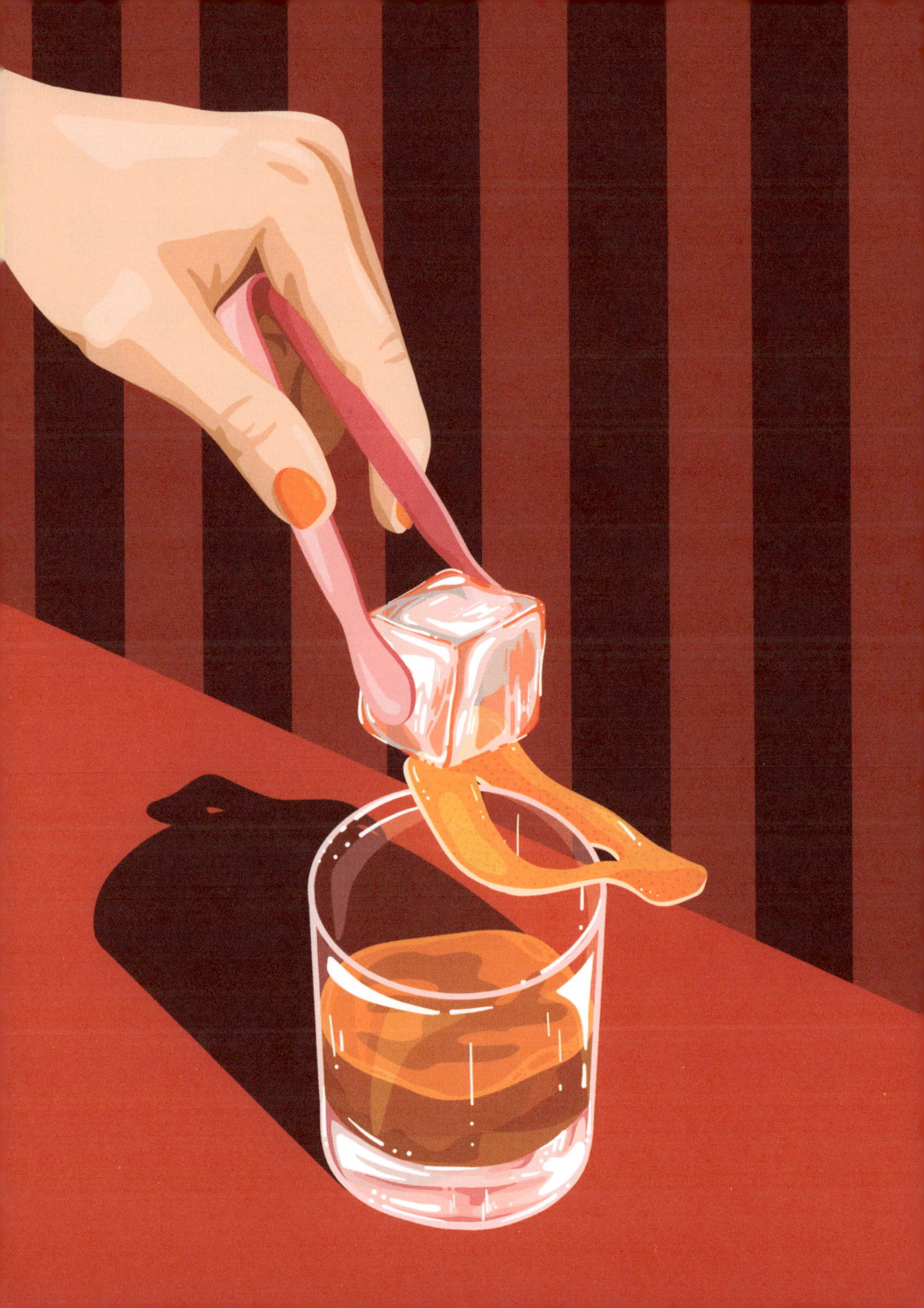

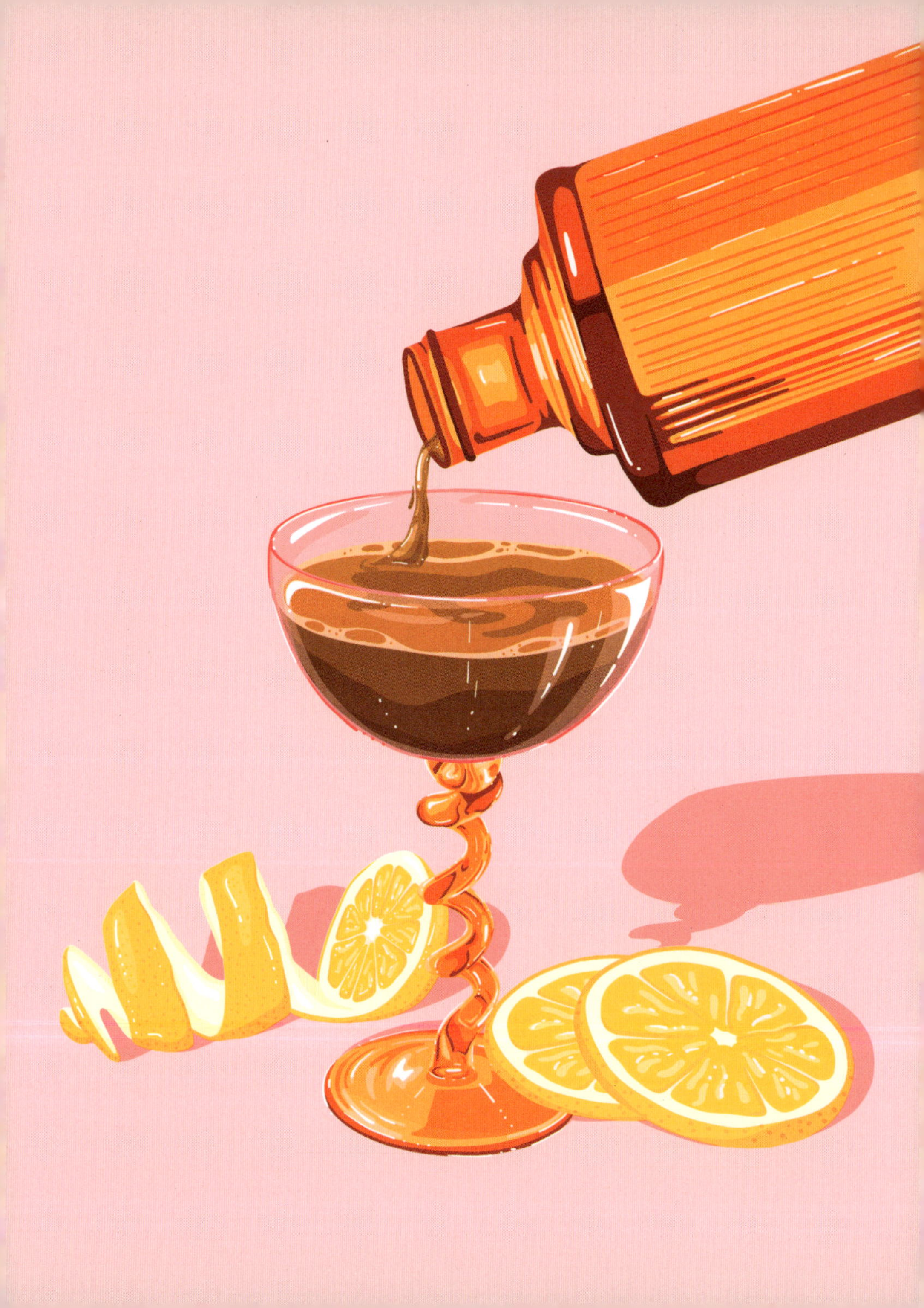

Jaggery Sour

MAKES 1 DRINK

In most recipes in this book that include jaggery syrup, it plays a supporting role, undergirding drinks with an earthy, caramel-like complexity that allows the other ingredients to shine. But this cocktail brings it to the forefront, mixing it with a nonalcoholic tequila and verjus to create a bright backdrop. Orange juice is a tricky ingredient to work with in beverages: it tastes great but lacks the concentrated acidity needed to create proper balance. I recommend using it alongside another citrus that supplements acidity—lemon, in this instance—while allowing the juiciness of the orange juice to do its job.

1½ ounces nonalcoholic blanco tequila

1 ounce verjus

¾ ounce Jaggery Syrup (see page 36)

½ ounce fresh lemon juice

½ ounce fresh orange juice

In a shaker, combine the drink ingredients. Fill with ice and shake vigorously for 15 seconds. Strain into a chilled coupe or small glass and serve.

Mugi Manhattan

MAKES 1 DRINK

◆

This recipe isn't the only Manhattan riff you'll find in this book, but it's for sure the least faithful to the original. It doesn't even try to act like it has whiskey or vermouth in it, but it tastes like the boozy classic just the same. Here the mugi concentrate offers the grainy notes typically found in whiskey while the red hibiscus and maple syrup combine to form something that resembles sweet vermouth.

---

2 ounces Mugi Concentrate (see page 41)

½ ounce Red Hibiscus Concentrate (see page 42)

¼ ounce dark maple syrup

Garnish: orange peel

In a small shaking tin or mixing glass, combine the drink ingredients. Fill with ice and stir gently for 20 seconds. Strain into a coupe. Express the orange peel over the top of the drink, then perch it on the rim of the glass and serve.

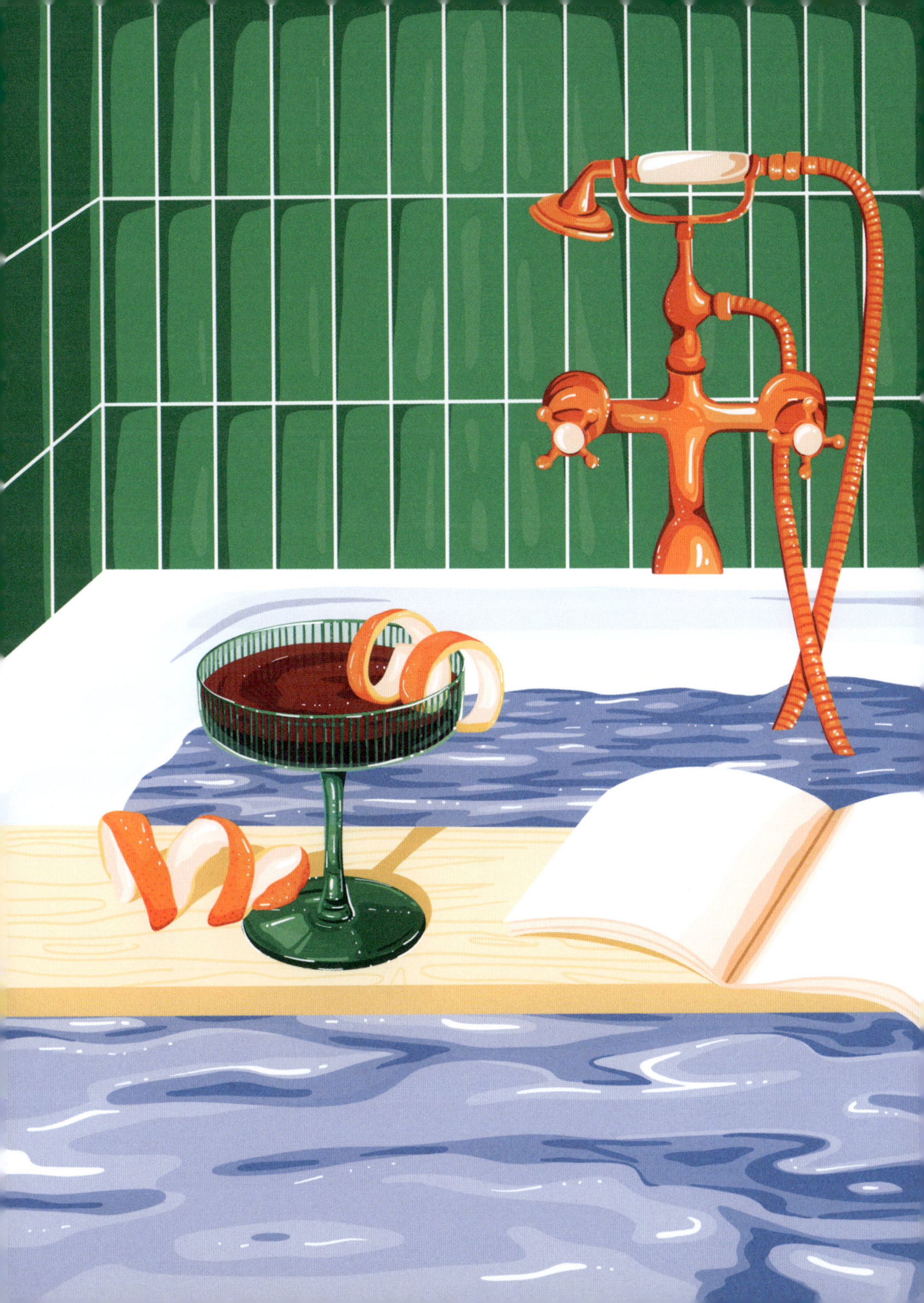

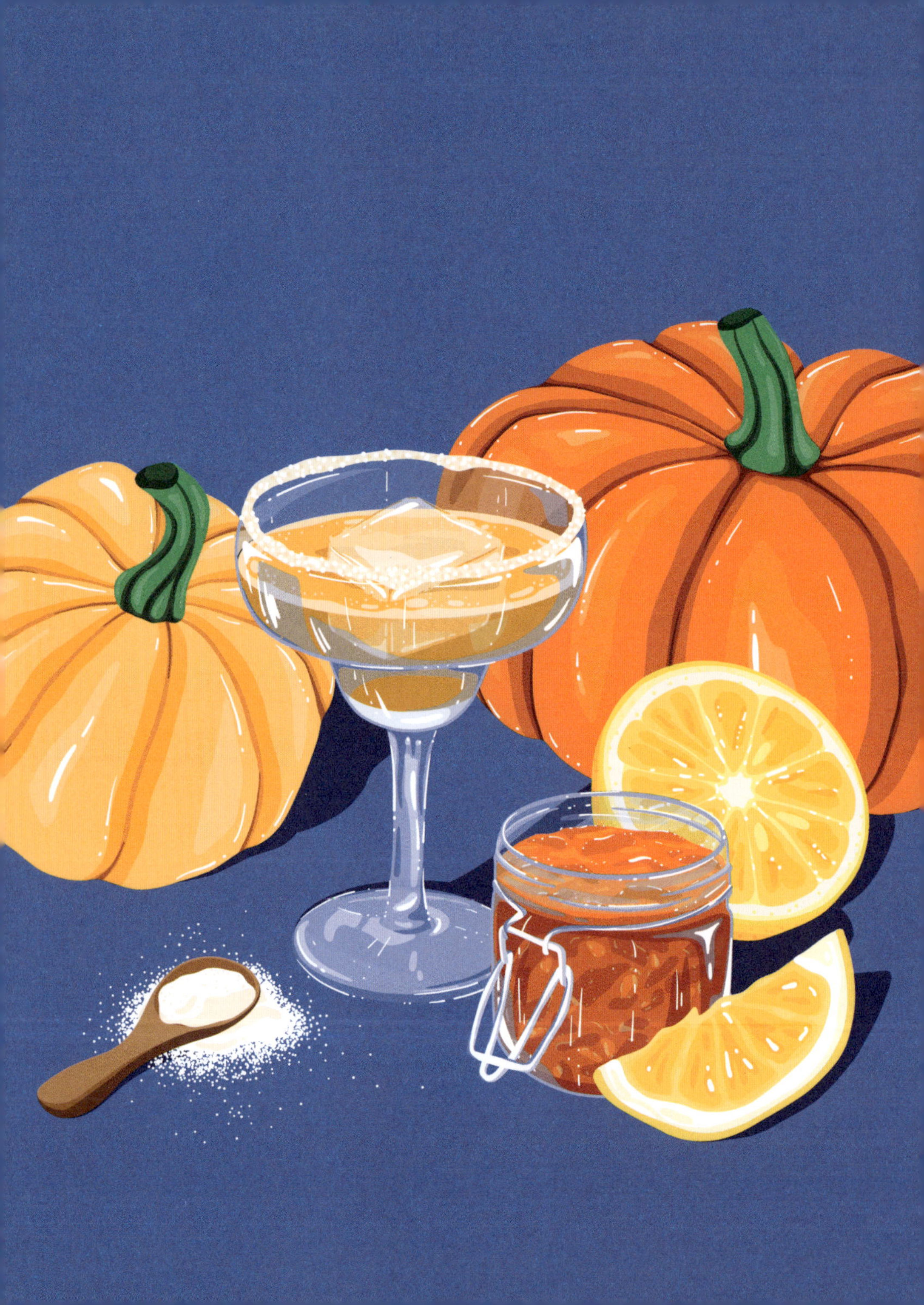

Pumpkin Spice Margarita

MAKES 1 DRINK

■

I really don't know why pumpkin spice is so triggering for some people—it's just a spice blend! Let people enjoy the things they like! Personally, I enjoy how the clove, cinnamon, nutmeg, and other spices typically found in pumpkin spice mixes play with the roasted agave notes from the nonalcoholic tequila in this autumnal margarita riff. The orange marmalade helps absorb some of the graininess while also delivering a lush texture when shaken into this drink.

Kosher salt

¾ ounce fresh lime juice

1½ ounces nonalcoholic blanco tequila

1 tablespoon orange marmalade

¼ teaspoon pumpkin spice blend

Pour about 2 tablespoons salt onto a small plate. Dip the rim of an old fashioned glass into a small amount of the lime juice and then into the salt to coat. Fill the glass with one large ice cube or a few small ice cubes. In a shaker, combine the tequila, marmalade, and pumpkin spice blend. Fill with ice and shake vigorously for 15 seconds. Strain into the prepared glass and serve.

Mugi Punch

SERVES 8

One of my favorite things about the hospitality industry is how through the crucible of nightly service, many colleagues become dear friends. One such friend, a teetotaler living in Chicago, texted me in need of a festive large-format drink for a holiday party. So I sent her the recipe for this autumnal punch that I can only describe as a mulled cider dialed up to 200. Here, I recommend you opt for a super sweet sparkling apple cider, such as the ubiquitous Martinelli's, to balance out the bitters, mugi concentrate, and a ginger-based nonalcoholic spirit. If you use a "fancier" cider, you run the risk of the drink being a bit too dry and spicy for most palates.

---

2 cups Mugi Concentrate (see page 41)

9 ounces chilled sparkling apple cider, such as Martinelli's

6 ounces chilled apple cider

3 ounces chilled cola

2½ ounces Tenneyson Black Ginger nonalcoholic spirit

6 dashes Angostura bitters or nonalcoholic bitters

Garnish: clove-studded apple slices (see Note) and whole star anise pods

In a large bowl, combine the drink ingredients and stir gently to combine. Add 4 to 6 large ice cubes or 2 cups regular ice. Scatter the apple slices and star anise pods over the top of the punch. Ladle into whatever glasses you like and serve.

NOTE: To make clove-studded apple slices, thinly slice an apple (any variety) and dip the slices in lemon juice to keep them from browning. Push 3 whole cloves into the flesh of each apple slice and drop them into the punch right before serving.

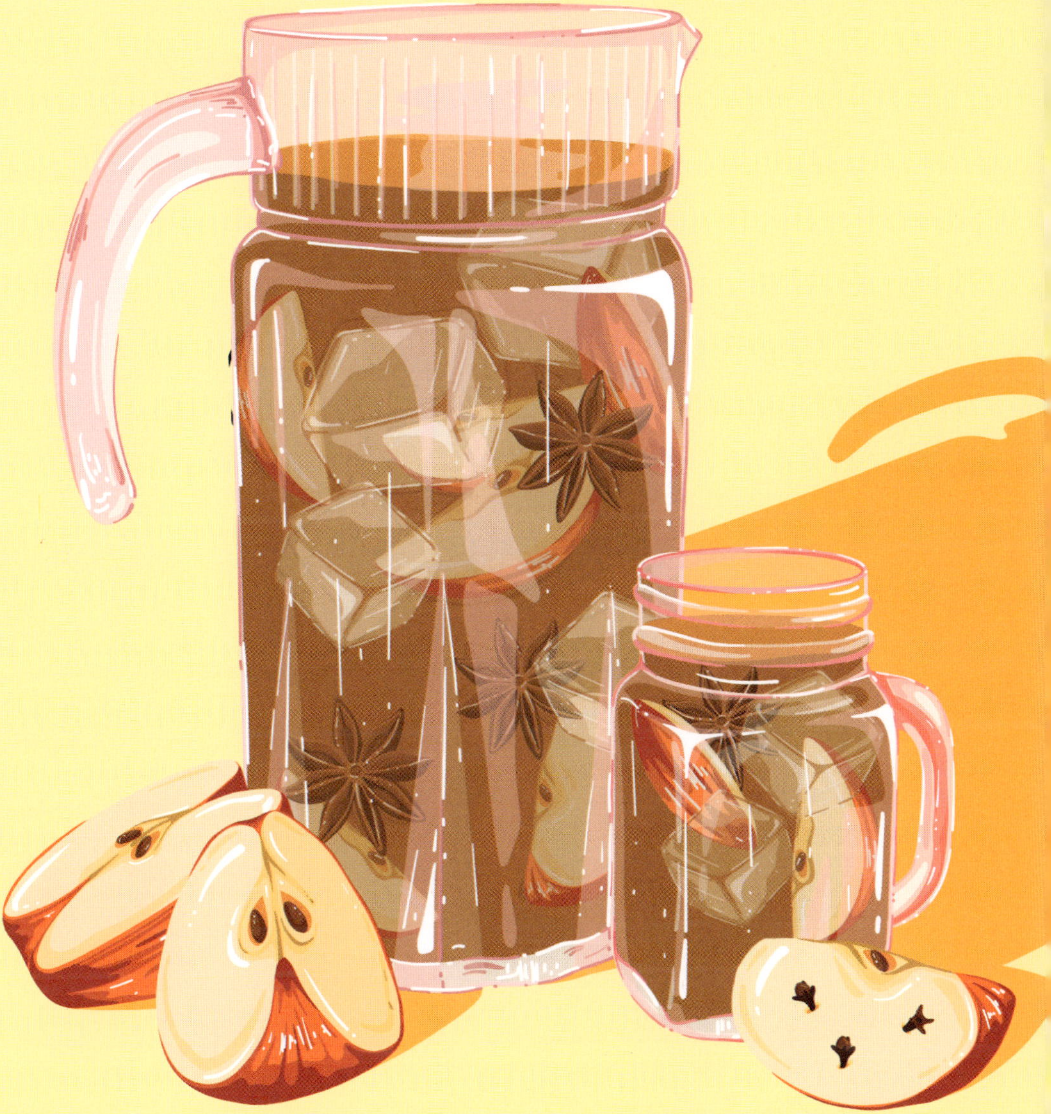

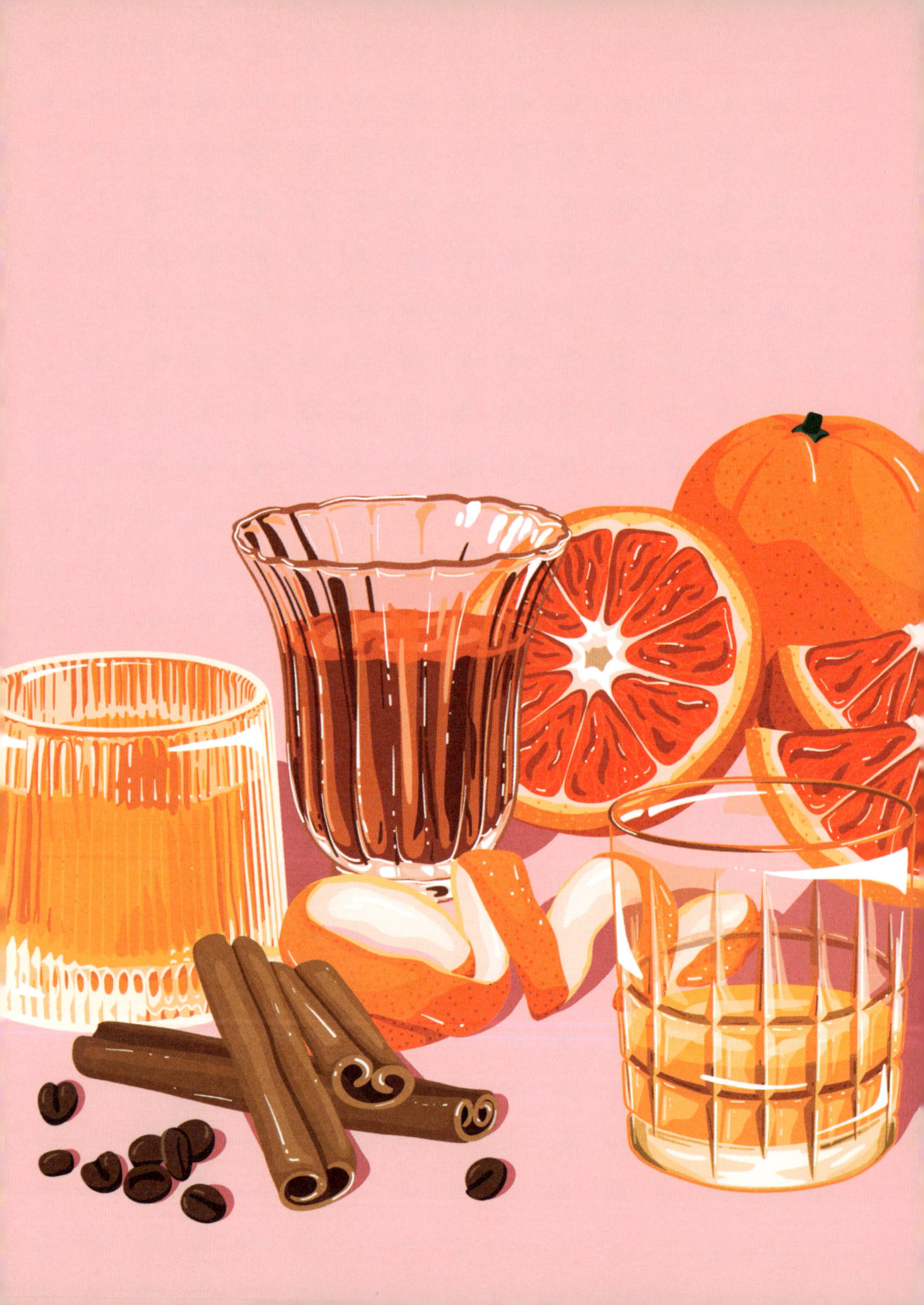

BITTER

Bitterness is such a fascinating sensation. Unlike sweetness, saltiness, acidity, and umami, which all help to tell us that the food we're eating contains nutrients such as sugar, fat, and protein, we detect bitterness as a warning sign for the presence of poison, triggering a strong negative reaction upon tasting bitter foods and drinks that might look otherwise perfectly edible. For this reason, many food items that taste bitter are considered acquired tastes—and in drinks, that typically means they have a more challenging flavor profile with a bit of a "bite" from the bitter ingredients. Negronis, Aperol Spritzes, even the gin and tonic are classic bitter drinks comparable to these, all of which I see as great accompaniments to food, helping to settle the stomach before or after a rich meal. Some of them make perfect nightcaps, too.

Tart Negroni

MAKES 1 DRINK

One of the first classics the nonalcoholic drink pioneers nailed down properly was the nonalcoholic Negroni, sometimes cutely renamed as a "no-grony," or, less cutely, "NA-grony." Nomenclature notwithstanding, we can use nonalcoholic vermouth paired with the life-giving manna that is the syrup that Luxardo cherries come packed in. A substantial measure of red hibiscus triples down on the redness of this drink and also delivers a huge hit of acidity and tannins.

1½ ounces nonalcoholic sweet vermouth

1 ounce Luxardo cherry syrup

1 ounce Red Hibiscus Concentrate (see page 42)

In a small shaking tin or mixing glass, combine the drink ingredients. Fill with ice and stir gently for 20 seconds. Strain into a coupe and serve.

BITTER | 131

Monaco

MAKES 1 DRINK

I was last in Paris about a decade ago for a family reunion. Some not-great family drama going on at the time meant I spent most of the trip in a particularly inebriated state. I have a hazy memory of sitting in a sidewalk café in the Marais with my husband and seeing—to the best of my recollection—a "Monaco" (a drink I'd never heard of) listed on the menu (with no explanation). Obviously, I ordered it immediately. I was delivered a mixture of light beer and Campari . . . or maybe it was Aperol. I cannot for the life of me find any documentation of this drink, but the idea of dousing an uninteresting beer with a hit of bright bitter stuck with me. I've re-created the memory here using entirely nonalcoholic ingredients—which is arguably much better for the psyche.

---

12 ounces chilled nonalcoholic IPA

1 ounce nonalcoholic bitter aperitif, such as Wilfred's

Garnish: orange wedge

In a tall glass, combine the drink ingredients. Garnish with the orange wedge and serve.

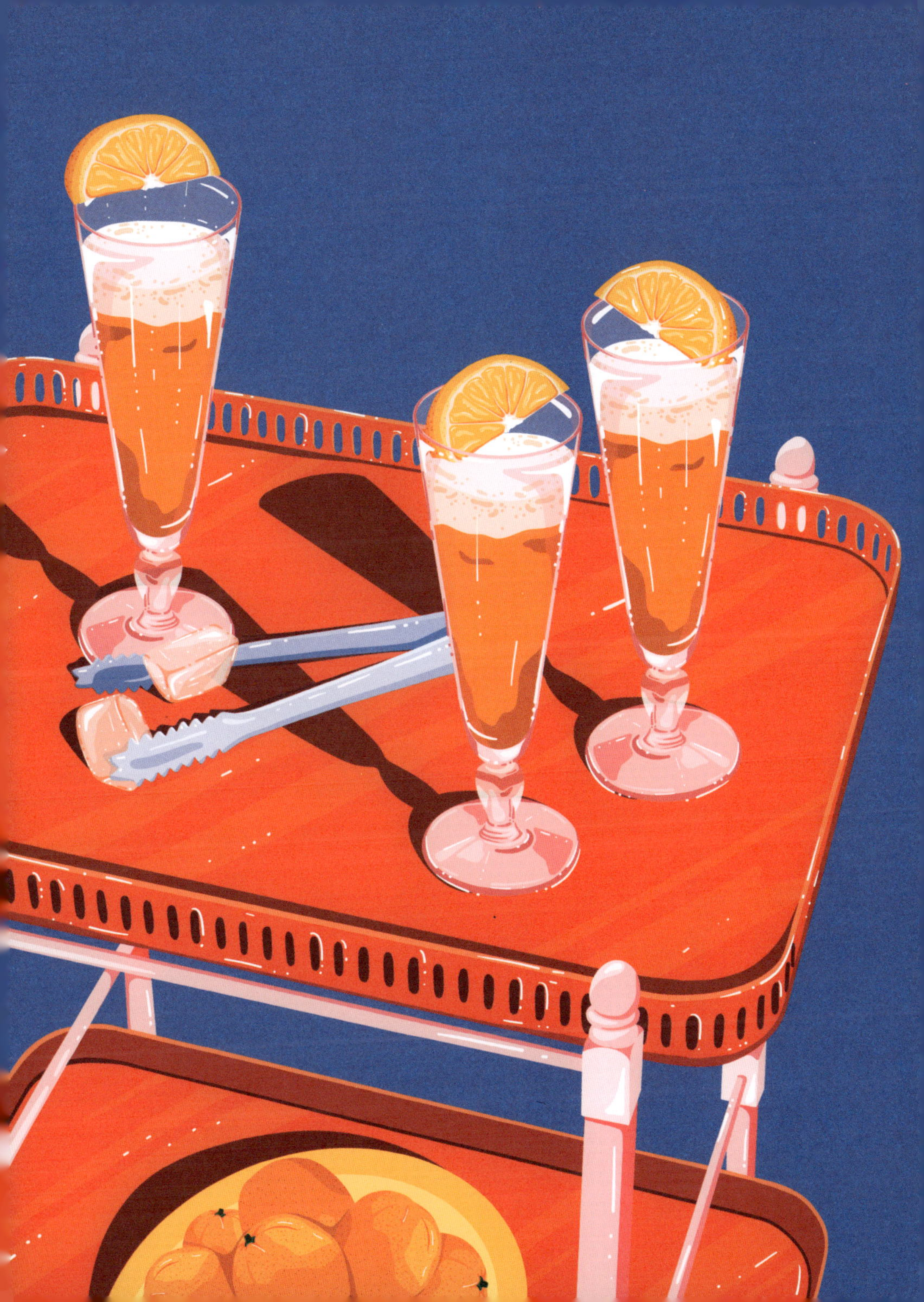

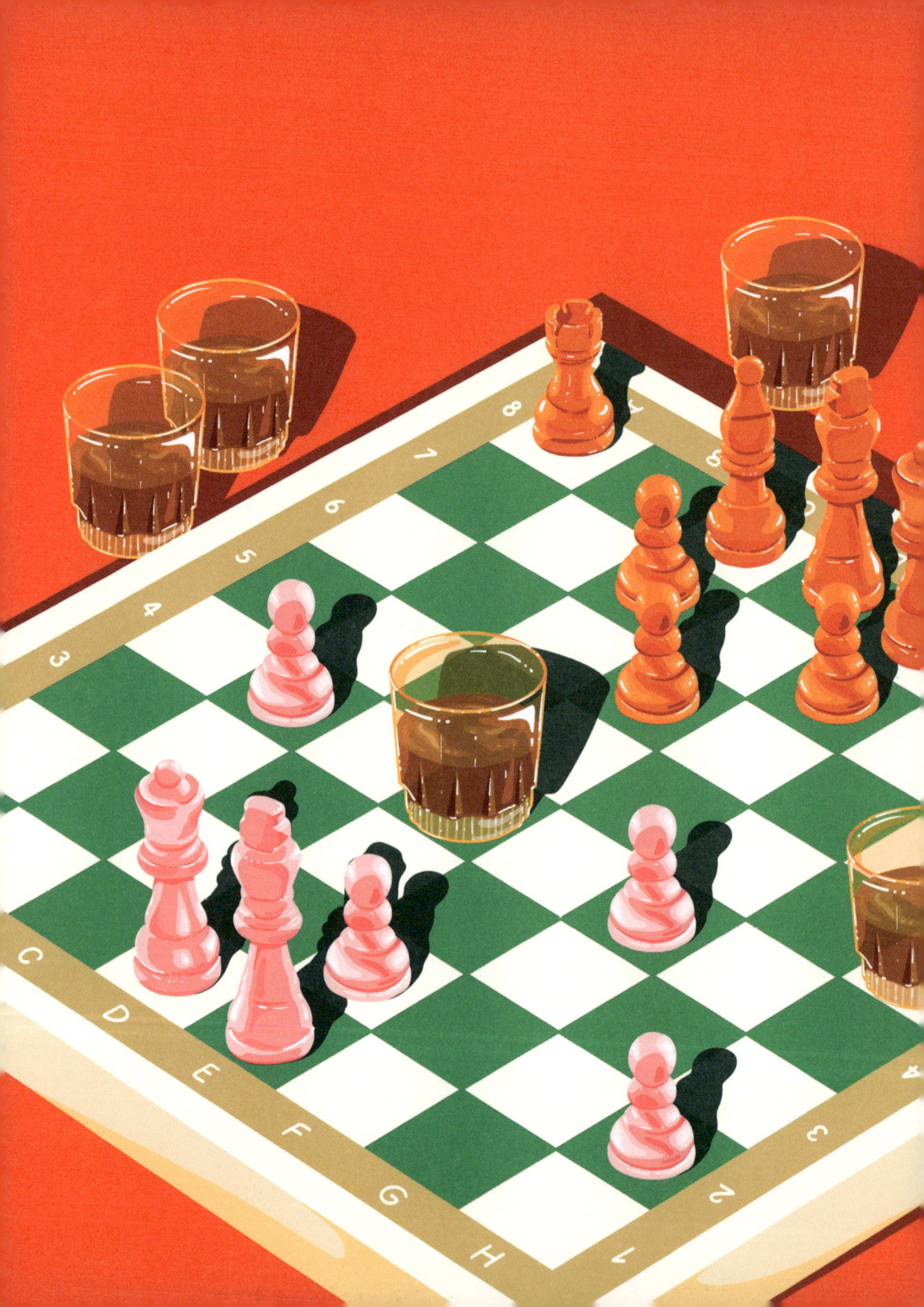
8
7
6
5
4
3
C
D
E
F
G
H
1
2
3
4

Digestivo Shots

SERVES 4

The phenomenon of "taking shots" is a stark illustration that alcohol is often used solely for its pharmacological effects. And that's perfectly acceptable! I love drugs and think all of them should be legal, regulated, and safe to use. While we wait—perhaps in vain—for the day when we can buy LSD at CVS, we can put together *these* shots, which pack a doozy of flavor. Serving them at room temperature demonstrates how warmer drinks tend to be stronger on the palate than cold ones. Of course, you can literally shoot them down quickly if you like, but I find these are best to sip on at the end of a long, indulgent meal. The bitterness and heavy ginger notes are great stomach-settlers.

---

3 ounces Ultra Gin (see page 43) or plain nonalcoholic gin

3 ounces Tenneyson Black Ginger nonalcoholic spirit

In a small shaking tin or mixing glass, combine the drink ingredients. Pour among four old fashioned glasses, dividing evenly, and serve.

BITTER | 135

Proxy Blush

MAKES 1 DRINK

Despite their best efforts, I'm sorry to say I don't find nonalcoholic red wines to be all that delicious. They're made by taking regular wine and removing the alcohol, which leaves the wine tasting a little cooked and hollow. The best approximations of red wine are drinks that build the same flavor profile—fruit, tannins, acidity, and complexity—from the ground up, and they're generally referred to as "proxies." I recommend checking out some of those products, but for those with a more DIY inclination, this recipe does a bang-up job of standing in for a nice glass of red.

---

1 ounce Red Hibiscus Concentrate (see page 42)

1 ounce fresh grapefruit juice

½ ounce nonalcoholic bitter aperitif, such as Wilfred's

½ ounce Rooh Afza syrup

4 ounces chilled nonalcoholic sparkling wine

In a small shaking tin or mixing glass, combine the red hibiscus concentrate, grapefruit juice, aperitif, and Rooh Afza syrup. Fill with ice and stir gently for 20 seconds. Strain into a wine glass, top with the sparkling wine, and serve.

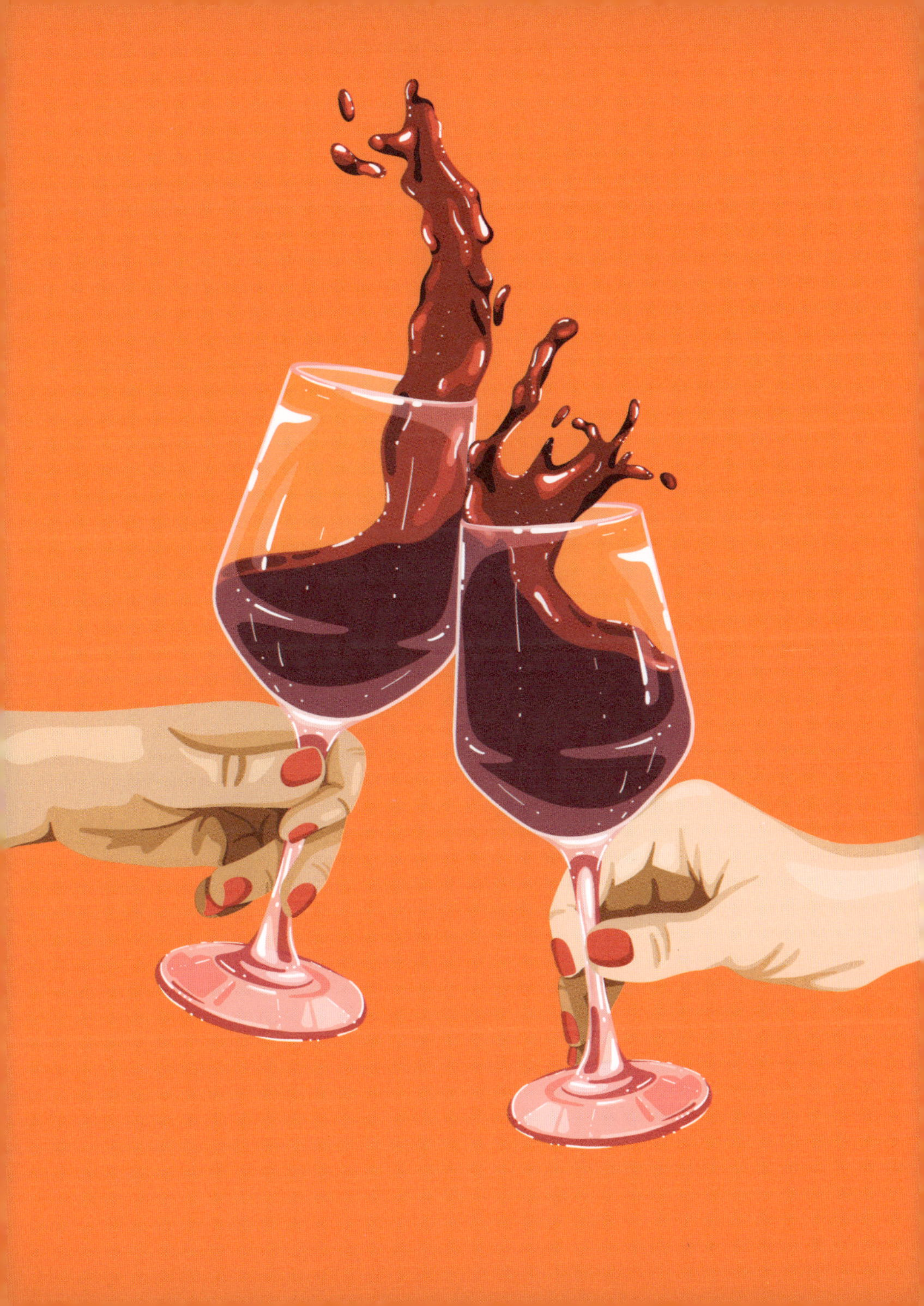

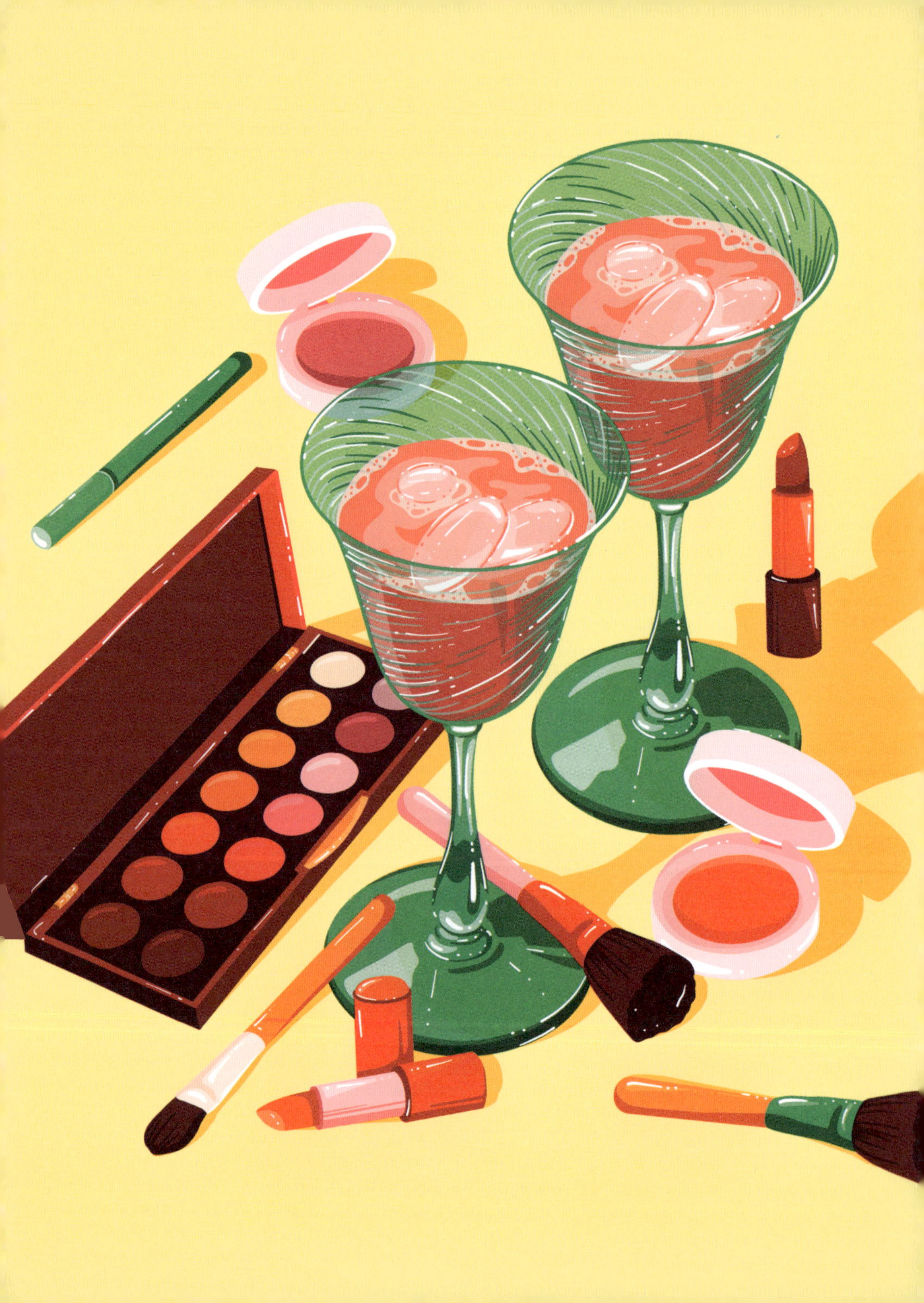

Negroni Sbagliato (for Two)

MAKES 2 DRINKS

Brooklyn distillery St. Agrestis makes one of my favorite nonalcoholic beverages, the Phony Negroni. It's a bottled, slightly carbonated nonalcoholic Negroni, making it easy to just pour one out and call it a day—and while that's something I do quite often, that's not as much fun as mixing it up with a few extras. Here, we turn it into a nonalcoholic Negroni Sbagliato, a drink now famous the world over thanks to a fun, sapphic, viral moment. One for you and a loved one each to sip on.

---

1 bottle St. Agrestis Phony Negroni

4 ounces chilled nonalcoholic sparkling wine

1 ounce Grapefruit Syrup (see page 37)

Divide the drink ingredients between two wine glasses. Add ½ cup ice to each. Stir briefly to combine and serve.

A Definitive Manhattan

MAKES 1 DRINK

I find that converting drinks to nonalcoholic by simply swapping in nonalcoholic spirits for their traditional counterparts does not always lead to a satisfying drink. Here, though, we have pretty much a one-for-one re-creation of the classic. I take advantage of flavor-enhanced nonalcoholic whiskey plus nonalcoholic sweet vermouth—I like the version from Greek producer Roots, which is almost indistinguishable from traditional sweet vermouths.

---

2 ounces Super Whiskey (see page 43) or plain nonalcoholic whiskey

1 ounce nonalcoholic sweet vermouth, such as Roots Divino Aperitif Rosso

4 dashes orange bitters or nonalcoholic orange bitters

4 dashes Angostura bitters or nonalcoholic bitters

Garnish: Luxardo cherries

In a small shaking tin or mixing glass, combine the drink ingredients. Fill with ice and stir gently for 20 seconds. Strain into a coupe and garnish with Luxardo cherries on a pick, then serve.

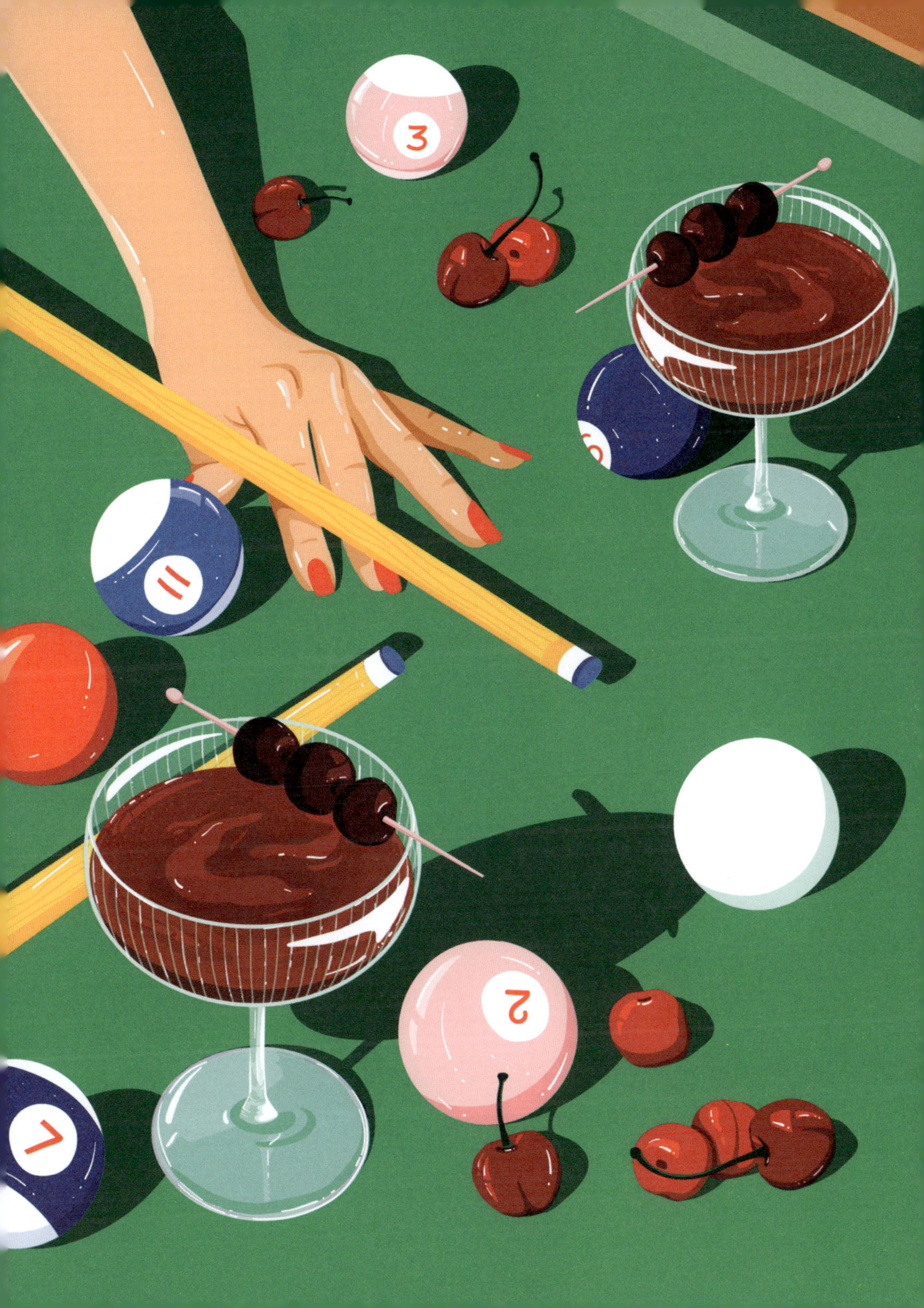

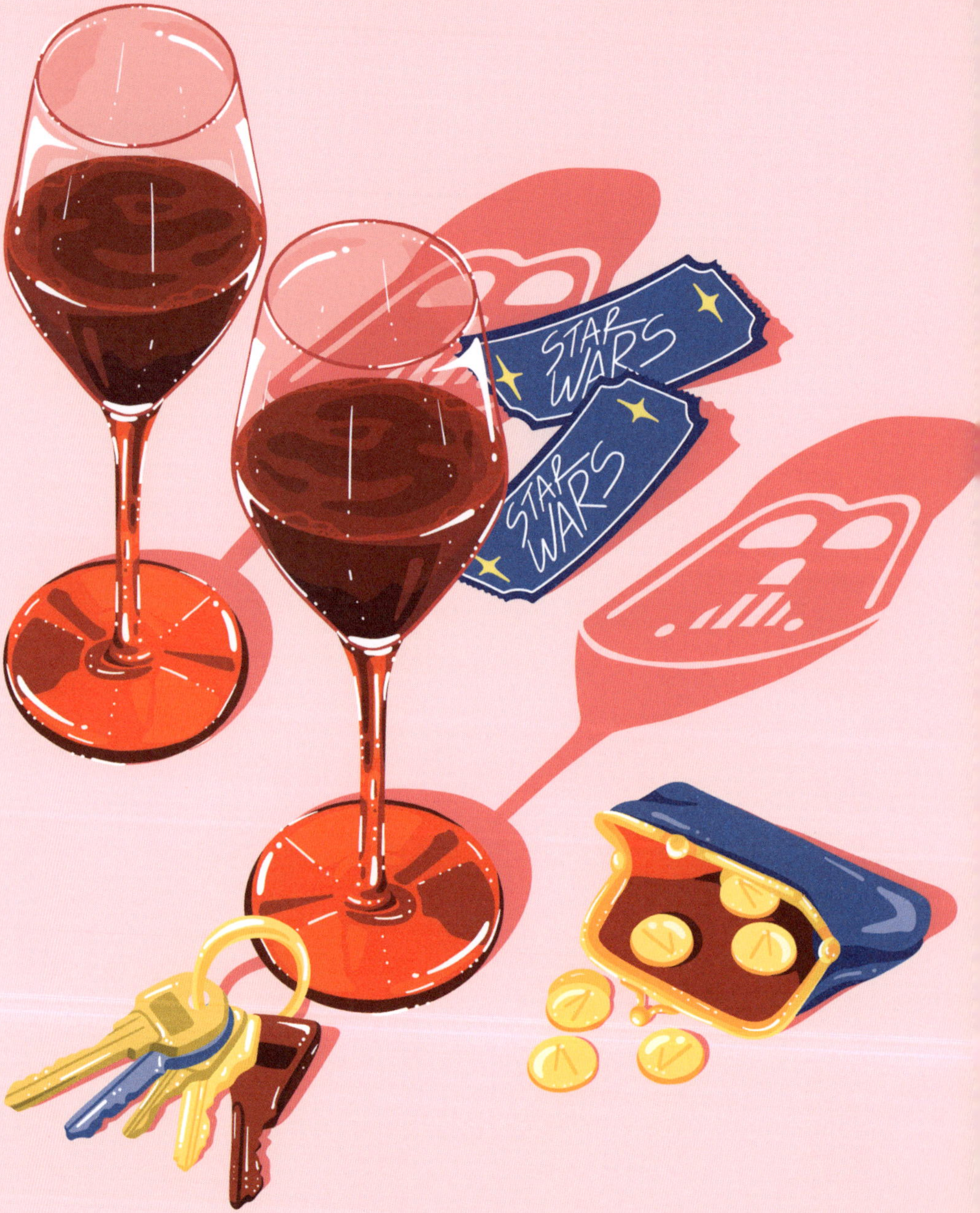
STAR WARS
STAR WARS

Darth Spritz

MAKES 2 DRINKS

This drink is a stripped-down version of something I created for the opening cocktail menu at Café Mars, a delightfully off-kilter Italian restaurant in Brooklyn. There, it contains squid ink to make the cocktail opaquely black, but that's tough to find if you're not a professional chef, so I omitted it here. (If you have some lying around, have at it!) This drink is named for that dark color—but I also love referencing the iconic *Star Wars* villain because I feel like a lot of nonalcoholic cocktail names are cutesy and childish. I wanted something people would feel a little bit dangerous ordering, even if Darth Vader isn't exactly the kind of fictional character whose behavior we should celebrate.

---

1 bottle St. Agrestis Amaro Falso

4 ounces chilled nonalcoholic sparkling wine

2 ounces chilled sparkling water

1 ounce Tenneyson Black Ginger nonalcoholic spirit

4 dashes Angostura bitters or nonalcoholic bitters

Divide the drink ingredients between two wine glasses and add ½ cup ice to each glass. Stir briefly to combine and serve.

BITTER | 143

A Definitive Nonalcoholic Gin & Tonic

MAKES 1 DRINK

◆

The gin and tonic is one of those drinks that can feel very personal. Despite only being two ingredients, there seem to be as many ways to make one "properly" as there are galaxies in the universe. Now, a nonalcoholic version enters the canon—though it takes a few more ingredients to get there. Lime syrup not only adds citrus aromatics but also, thanks to the rather pronounced bitterness of the peels, makes this drink feel a bit more sturdy. The Ultra Gin is essential to balance the drink's dilution.

---

5 ounces chilled tonic water

2 ounces Ultra Gin (see page 43) or plain nonalcoholic gin

¾ ounce fresh lime juice

½ ounce Lime Syrup (see page 37)

2 dashes orange bitters or nonalcoholic orange bitters

Garnish: lime wedge

Fill a tall glass with ice and add 2 ounces of the tonic water. In a shaker, combine the gin, lime juice, lime syrup, and bitters. Shake without ice for 5 seconds, then pour into the prepared glass. Top with the remaining 3 ounces tonic water and garnish with a lime wedge, then serve.

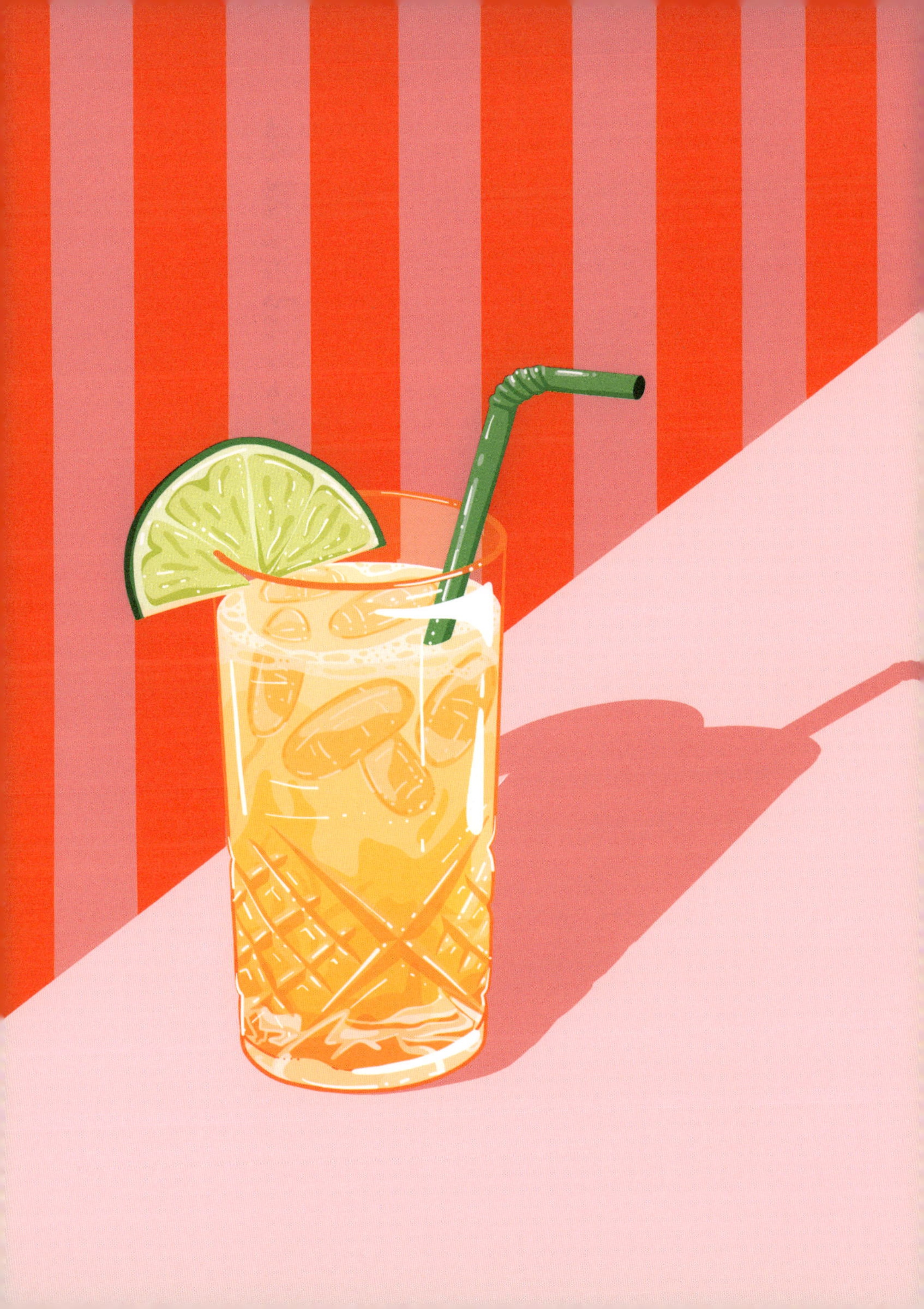

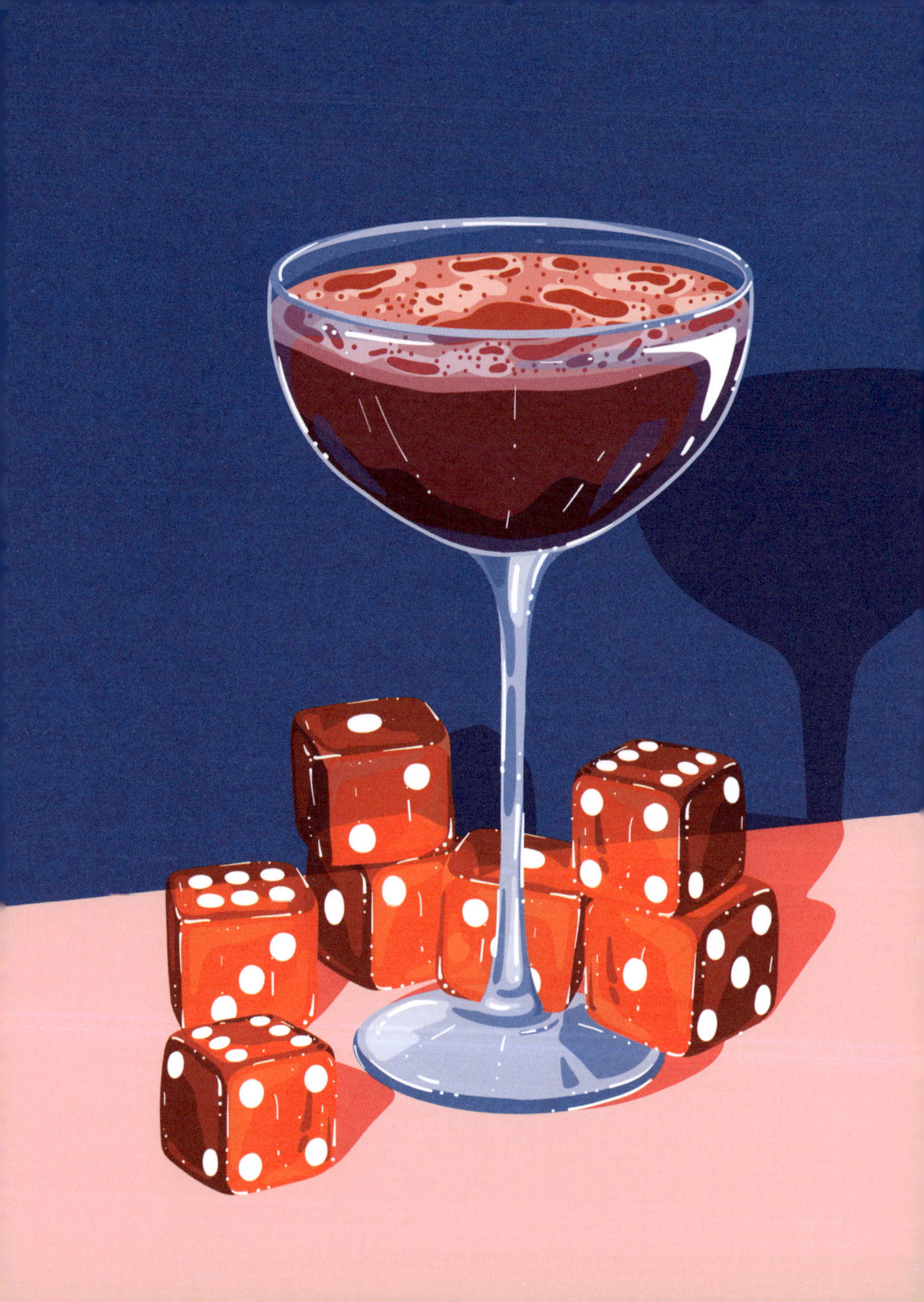

Polyberry Daiquiri

MAKES 1 DRINK

This drink was inspired by my love for the Strawberry Daiquiri, which began long, long ago with the virgin version I would order at my family's favorite Indian restaurant when I was a kid. That sentence is really weird on a lot of levels if you think about it, but let's move on. Ghia is a nonalcoholic aperitif inspired by summers on the Mediterranean and has some similarity to sweet-bitter Campari with added notes of lemon balm and orange. The rum extract offers just enough rum-like sugar cane and molasses flavor to augment the bright fruity notes from the Ghia and berries but is extremely concentrated, which allows you to alter the flavor of the drink without changing its dilution.

---

2 ounces Ghia nonalcoholic aperitif

1 ounce Polyberry Syrup (see page 39)

¾ ounce fresh lime juice

⅛ teaspoon rum extract

In a shaker, combine the drink ingredients. Fill with ice and shake vigorously for 15 seconds. Strain into a coupe and serve.

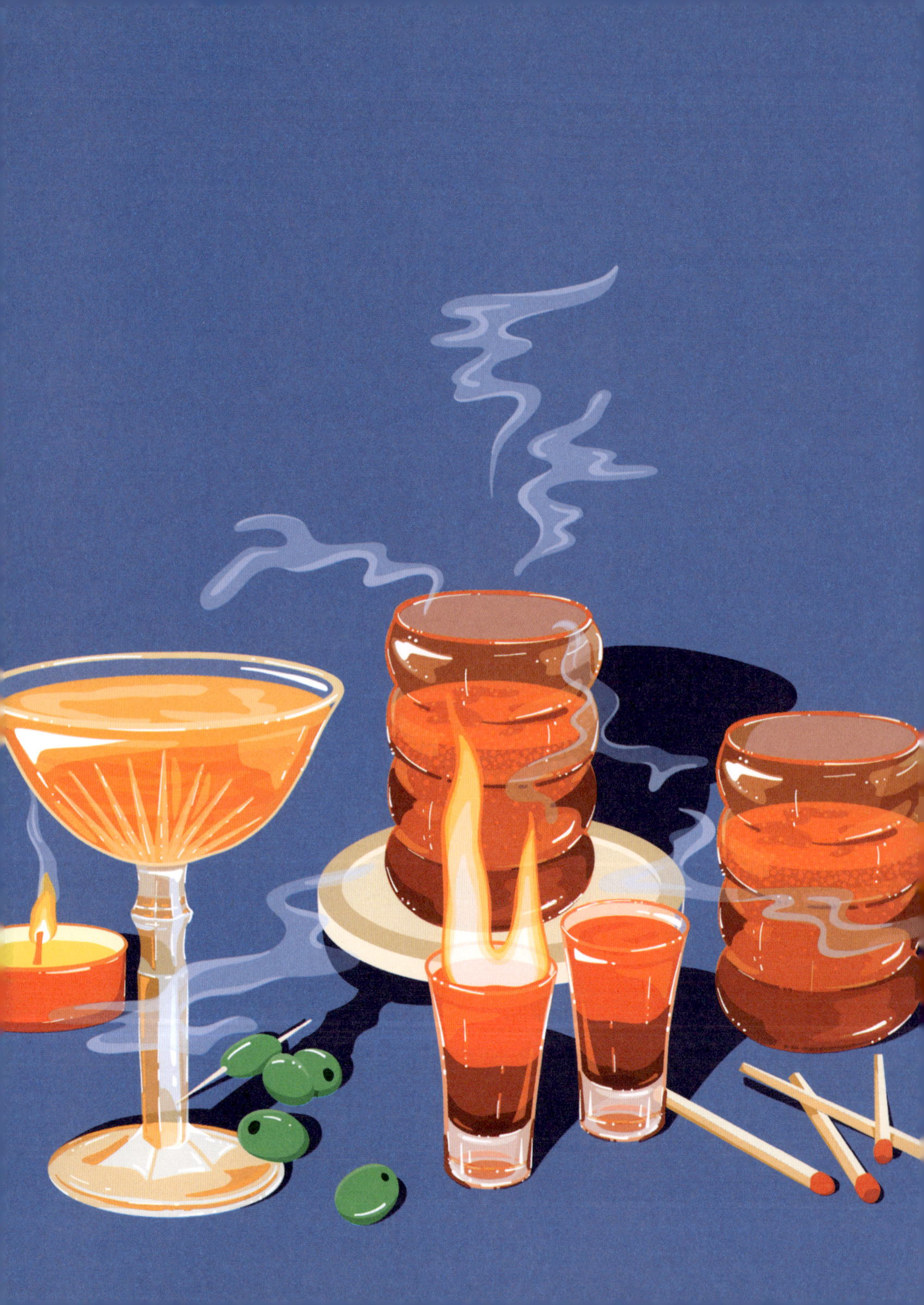

SMOKY

In spite of, or perhaps because of, the fact that we have limited avenues for incorporating smoky flavors into nonalcoholic cocktails, it makes the effort to devise smoke-inflected nonalcoholic cocktails that much more rewarding. Classic cocktails with smoky Scotch such as the Penicillin and Rob Roy are some of the inspiration for the drinks in this section. Smoky Lapsang Souchong tea is a neat trick, but there are also a few smoky nonalcoholic spirits called for to bring this woody campfire element. These drinks run the gamut from refreshing to intense and are great to drink on a cold, rainy evening spent indoors with loved ones.

Mugi Toddy

MAKES 1 DRINK

◆

I first visited Japan in the '90s as a dorky teenager obsessed with anime and video games. I also wanted to know everything about this fascinating country. One of the ways I did this was by putting coins into one of the nation's astonishingly ubiquitous vending machines and pressing buttons at random. One such result was a bottle of chilled, unsweetened mugicha, made from roasted barley. As a thirteen-year-old, it was not sweet enough to delight me, but over the years I have come to love this stuff. On my most recent trip to Japan, I think I drank about 900 bottles—in Japan, you are never more than a two-minute walk from a vending machine. Despite chilled being my temperature of preference for straight mugicha, it works great as the base for this hot toddy.

---

6 ounces boiling water

6 ounces Mugi Concentrate (see page 41)

1 ounce nonalcoholic whiskey

½ ounce Jaggery Syrup (see page 36)

Garnish: lemon wedge

In a heatproof mug, combine the drink ingredients and stir briefly to combine. Garnish with the lemon wedge and serve.

SMOKY | 151

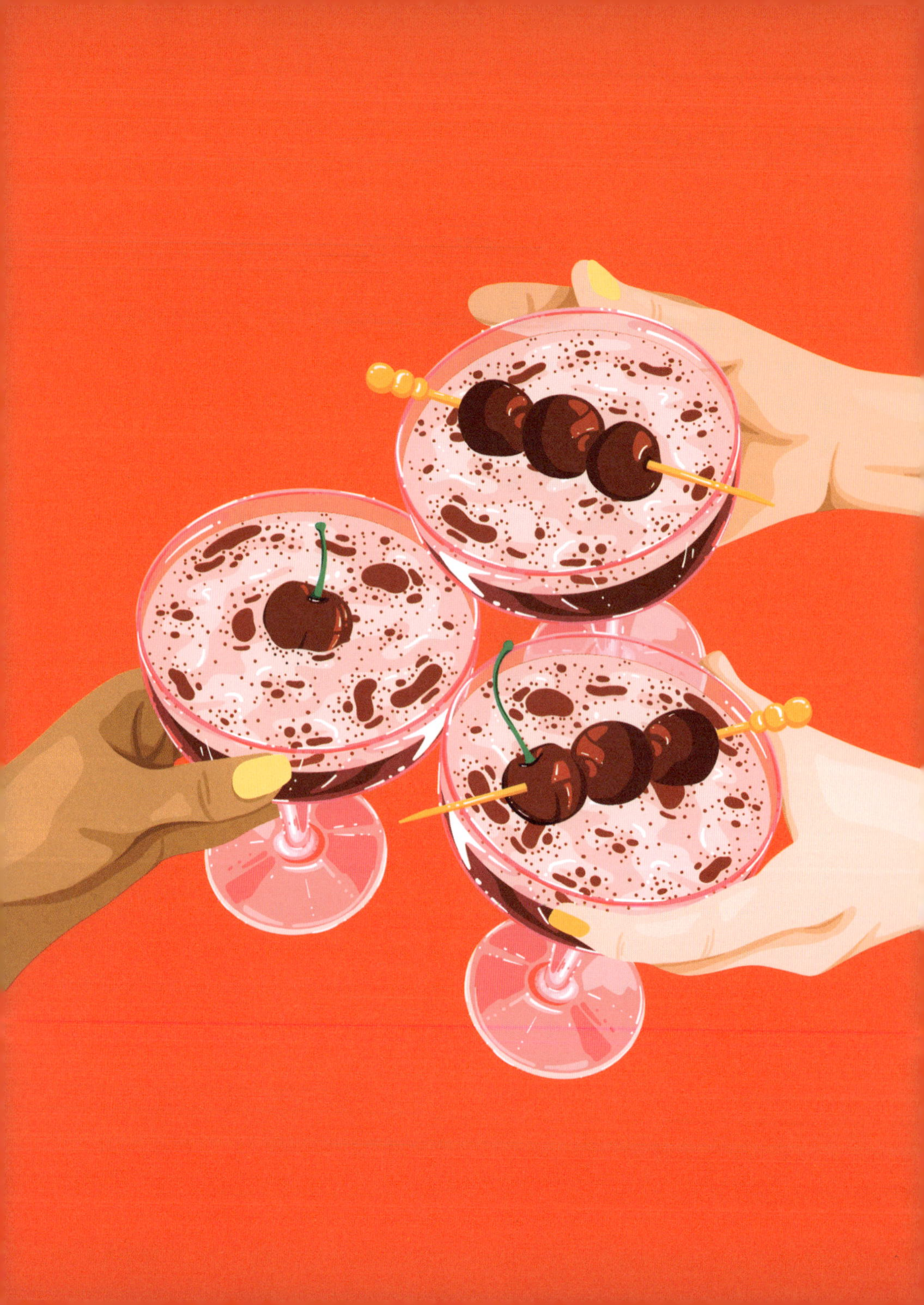

Lapsang-Luxardo

MAKES 1 DRINK
■

In my second book, *Saved by the Bellini*, I created a drink in honor of the '90s group En Vogue, whose *Funky Divas* album was one of the first I owned (on cassette, thankyouverymuch). Free Your Mind was an alcohol-free (Get it?) mixture of smoky Lapsang Souchong tea, watermelon, and Luxardo cherry syrup. It required a fine straining of the tea, which is infused into the watermelon juice during shaking. Here, that (tasty but precious) drink is rebuilt with Lapsang concentrate, making it both more delicious and a bit easier to throw together. The small pour of tonic water delivers a subtle bitterness plus carbonation to balance out the richer notes of the watermelon and Luxardo syrup.

---

1 ounce Lapsang Concentrate (see page 41)

1 ounce fresh watermelon juice

½ ounce fresh lime juice

½ ounce Luxardo cherry syrup

1 ounce chilled tonic water

Garnish: Luxardo cherries

In a shaker, combine the Lapsang concentrate, watermelon juice, lime juice, and Luxardo syrup. Fill with ice and shake vigorously for 15 seconds. Strain into a coupe and top with the tonic water. Garnish with the cherries on a pick and serve.

Berry Bramble

MAKES 1 DRINK

◆

If you're familiar with the classic Bramble cocktail, you might think calling it a "Berry Bramble" is somewhat redundant, given the drink is made with blackberry liqueur, gin, and lemon juice. And you'd be right! But I'd imagine most people aren't as aggressively steeped in cocktail arcana as I am, and that's fine. Rather than using gin, I opt for nonalcoholic whiskey supported by a dose of nonalcoholic red wine. By itself, I don't think nonalcoholic red wine is all that great (which is why I made my own; see page 136) but it is a useful tool when mixing drinks because it gives complexity and acidity and dyes this drink with a nice violet hue.

1½ ounces nonalcoholic red wine

1 ounce Super Whiskey (see page 43) or plain nonalcoholic whiskey

1 ounce Polyberry Syrup (see page 39)

Garnish: blackberries and mint

Fill a shaker with ice and shake vigorously for 30 seconds until the ice is crushed. Pour the crushed ice into an old fashioned glass. In the shaker, combine the drink ingredients. Fill with ice and shake vigorously for 15 seconds. Strain into the prepared glass. Garnish with berries and mint and serve.

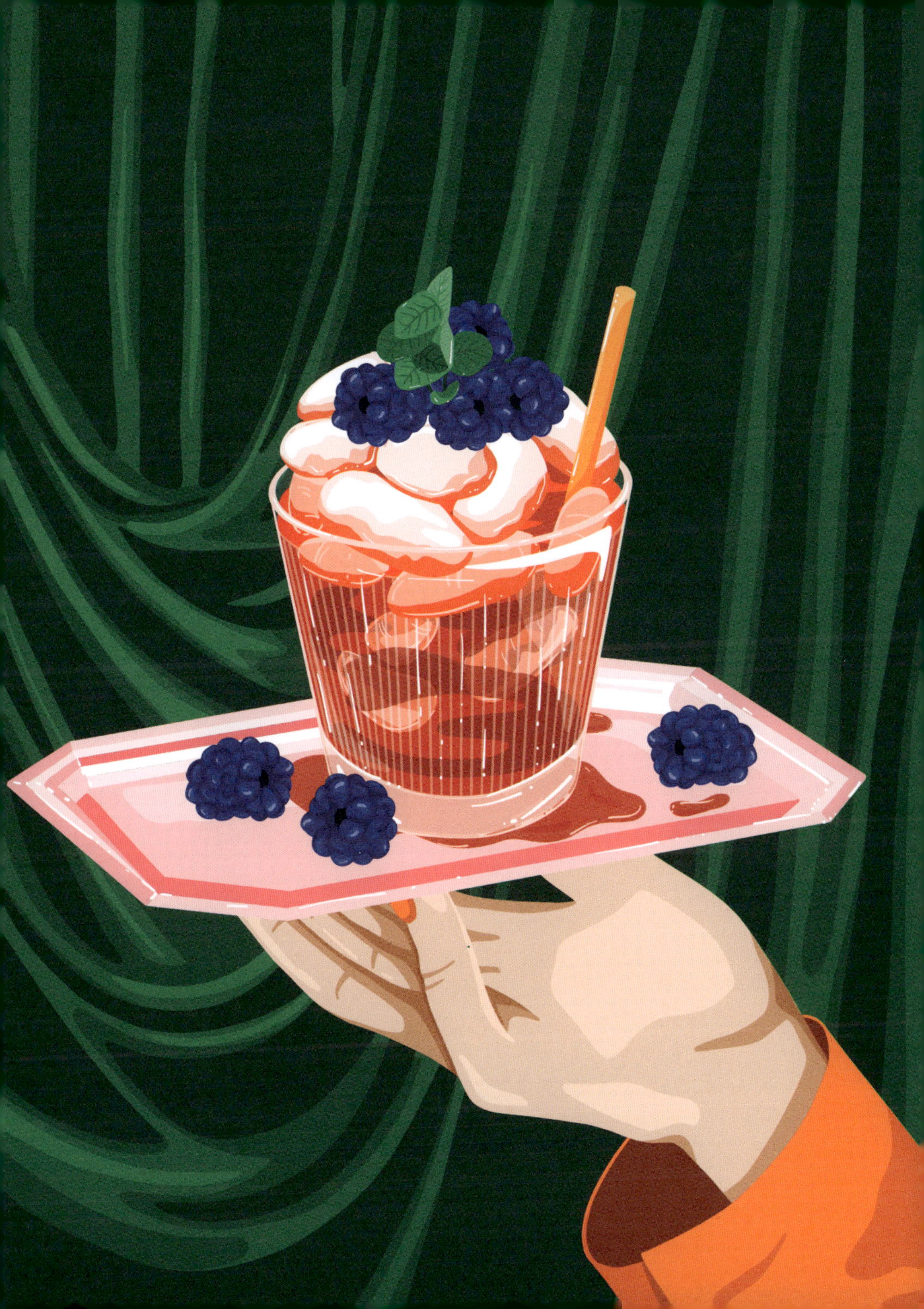

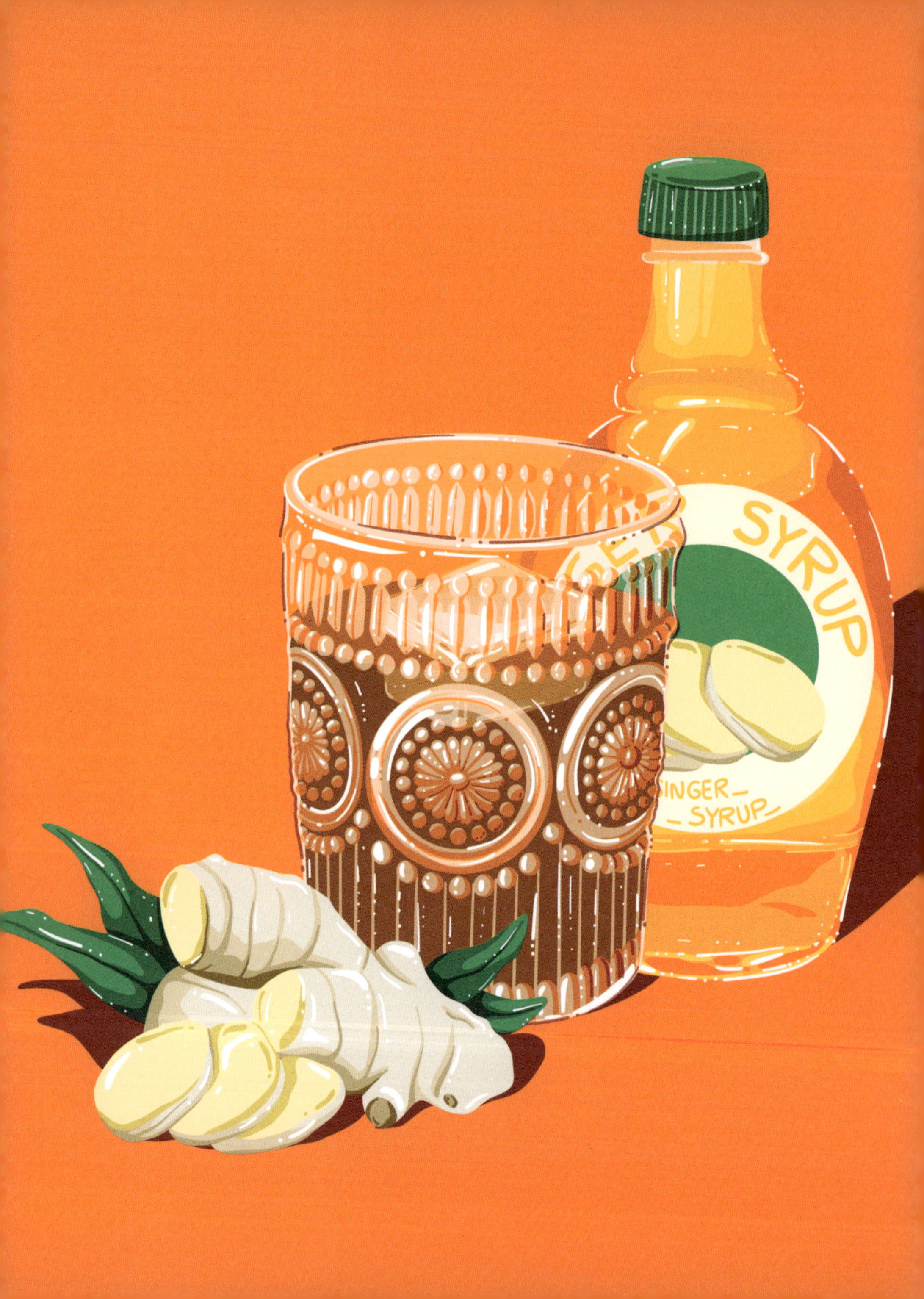
SYRUP
SYRUP

Smoked Cola Old Fashioned

MAKES 1 DRINK

◆

2 ounces Lapsang Concentrate (see page 41)

1 ounce chilled cola

¼ ounce Ginger Syrup (see page 38)

2 dashes orange bitters or nonalcoholic orange bitters

I wish a cola manufacturer would make a smoky version of their cola and sell it, but alas. I'm taking matters into my own hands to satisfy my oddly frequent cravings for cola's notes of cinnamon and vanilla against a backdrop of smoke. You might think it's a little weird to call a drink made with soda an "Old Fashioned," but we're not adding enough of it to make the drink notably fizzy. Plus, I've noticed that the current nonalcoholic cocktail canon is sorely lacking in Old Fashioned–inspired drinks, and I'm happy to add this one to the list.

In an old fashioned glass with one large ice cube or a few small ice cubes, combine the drink ingredients. Stir gently for 20 seconds and serve.

New New York Sour

MAKES 1 DRINK

My affection for the New York Sour—a standard whiskey sour with a float of red wine on top—is rooted in my memory of a fundraising dinner hosted by my then-employer, Momofuku. It was the week following Hurricane Sandy; my apartment didn't have power, and my husband and I were essentially living out of one of the group's restaurants in midtown Manhattan. I was in an understandable haze and when it came time to float the red wine over the tray of drinks, I could not steady my hands adequately—they ended up all sloppy and muddled. Tasted great, though! This version is a slightly modified version of the classic, but with lemon syrup to help bump up aromatics and texture. If the idea of raw egg white skeeves you out, you can omit it, but the texture will not be the same and it will be much harder to layer on the wine.

---

1 ounce nonalcoholic whiskey

1 ounce Lemon Syrup (see page 37)

¾ ounce fresh lemon juice

1 large egg white

¾ ounce nonalcoholic red wine

In a shaker, combine the whiskey, lemon syrup, lemon juice, and egg white. Shake without ice for 5 seconds. Fill with ice and shake vigorously for 15 seconds. Strain into an old fashioned glass with one large ice cube or a few small ice cubes. Pour the red wine over the top and serve.

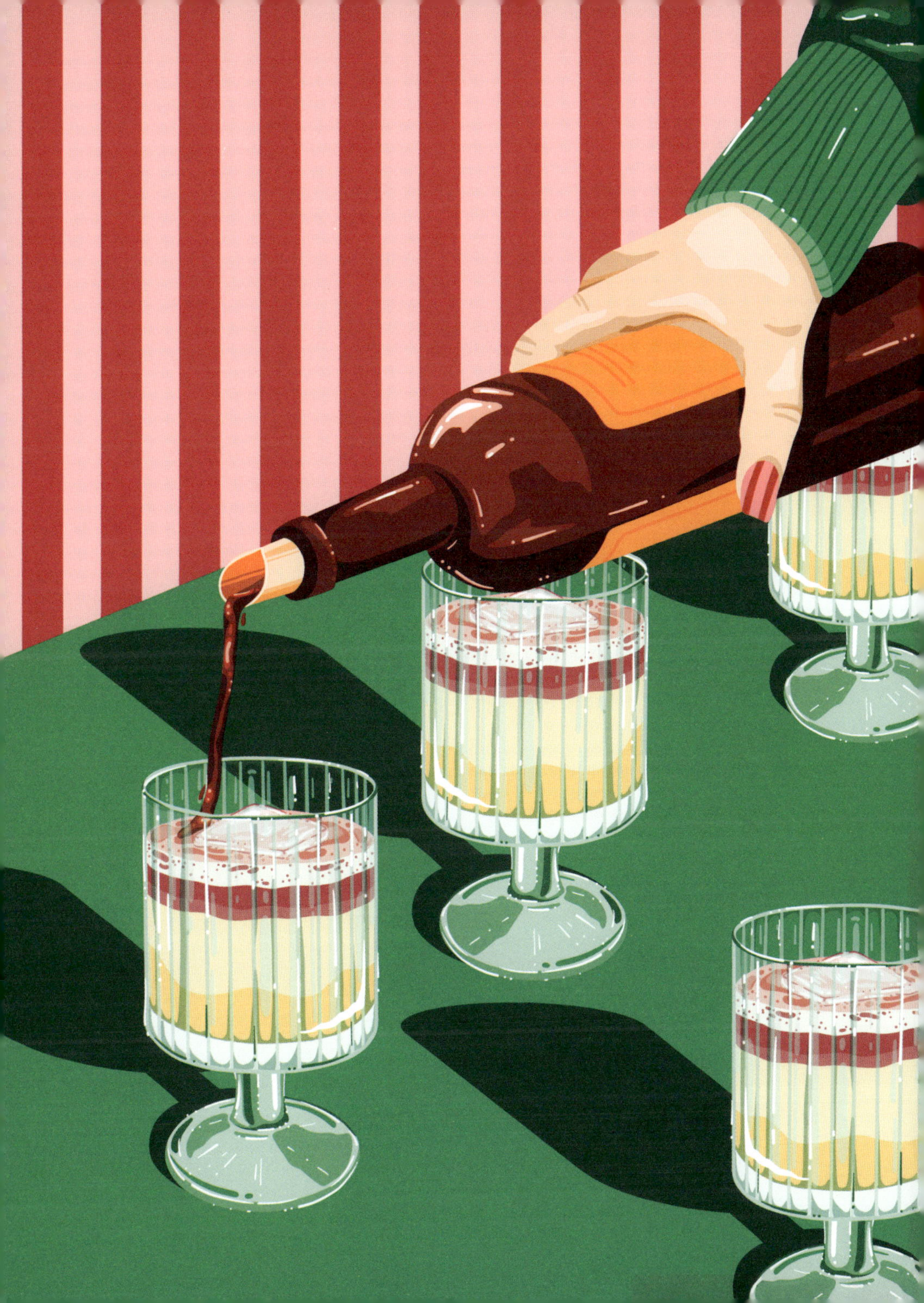

A Not-So-Definitive Old Fashioned

MAKES 1 DRINK

◆

Much like the martini and gin and tonic, the Old Fashioned can be infinitely riffed to suit anyone's individual tastes. Many prefer it sweetened with a sugar cube instead of sugar syrup. Others replace the traditional American whiskey with other spirits like Scotch, rum, or even brandy. In this particular riff, Lapsang concentrate plus super whiskey merge to become something resembling a generic whiskey: a little smoky like Scotch and a little grainy-toasty like bourbon. Jaggery syrup takes the place of a plain sugar or brown sugar syrup typically used to sweeten an Old Fashioned, and a grapefruit peel—not commonly deployed as a garnish—brightens up the otherwise dark-and-moody cocktail.

2½ ounces Lapsang Concentrate (see page 41)

½ ounce Super Whiskey (see page 43) or plain nonalcoholic whiskey

½ ounce Jaggery Syrup (see page 36)

2 dashes orange bitters or nonalcoholic orange bitters

2 dashes Angostura bitters or nonalcoholic bitters

Garnish: grapefruit peel

In an old fashioned glass with one large ice cube or a few small ice cubes, combine the drink ingredients. Stir gently for 20 seconds. Express the grapefruit peel over the top of the drink, then perch it on the rim of the glass and serve.

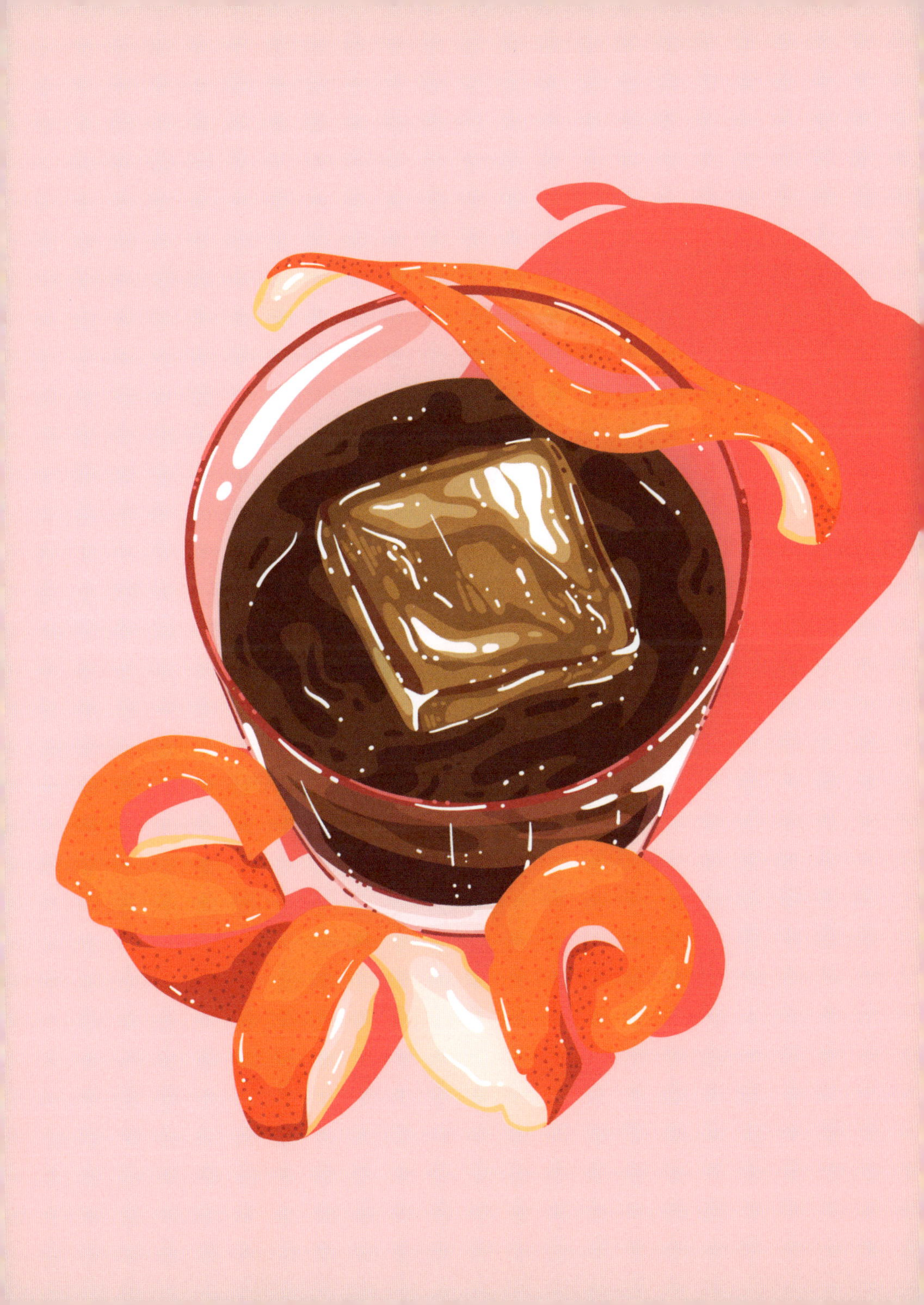

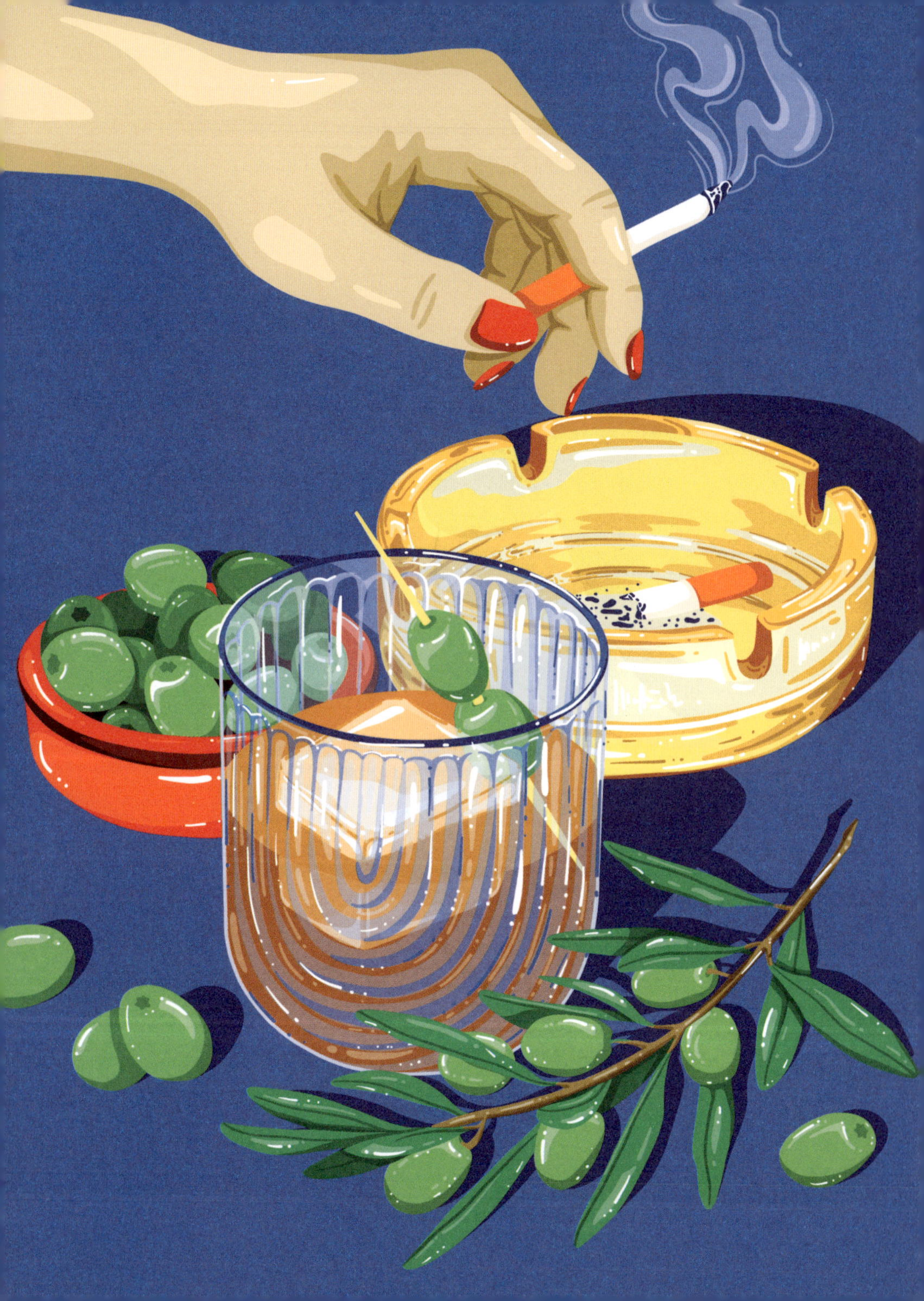

Dirty Old Fashioned

MAKES 1 DRINK

●

On paper, this drink bears very little similarity to the classic Old Fashioned, but in the glass, it bears an unmistakable (though admittedly rather odd) resemblance. New York City drinks company (parentheses) makes two vinegar-based spirits I really love. Instead of trying to mimic an existing spirit, they simply crafted something delicious. The spirit called After is made with angelica, cherry bark, and chamomile, among other ingredients. I think this stuff is good enough to sip neat, but when combined with yuzu and olive brine, you get a salty, tart, and smoky drink that's complexly satisfying but simple to make.

---

2 ounces (parentheses) After nonalcoholic spirit

½ ounce yuzu juice

¼ ounce olive brine

Garnish: olives

In an old fashioned glass with one large ice cube or a few small ice cubes, combine the drink ingredients. Stir gently for 20 seconds. Garnish with olives on a pick and serve.

Pickup Toddy

MAKES 1 DRINK

●

Despite the word "toddy" generally referring to a hot drink made with spirits, sugar, and other cocktail-coded ingredients, one of the most popular tools for making cold brew coffee calls itself "Toddy." To honor this semantic overlap, I'm mixing cold brew coffee with a healthy slug of apple cider and a touch of the vinegar-based boutique botanical spirit made by NYC-based producer (parentheses). They make two versions: Before, which is more aperitif-y, and After, used here, which has nightcap-like notes of black cardamom and peppermint. If you can't find it, you can swap out the After for another dark botanical nonalcoholic spirit of your choosing, but I recommend making the effort.

---

6 ounces apple cider

2 ounces cold brew coffee concentrate

½ ounce (parentheses) After or other nonalcoholic dark spirit

Garnish: freshly grated nutmeg

In a small pan, combine the drink ingredients. Place over medium heat until the mixture is just steaming, about 5 minutes, then pour it into a heatproof mug. Grate nutmeg over the top and serve.

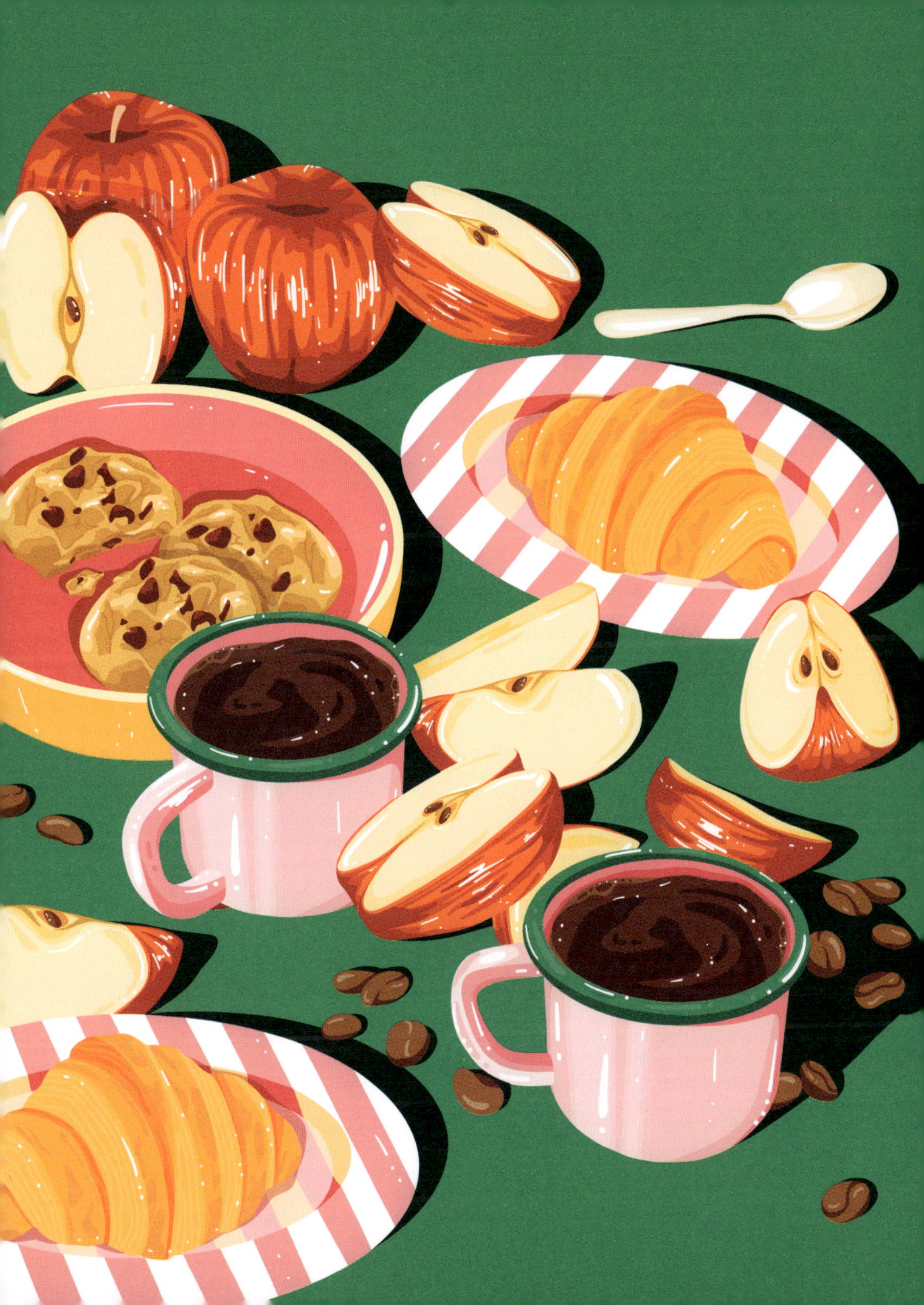

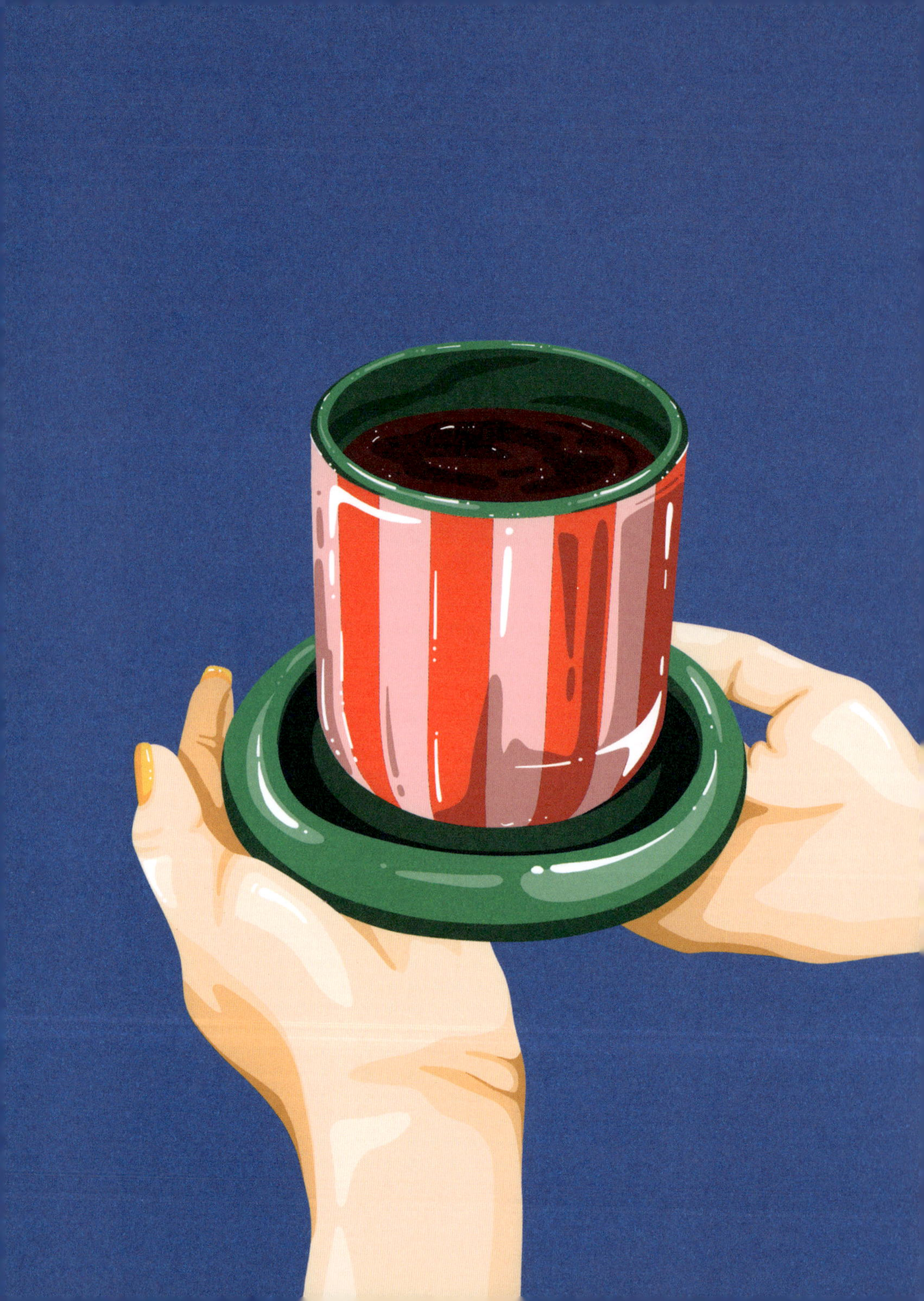

Hot Curcu

MAKES 1 DRINK

◆

Many nonalcoholic spirits love to associate themselves with "functional benefits" like enhanced mood, improved cognition, and better sleep. Curcumin is one of the active compounds in turmeric, and a decent amount of evidence supports claims that it can address a variety of health issues, but until enough placebo-controlled studies take place, my point of view is that the only benefit of any nonalcoholic beverage is that it should taste amazing. Hopefully you'll agree this invigoratingly complex three-ingredient (okay, four, if you count the boiling water) hot toddy does, indeed, taste amazing. Study complete!

---

6 ounces boiling water

5 ounces Lapsang Concentrate (see page 41)

1½ ounces Turmeric Syrup (see page 39)

½ ounce fresh lime juice

In a heatproof mug, combine the drink ingredients. Stir gently to combine and serve.

Fireplace Punch

SERVES 10

♦♦

Despite what some individuals and industries want us to believe, human activity has indeed led to a spike in global temperatures. Case in point: One Christmas Eve in the early aughts, my family wanted to enjoy a cozy fire even though the temperature was sixty-five degrees in the Northeast. So, of course, a fire we made, and we opened all the windows in the house, too. This was absurd, and I do not recommend trying it yourself. Instead, make this hearty, smoky punch. It will give you all the coziness of a warm fire no matter what temperature it is outside.

---

16 ounces Lapsang Concentrate (see page 41)

16 ounces chilled nonalcoholic dark beer, such as porter or stout

8 ounces Super Whiskey (see page 43) or plain nonalcoholic whiskey

4 ounces Ginger Syrup (see page 38)

2 ounces Pepper Syrup (see page 38)

8 dashes orange bitters or nonalcoholic orange bitters

In a large punch bowl or pitcher, combine the drink ingredients. Add 4 to 6 large ice cubes or 2 cups regular ice. Stir briefly to combine and serve in old fashioned glasses.

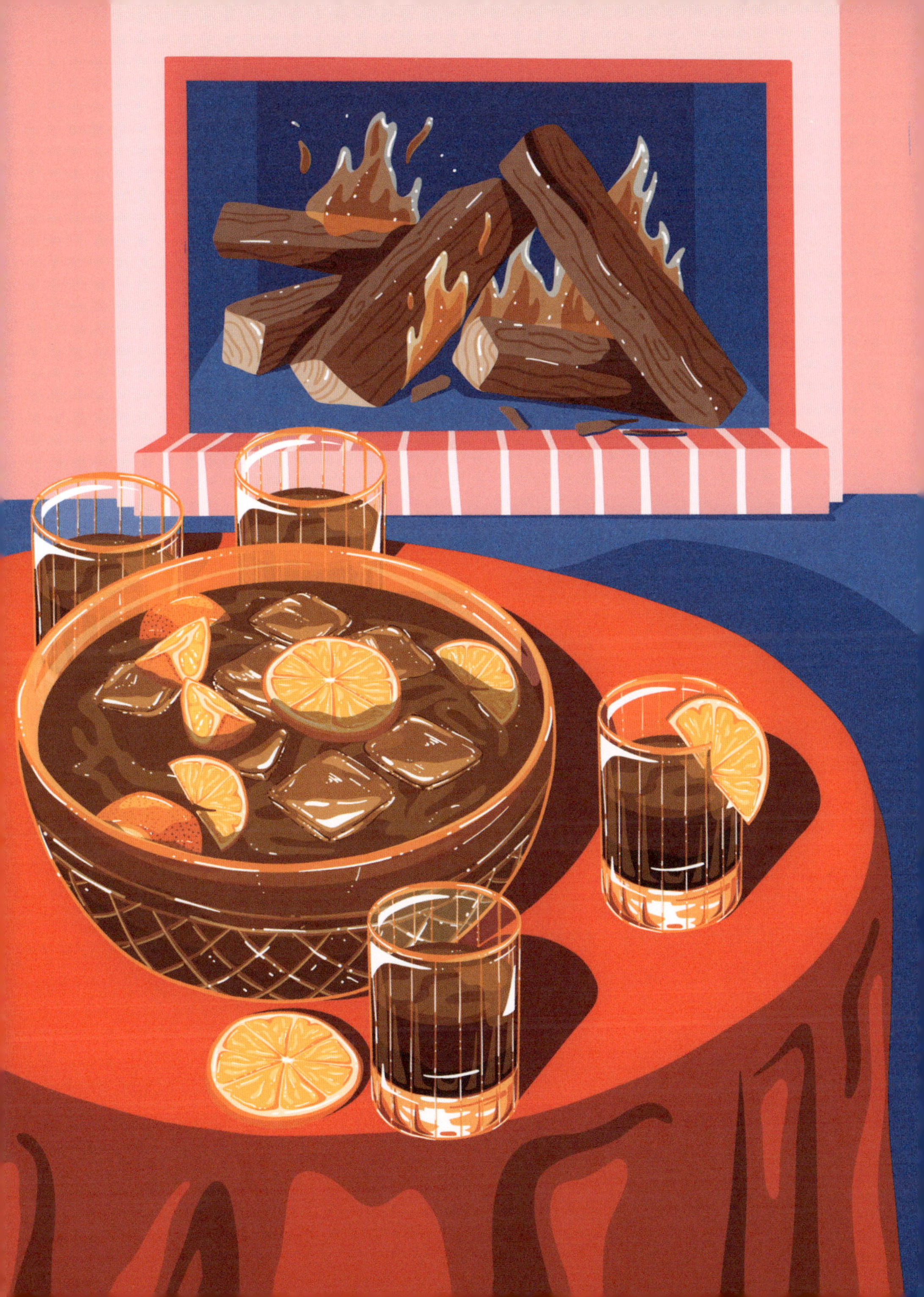

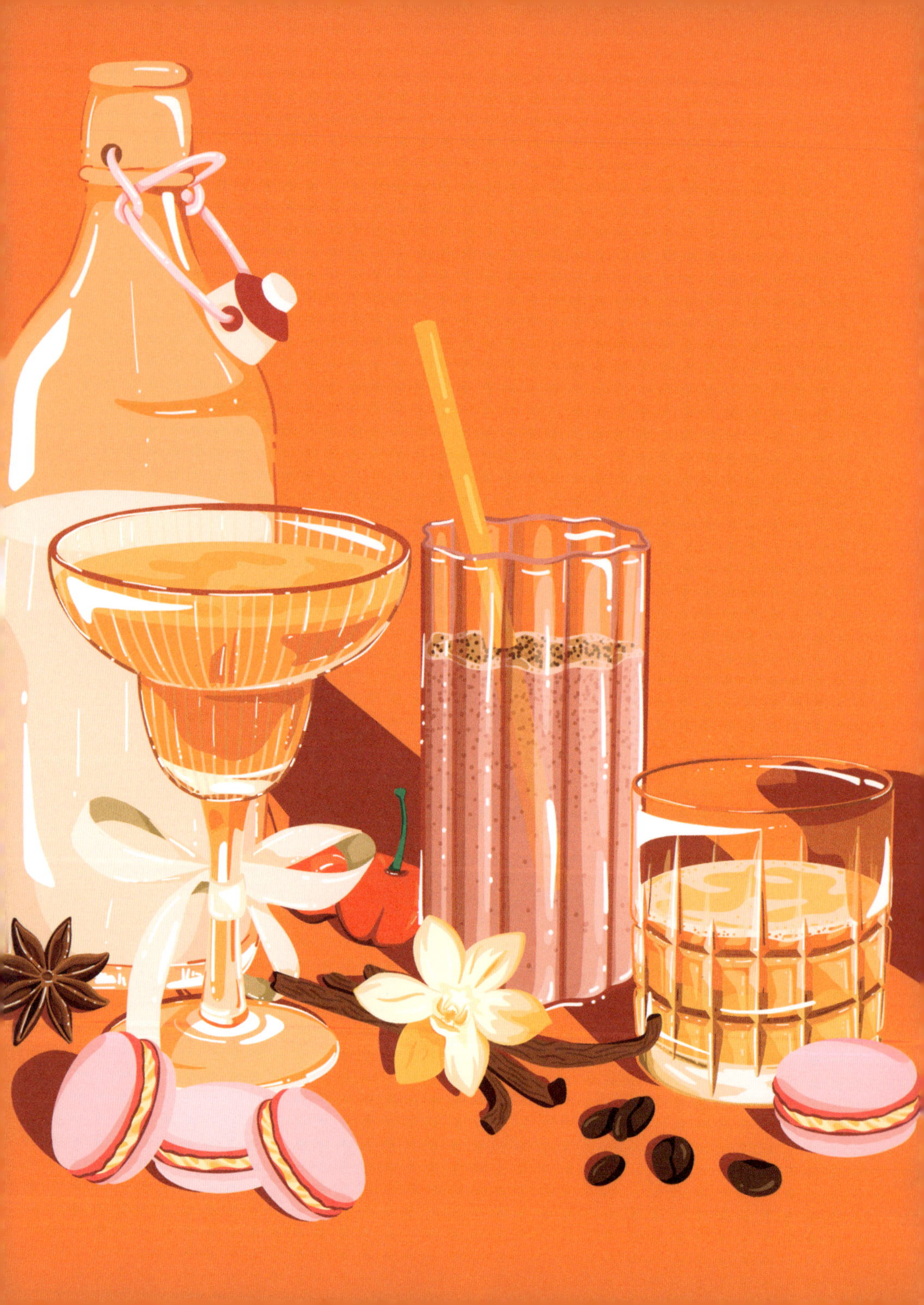

VELVETY

Rich, creamy textures are more commonly found in the realm of desserts than cocktails, but the luxurious texture supplied by fat-containing ingredients such as nuts and dairy deserve their place in cocktails. If overused, we may be left with a drink more like a milkshake than a cocktail, but when applied judiciously the texture and richness fats bring to drinks can create satisfying experiences and also allow a degree of aeration and fluffiness. Eggnog and the Ramos Gin Fizz are two classic velvety cocktails. The alternatives found in this section are best served after dinner, or whenever you want something rich, fluffy, and intriguing.

Miso Flip

MAKES 1 DRINK

You have to be careful with salt in cocktails. Even in things that don't taste perceptibly salty, salt helps to accentuate flavors and even out harsh bitter notes. But if you use too much, things can get revolting, real fast. For this drink make sure you find a "light" or "white" miso, which is the most subtly flavored. Its saltiness helps dial up the rich, roasty flavors found in the nonalcoholic stout and jaggery syrup. With the addition of a whole egg, this drink is almost a self-contained meal!

4½ ounces chilled nonalcoholic stout or porter beer

¾ ounce Jaggery Syrup (see page 36)

1 tablespoon light or white miso

1 large egg

Garnish: freshly ground black pepper

In a shaker, combine ½ ounce of the beer, the jaggery syrup, miso, and egg. Shake without ice for 5 seconds. Fill with ice and shake vigorously for 15 seconds. Strain into a chilled small glass, then top with the remaining 4 ounces beer. Garnish with ground black pepper and serve.

Bocce Boule

MAKES 1 DRINK

I was introduced to the Bocce Ball cocktail when I was writing a piece for the drinks website PUNCH. It's one of those forgotten disco cocktails that might have been popular in the '70s, but has fallen by the wayside as more "serious" drinks were elevated to the canon. The classic is a dead-simple combo of orange juice, sparkling water, and amaretto liqueur—and now some brave bartenders are reaching back and dusting off memories we almost forgot about, triggering a resurgence. Here, nutty orgeat syrup, white hibiscus, and orange bitters stand in for the amaretto liqueur. I highly recommend using freshly squeezed orange juice, as it will froth nicely in the shaker.

---

2 ounces fresh orange juice

1½ ounces orgeat syrup

¾ ounce White Hibiscus Concentrate (see page 42)

4 dashes orange bitters or nonalcoholic orange bitters

4 ounces chilled sparkling water

In a shaker, combine the orange juice, orgeat, white hibiscus concentrate, and orange bitters. Fill with ice and shake vigorously for 15 seconds. Pour the sparkling water into a chilled small glass, then strain the drink over the top and serve.

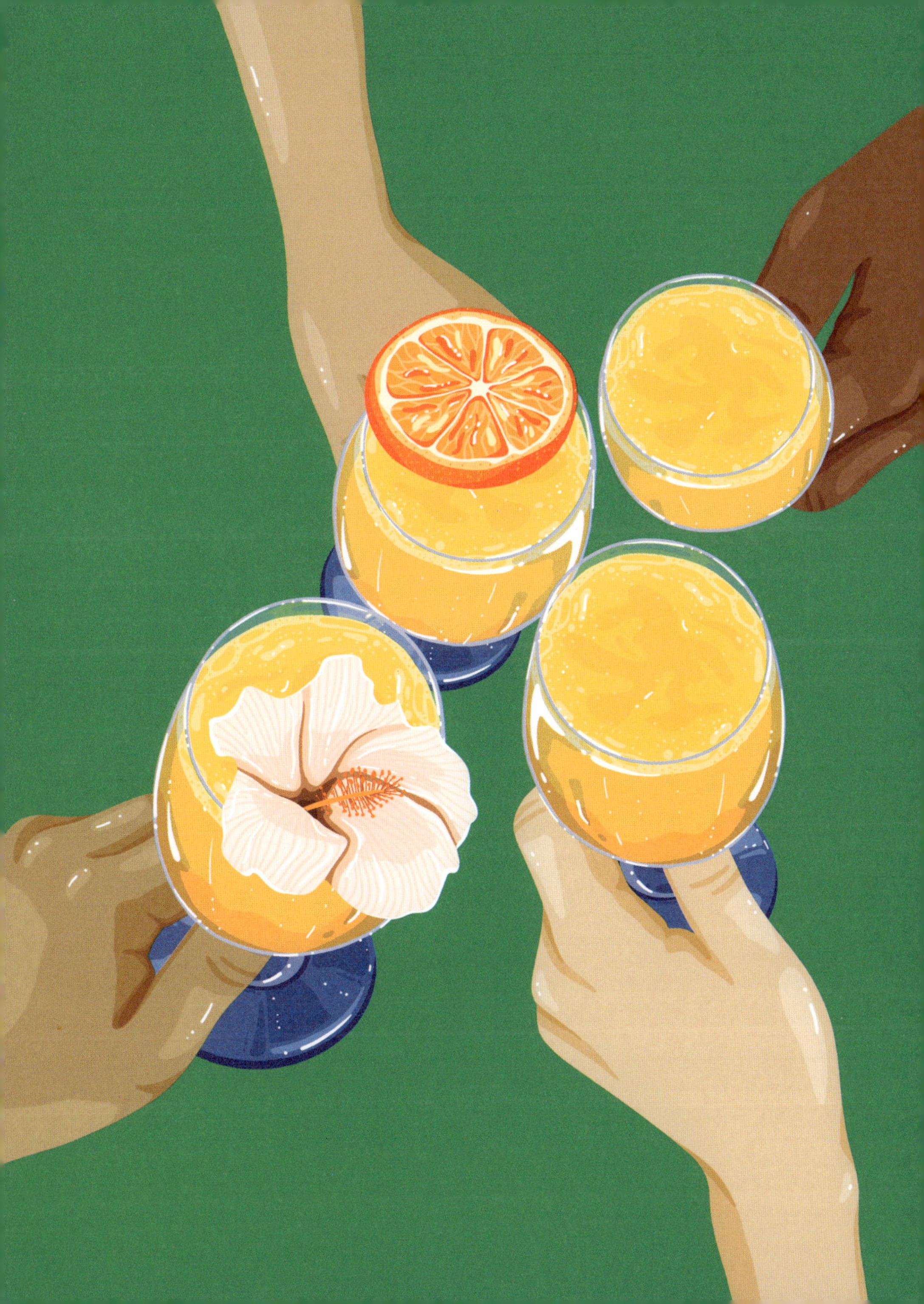

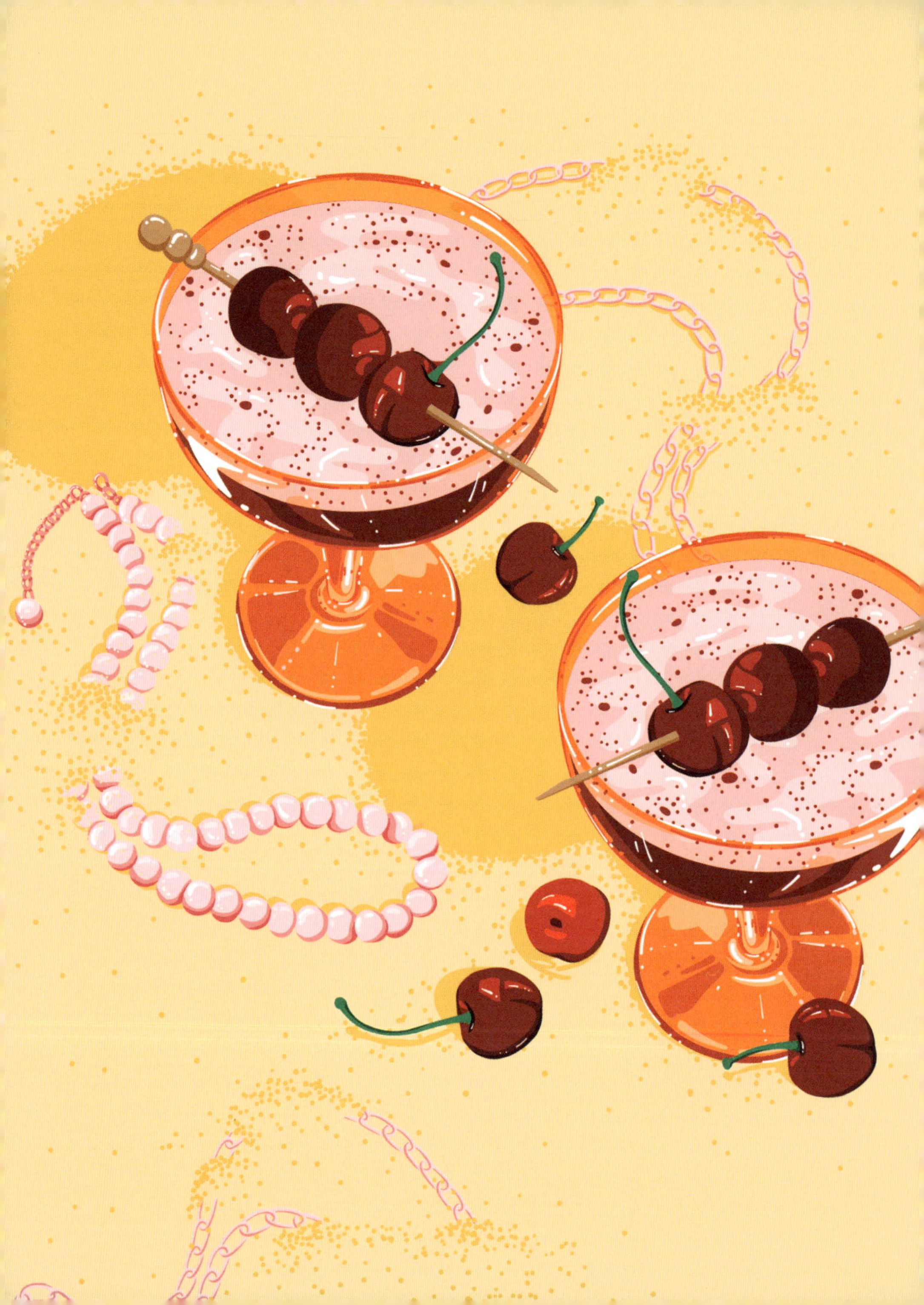

Lost-and-Found Lake

MAKES 1 DRINK

The Lost Lake is a classic Tiki cocktail made with passion fruit, rum, lime, and Campari. One of my favorite nonalcoholic alien spirits is Ghia, which bears a lot of similarity to Campari, thanks to its red color and bitter botanical profile—but to drive the point home, I'm adding a few dashes of cherry-and-anise-flavored Peychaud's bitters. Rica, a food producer from the Dominican Republic, makes a passion fruit juice that is head and shoulders above everything else I've tried, and while it's not a crime to use another brand of passion fruit juice, this is one of the few instances where using a specific brand is important.

1½ ounces Ghia nonalcoholic aperitif

1 ounce Rica passion fruit juice

½ ounce orgeat syrup

2 dashes Peychaud's bitters or nonalcoholic bitters

Garnish: Luxardo cherries

In a shaker, combine the drink ingredients. Fill with ice and shake vigorously for 15 seconds. Strain into a coupe, garnish with Luxardo cherries on a pick, and serve.

Ethereal Angel

MAKES 1 DRINK

◆

In the minds of many bartenders, Japan holds near-mythic status. Japanese bars and the bartenders who work in them produce some of the most meticulous, beautiful, and austerely simple cocktails. If you order a Bloody Mary at one of these bars, you will likely be served something that only vaguely resembles the gloopy brunchtime drink you know and love. Instead of canned tomato juice, many Japanese bartenders blend fresh tomatoes with vodka à la minute, which results in a pink, frothy marvel. This nonalcoholic version requires you to strain out the flecks of skin and then re-whip the drink, but I wouldn't ask you to make the extra effort if it wasn't absolutely worth it.

---

6 large cherry tomatoes

2 ounces Ultra Gin (see page 43) or plain nonalcoholic gin

Garnishes: flaky sea salt, such as Maldon, and freshly ground black pepper

In a blender, combine the tomatoes and gin. Blend on high speed until smooth, about 45 seconds. Strain through a fine-mesh sieve into an airtight container. Chill in the refrigerator for at least 4 hours or up to 3 days.

To serve, whip the mixture in the blender on high until frothy, about 10 seconds. Pour into a tall glass. Sprinkle with flaky salt and a few turns of black pepper over the top.

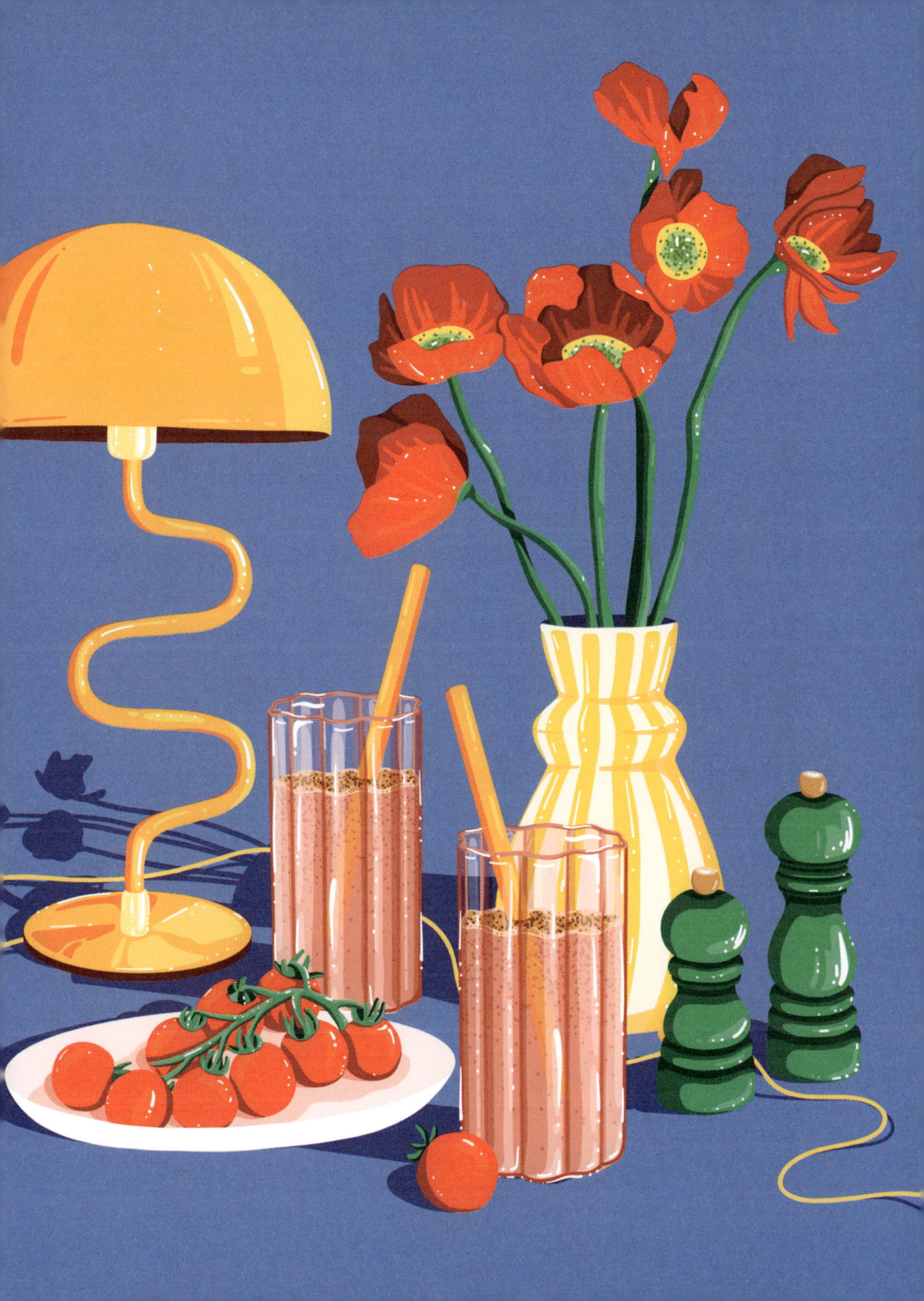

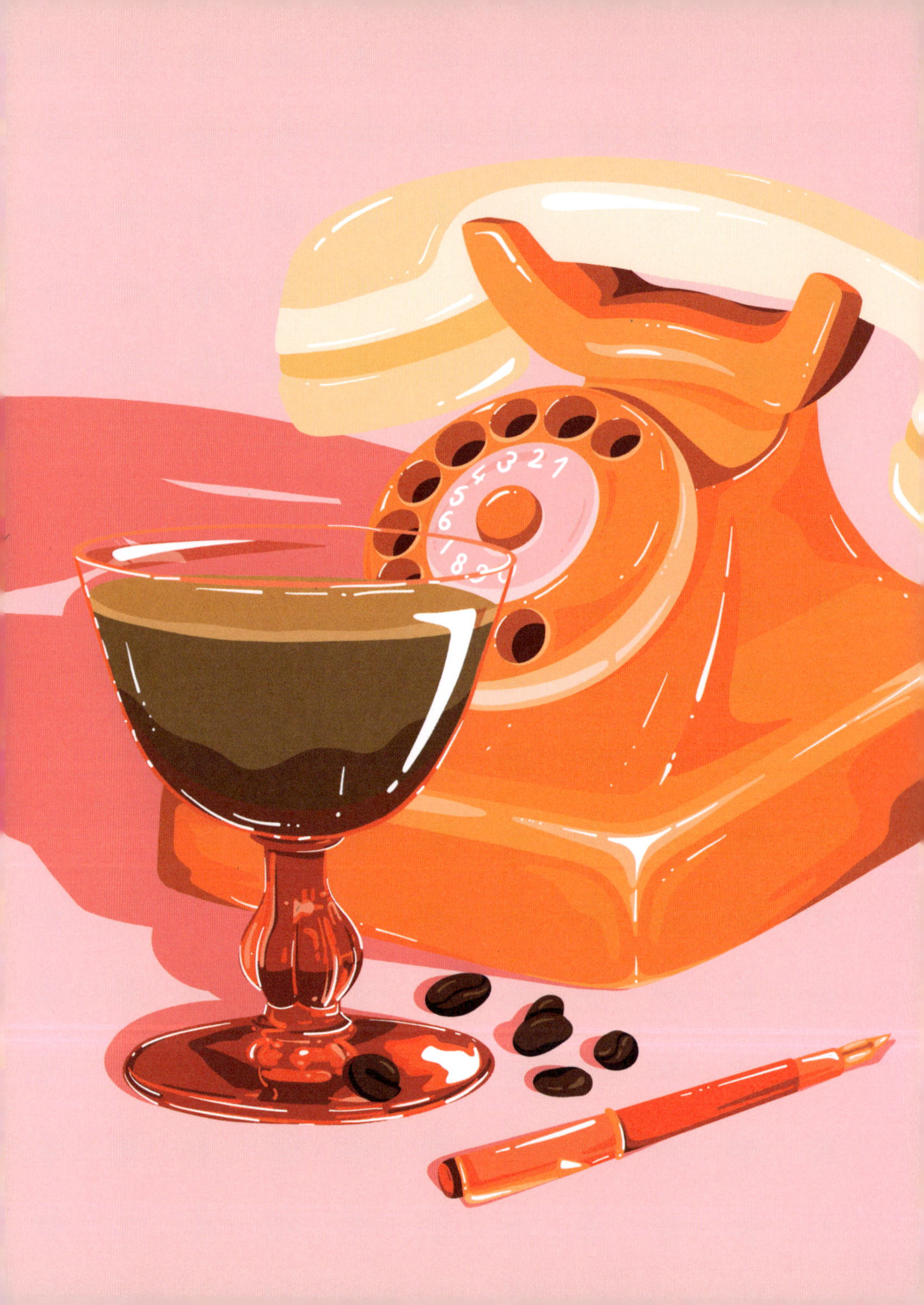

Coco-Coffee

MAKES 1 DRINK

The Puerto Rican coconut cream Coco López sits next to Luxardo cherries as an ingredient so primally delicious it goes right to your lizard brain, bypassing all conscious thought and reason to deliver a sledgehammer of hedonistic pleasure. I might be overselling it, especially if you're not fond of coconut, but Coco López is really, really good. Don't confuse it for standard coconut cream, which is fine in its own right, but . . . it's not Coco López. This ingredient is typically used in drinks like piña coladas (and a surprising number of shrimp recipes, according to the product's website). But here it's shaken with some cold brew coffee and a little Super Whiskey. I'd say this drink is a nonalcoholic shakerato, but the number of people who know that drink is quite limited, so I'm just calling it delicious.

---

2 ounces cold brew coffee concentrate

½ ounce Coco López

½ ounce Super Whiskey (see page 43) or plain nonalcoholic whiskey

In a shaker, combine the drink ingredients. Fill with ice and shake vigorously for 15 seconds. Strain into a coupe and serve.

VELVETY

Tahini Dreamsicle

MAKES 2 DRINKS

The nostalgic appeal of the creamy orange-vanilla Dreamsicle dessert is irresistible to me. Bust out the blender for this rich yet refreshing liquid version of the childhood favorite made a touch more mature by the inclusion of tahini, a Middle Eastern sesame paste. You may not typically think of tahini when choosing things to drink, but when used judiciously, it brings a nutty, rich dimension. If you swap out the regular whole milk for a nondairy milk of your choice, this drink can be made vegan.

---

1 cup chilled whole milk or nondairy milk, such as almond or oat

2 ounces fresh orange juice

1 ounce Orange Syrup (see page 37)

2 tablespoons tahini

1 teaspoon pure vanilla extract

1 teaspoon rum extract

In a blender, combine the drink ingredients along with 2 cups ice. Blend on medium speed until the ice is crushed and the drink is smooth, about 20 seconds. Pour into old fashioned glasses and serve.

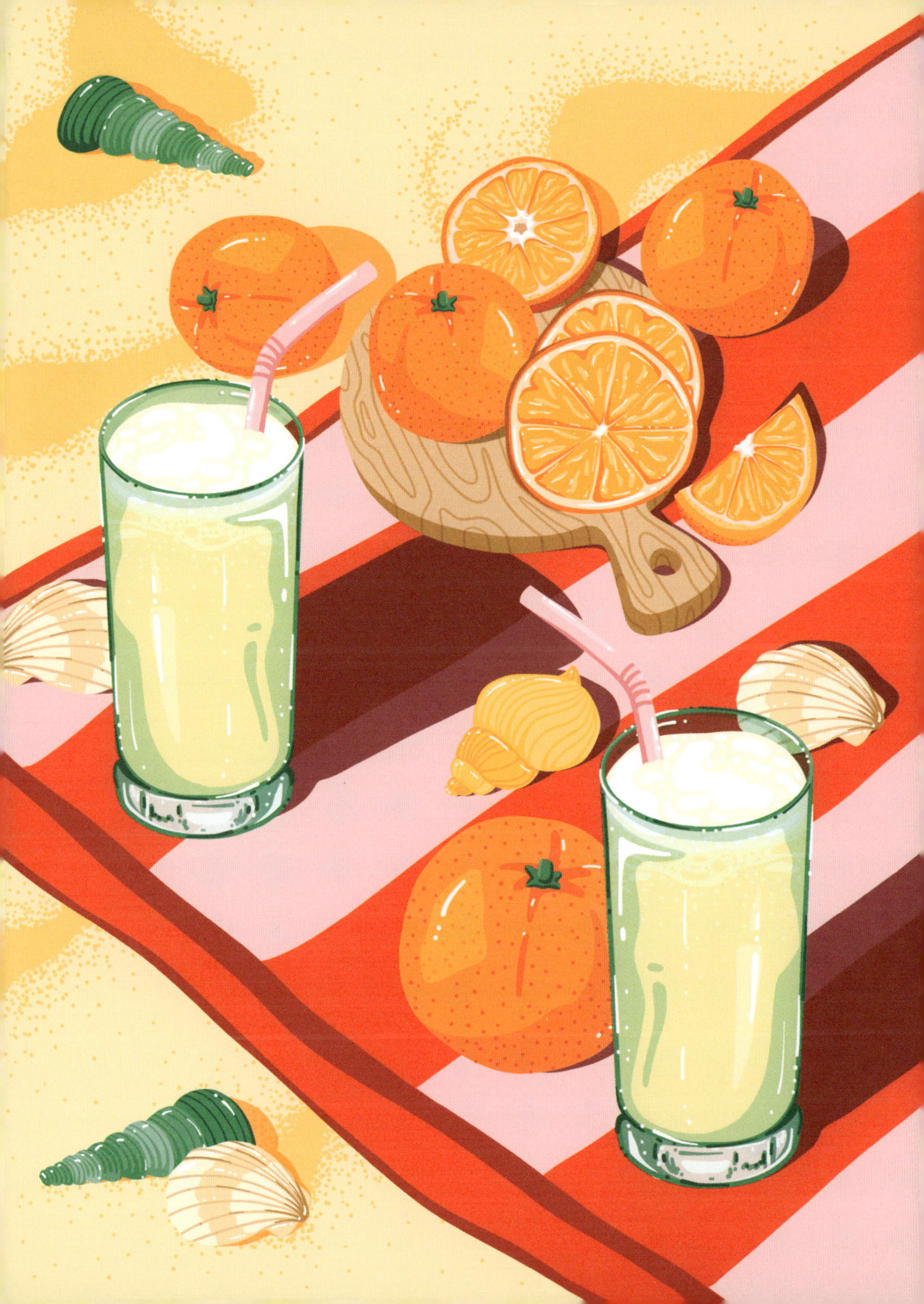

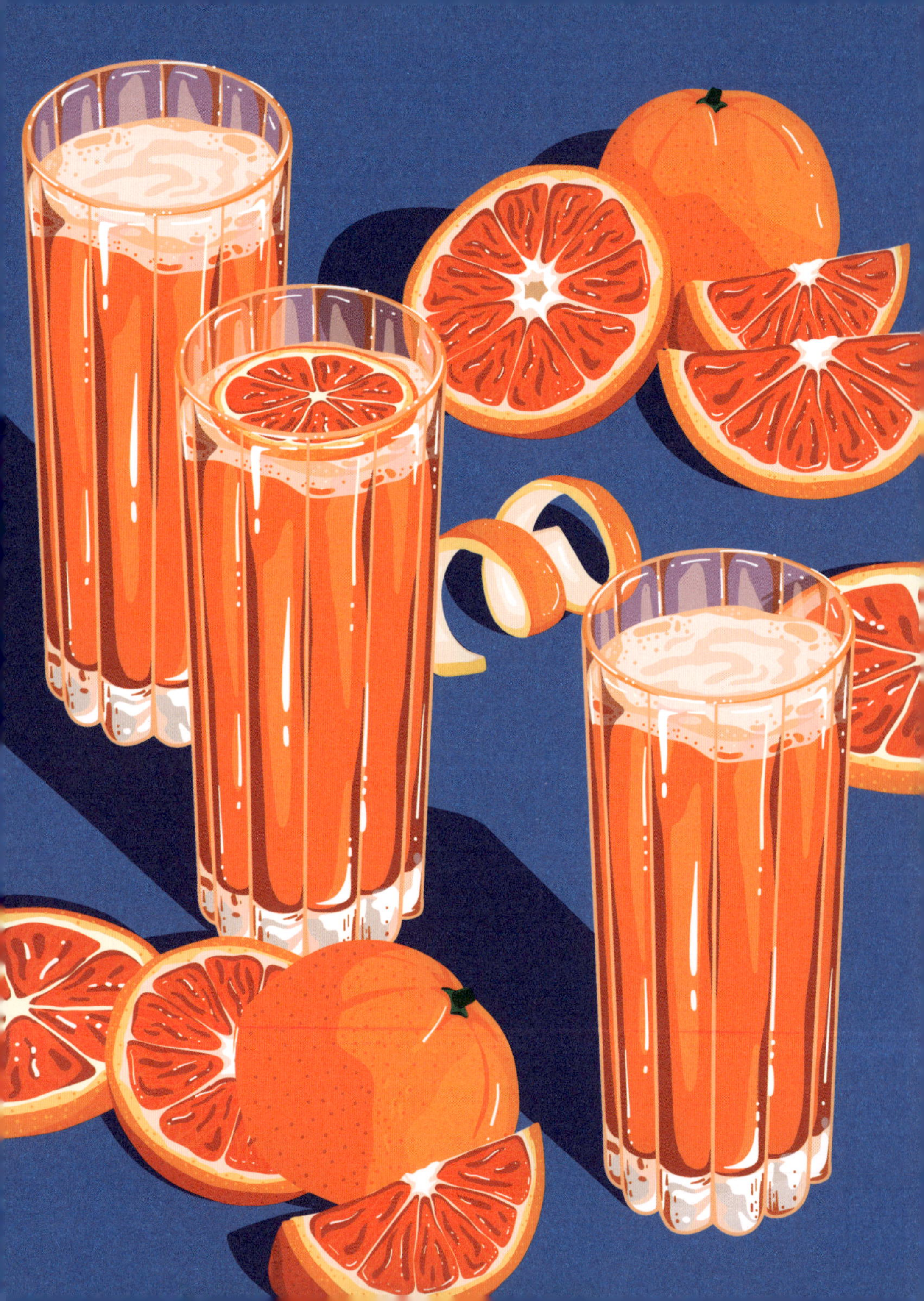

Blood Orange Ramos

MAKES 1 DRINK

◆

Thanks to clever nineteenth-century marketing, the Ramos Gin Fizz is a legendary drink made with gin, egg white, cream, lemon juice, and orange blossom water and topped with sparkling water. It's known for being arduous to make, but I never really found that to be true. It does require the extra step of dry shaking (shaking without ice) to emulsify the egg white, but that does not make it much harder than every other shaken drink in existence. Instead of using the plain soda that's called for in the classic Ramos recipe, here I've substituted Sanbittèr, a bitter Italian soda with a brilliant ruby hue. Blood oranges are a gamble; despite their name, they're not always red. But the Sanbittèr and nonalcoholic sweet vermouth do the heavy lifting in the color department.

---

1 ounce Ultra Gin (see page 43) or plain nonalcoholic gin

1 ounce fresh blood orange juice

1 ounce Orange Syrup (see page 37)

½ ounce nonalcoholic sweet vermouth

½ ounce fresh lemon juice

¼ teaspoon orange blossom water

2 dashes Peychaud's bitters or nonalcoholic bitters

1 large egg white

1 (100mL) bottle Sanbittèr

Garnish: blood orange wheel

In a shaker, combine the gin, blood orange juice, orange syrup, sweet vermouth, lemon juice, orange blossom water, bitters, and egg white. Shake without ice for 5 seconds. Fill with ice and shake vigorously for 15 seconds. Strain into a tall glass, then top with the Sanbittèr. Garnish with a blood orange wheel and serve.

Nog of Virtue

SERVES 10

♦♦

I don't believe adhering to a vegan diet or avoiding alcohol makes anyone morally superior, but if that aligns with your values, then, boy, do I have the holiday nog for you! And even if not, you should still make it—because it's good! In place of eggs and cream, here you'll find nondairy milk, Coco López, and an egg replacer powder that brings a smooth, creamy texture and also aerates nicely—an important feature of any good nog, egg or otherwise. You can make this drink in advance if you're planning ahead for a festive wintertime gathering; just don't forget to give it a good stir before serving. Frothing in a cocktail shaker is a low-impact way to liven up the texture, but if you have a milk frother, feel free to use that—or better yet, bring out the big guns and blend the batch on high speed for 30 seconds.

---

2 (2-inch) pieces cinnamon stick

1 teaspoon whole cloves

2 whole star anise pods

4 cups nondairy milk of your choice

1 teaspoon pure vanilla extract

½ cup Coco López

2 ounces Pepper Syrup (see page 38)

1 ounce dark maple syrup

2 tablespoons egg replacer powder

Garnish: freshly grated nutmeg

In a medium saucepan, combine the cinnamon sticks, cloves, and star anise. Cook over medium heat until fragrant, about 5 minutes. Add 2 cups of the nondairy milk, reduce the heat to low, and bring to a simmer. Remove from the heat and let cool to room temperature, about 30 minutes, then remove the spices with a slotted spoon or tongs.

Stir in the remaining 2 cups nondairy milk along with the vanilla, Coco López, pepper syrup, and maple syrup. Add the egg replacer powder in a slow, steady stream, whisking constantly to ensure no clumps form. Transfer to an airtight container and chill in the refrigerator for at least 4 hours or up to 1 week.

To serve, pour 4 to 5 ounces into a shaker and shake without ice for 5 seconds to make the drink frothy. Pour into teacups or old fashioned glasses and grate nutmeg over the top to garnish.

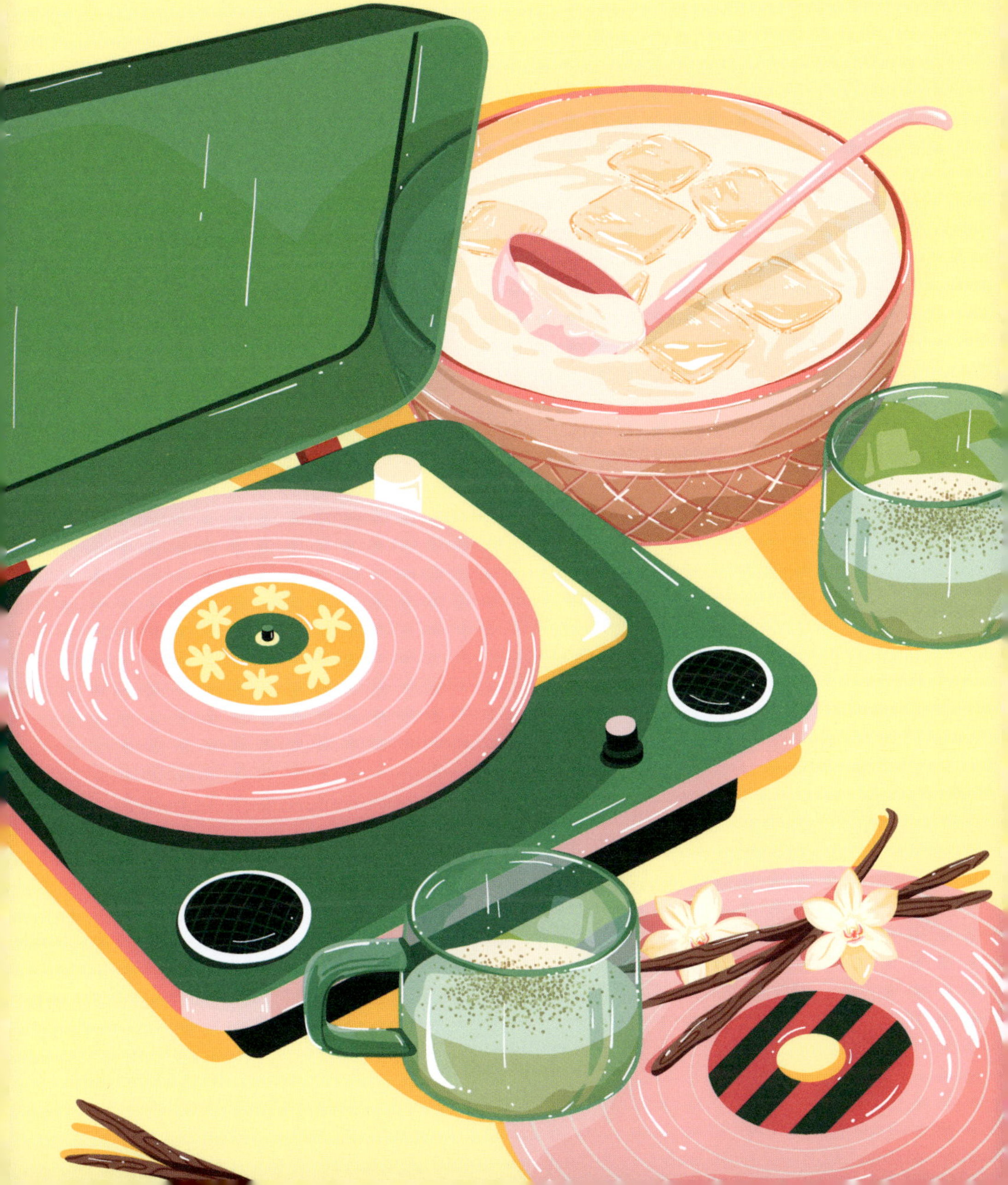

ACKNOWLEDGMENTS

Enormous gratitude to those whose hard work and collaboration made this book possible:

My literary agent, Nicole Tourtelot; my editor, Amanda Englander; and this book's illustrator, LOZO Illustration.

There are no words that can fully capture what it's meant to have the love and support of my husband, Michael Remaley, during our eighteen years together. I love you. Thank you.

Thank you to the rest of the team at Union Square & Co., especially Renée Bollier, Lisa Forde, and Ivy McFadden.

To those people whose indirect support and inspiration made this book possible:

My family, including Ned deBary, Paul and Stefana deBary, and George and Joan Hellman, as well as my comically large extended family of cousins, aunts, uncles, and globe-spanning network of relatives whom I also call cousins for the sake of simplicity. Not to mention my wonderful Stiepock family.

Friends who might as well be family at this point: Jonathan and Amy Poppers-Rousell; Leslie and Charles Rousell; Youngmi Mayer; Alex Pemoulié; Buzzy Cohen; Noa Gottleib; Hannah and Denny Lee; Kerrin Egalka; Karen Fu; Rita Su; Julia Bainbridge; and Nicole Allen.

INDEX

A
Amaro Falso
    Darth Spritz, 143
Aplós
    Corpse Reviver Reviver, 78
    Garden Soother, 47
Apricot Spritz, 94

B
Basil Smash, 70
beer, 27
    Berry Michelada, 97
    Fireplace Punch, 168
    Miso Flip, 173
    Monaco, 132
berries. See Polyberry Syrup
bitter aperitif, 26
    Monaco, 132
    Proxy Blush, 136
    Slushy Minty Mary, 102
bitters, 30–31
black pepper, 32
    Pepper Syrup, 38

C
cherries, 31
    Cherry-Cola Temple, 90
    Lapsang-Luxardo, 153
    Tart Negroni, 131
cider
    Cider Shandy, 109
    Mugi Punch, 126
    Pickup Toddy, 164
citrus fruits, 28
Citrus Syrups, 37
Coco López
    Coco-Coffee, 181
    Nog of Virtue, 186
cola, 29
    Cherry-Cola Temple, 90
    Cider Shandy, 109
    Smoked Cola Old Fashioned, 157
cold brew coffee, 31
    Coco-Coffee, 181
    Pickup Toddy, 164
Cucumber Collins, 48

E
eggs, 31–32
    Blood Orange Ramos, 185
    "Midori Sour," 101
    Miso Flip, 173
    New New York Sour, 158
elderflower liqueur
    Barley Bomber, 113
    Honeysuckle 75, 60
    Lychee Hugo Spritz, 50
    Vernal Equinox Punch, 59

F
fruit preserves, 32–33

G
Ghia
    Lost-and-Found Lake, 177
    Polyberry Daiquiri, 147
gin
    Basil Smash, 70
    Blood Orange Ramos, 185
    Corpse Reviver Reviver, 78
    Cucumber Collins, 48
    A Definitive Nonalcoholic Gin & Tonic, 144
    A Definitive Nonalcoholic Martini, 56
    Digestivo Shots, 135
    Ethereal Angel, 178
    Ultra Gin, 43
    Vernal Equinox Punch, 59
Ginger Syrup, 38
    Amoxicillin, 74
    Fireplace Punch, 168
    Moderate Mule, 53
    Smoked Cola Old Fashioned, 157
grapefruit
    Deep Purple, 67
    Grapefruit Syrup, 37
    Negroni Sbagliato (for Two), 139

grapefruit *(continued)*
    Proxy Blush, 136
    Senchu-Hi, 83
Green Tea Concentrate, 40
    Green Lightning, 64
    Senchu-Hi, 83

H

hibiscus concentrate
    Arctic Cooler, 84
    Bocce Boule, 174
    Honeysuckle 75, 60
    Mugi Manhattan, 122
    Proxy Blush, 136
    Red Hibiscus
        Concentrate, 42
    Slushy Minty Mary, 102
    Tart Negroni, 131
    White Hibiscus
        Concentrate, 42
honey. *See* Saffron Honey
honeydew, 29
    Honeydew Old
        Fashioned, 118
    "Midori Sour," 101
hop water, 30
hot sauce, 32

I

ice, 29

J

Jaggery Sour, 121
Jaggery Syrup, 36

K

kombucha, 28
    Fermented Passion, 80

L

Lapsang Concentrate, 41
    Amoxicillin, 74
    Fireplace Punch, 168
    Hot Curcu, 167
    Lapsang-Luxardo, 153
    A Not-So-Definitive Old
        Fashioned, 160
    Smoked Cola Old
        Fashioned, 157
lemon
    Arctic Cooler, 84
    Lemon Syrup, 37
    New New York Sour, 158
    Senchu-Hi, 83
lemon-lime soda, 30
lime
    Arctic Cooler, 84
    Basil Smash, 70
    Cameron's Kiss, 117
    A Definitive
        Nonalcoholic Gin &
        Tonic, 144
    Lime Syrup, 37
    Moderate Mule, 53
    Polyberry Daiquiri, 147
    Pumpkin Spice
        Margarita, 125
    Verjus Daiquiri, 69
liqueurs, 26
Lychee Hugo Spritz, 50

M

maple syrup, 33
    Mugi Manhattan, 122
    Vinegar Fizz, 110
"Midori Sour," 101
milk
    Nog of Virtue, 186
    Tahini Dreamsicle, 182
Mint Syrup, 40
    Green Lightning, 64
    Moderate Mule, 53
    Slushy Minty Mary, 102
Miso Flip, 173
"mocktail," note about, 15
Mugi Concentrate, 41
    Barley Bomber, 113
    Honeydew Old
        Fashioned, 118
    Mugi Manhattan, 122
    Mugi Punch, 126
    Mugi Toddy, 151

N

nonalcoholic, defined, 12
nonalcoholic cocktails
    characteristics, 13–14
    equipment, 19–21
    glassware, 22
    ingredients, 25–33
    recipe icons, 18
    science of, 15–16
    techniques, 23
nonalcoholic spirits, 15–16,
    25–26

O

orange
- Blood Orange Ramos, 185
- Bocce Boule, 174
- Golden Gimlet, 77
- Honey Sidecar, 73
- Orange Syrup, 37
- Tahini Dreamsicle, 182

orange blossom water, 33

orgeat, 33
- Bocce Boule, 174
- Cameron's Kiss, 117
- Lost-and-Found Lake, 177

P

(parentheses) After
- Dirty Old Fashioned, 163
- Pickup Toddy, 164

passion fruit
- Lost-and-Found Lake, 177

peaches
- Rocking Chair Punch, 89

pineapple, 28
- Citra Collins, 93
- Garden Soother, 47
- Honey Sidecar, 73
- Kitchen Sink Sling, 105
- Pineapple Elixir 2.0, 114

Polyberry Syrup, 39
- Arctic Cooler, 84
- Berry Bramble, 154
- Berry Michelada, 97
- Kitchen Sink Sling, 105
- Polyberry Daiquiri, 147

Pumpkin Spice Margarita, 125

R

Rooh Afza syrup
- Proxy Blush, 136
- Vetiver Blush, 98

S

Saffron Honey, 37
- Amoxicillin, 74
- Chamomile-Saffron Toddy, 55
- Golden Gimlet, 77
- Honey Sidecar, 73

salt, 32

Sanbittèr
- Blood Orange Ramos, 185
- Deep Purple, 67

sparkling water, 29

sugar, 32

syrups, 36–40

T

Tahini Dreamsicle, 182

tea
- Chamomile-Saffron Toddy, 55
- Rocking Chair Punch, 89
- tea concentrates, 40–41

Tenneyson Black Ginger
- Barley Bomber, 113
- Darth Spritz, 143
- Digestivo Shots, 135
- Mugi Punch, 126

tequila
- Citra Collins, 93
- Jaggery Sour, 121

Pumpkin Spice Margarita, 125

Slushy Minty Mary, 102

tomatoes
- Ethereal Angel, 178

tonic water, 30

Turmeric Syrup, 39
- Golden Gimlet, 77
- Hot Curcu, 167

V

verjus, 27
- Basil Smash, 70
- Jaggery Sour, 121
- "Midori Sour," 101
- Verjus Daiquiri, 69

vermouth, 26
- Blood Orange Ramos, 185
- A Definitive Manhattan, 140
- A Definitive Nonalcoholic Martini, 56
- Fermented Passion, 80
- Tart Negroni, 131

vinegar, 27

Vinegar Fizz, 110

W

water, 29

watermelon, 28–29
- Lapsang-Luxardo, 153
- Slushy Minty Mary, 102
- Vetiver Blush, 98

whiskey
- Amoxicillin, 74
- Apricot Spritz, 94

whiskey *(continued)*
   Barley Bomber, 113
   Berry Bramble, 154
   Cameron's Kiss, 117
   Coco-Coffee, 181
   A Definitive Manhattan, 140
   Fireplace Punch, 168
   Golden Gimlet, 77
   Moderate Mule, 53
   Mugi Toddy, 151
   New New York Sour, 158
   A Not-So-Definitive Old Fashioned, 160
   Rocking Chair Punch, 89
   Super Whiskey, 43

wine, 26–27
   Apricot Spritz, 94
   Berry Bramble, 154
   Corpse Reviver Reviver, 78
   Darth Spritz, 143
   Honeysuckle 75, 60
   Lychee Hugo Spritz, 50
   Negroni Sbagliato (for Two), 139
   New New York Sour, 158
   Proxy Blush, 136
   Rocking Chair Punch, 89
   Vernal Equinox Punch, 59
   Vetiver Blush, 98

Y

yuzu juice, 30
   Citra Collins, 93
   Dirty Old Fashioned, 163